2

**The Complete Encyclopedia of Cooking**

# Supercook

Marshall Cavendish · London Sydney New York

# Symbols in Supercook

**'Low-Calorie' Recipes**

The description 'low-calorie' has been given to recipes in *'Supercook'* which contain fewer calories than other comparable recipes in the book. For instance, the pudding recipes marked 'Low-cal' have the fewest calories when compared to other pudding recipes in *'Supercook'*. Some – but not all – of the recipes labelled 'Low-cal' would be suitable for people who are following strict slimming or low-calorie diets. Each recipe should be examined carefully to ascertain whether the ingredients are permitted for a particular special diet.

The labelling 'Low-cal' will be more helpful for those aiming to lose weight slowly by reducing their calorie intake slightly or those who frequently experiment with new recipes but wish to avoid a very high consumption of calories. These recipes can also guide the person entertaining for weight-conscious friends. However,

thought should also be given to what is to be served *with* the 'low-calorie' recipe. An over-enthusiastic combination of these recipes will not guarantee a low-calorie meal!

In deciding which recipes to consider in the 'low-calorie' category, each ingredient needs to be considered for its calorific contribution. Low-calorie ingredients such as vegetables, fruits, white fish and eggs may be combined with a moderate amount of fat or fat-containing foods and still be relatively 'low-calorie'. A generous combination of fats and fat-containing foods will produce a high-calorie recipe. Similarly, recipes which rely heavily on sugar, alcohol, flour or a combination of these foods with or without fat will be excluded from the 'low-calorie' rating.

In some recipes it may be possible to make further reductions in the amount of fats and sugars used, such as substituting low-fat yogurt for cream, or to grill [broil] food and drain off fat rather than frying, although the end results will differ slightly.

The calorie chart under the alphabetical heading CALORIES (p. 302) may be used to work out the approximate calorific value of individual recipes.

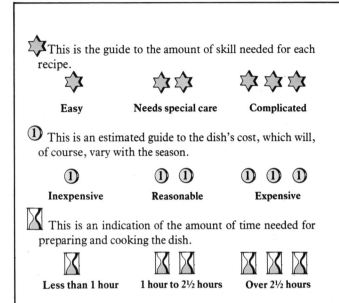

This is the guide to the amount of skill needed for each recipe.

**Easy**          **Needs special care**          **Complicated**

This is an estimated guide to the dish's cost, which will, of course, vary with the season.

**Inexpensive**          **Reasonable**          **Expensive**

This is an indication of the amount of time needed for preparing and cooking the dish.

**Less than 1 hour**          **1 hour to 2½ hours**          **Over 2½ hours**

Front Cover: Bombe Coppelia p. 206

Published by Marshall Cavendish House
58 Old Compton Street
London W1V 5PA

This Edition Published 1987

©Marshall Cavendish Ltd 1987, 1986, 1985, 1979, 1978, 1977, 1976, 1975, 1974, 1973, 1972, 58 Old Compton Street, London W1V 5PA

Printed and bound by
L.E.G.O. Spa Vicenza

Cataloguing in Publication Data

Supercook
1. Cookery
1. Cameron-Smith, Marye
641.5    TX717    79-52319

ISBN (for set) 0 85685 534 0
ISBN (this volume) 0 85685 536 7
Library of Congress catalog card number 78-52319.

# Recipes in Volume 2

# Béarnaise Sauce

*A rich egg-and-butter sauce sharpened with vinegar, Béarnaise (bay-ahr-nayz) is one of a number of sauces called* sauces au beurre. *Similar to Hollandaise Sauce, but thicker and sharper in taste, Béarnaise Sauce is served with fillet steak, other grilled [broiled]* red meat or fish and some shellfish.

ABOUT 5 FLUID OUNCES

5 tablespoons wine vinegar
1 shallot, or small onion,
   cut in 4 pieces
1 bay leaf
1 tarragon sprig
1 chervil sprig
4 peppercorns
4 oz. [½ cup] butter
2 large egg yolks
⅛ teaspoon salt
⅛ teaspoon cayenne pepper
1 teaspoon mixed chopped
   tarragon and chervil

Put the vinegar in a small saucepan with the shallot, or onion, the bay leaf, tarragon, chervil and peppercorns. Simmer over low heat until the vinegar is reduced to 1 tablespoon. Strain and set aside.

In a small bowl beat the butter until it is soft. In another bowl beat the egg yolks with a wire whisk or wooden spoon. Add a heaped teaspoon of softened butter and the salt to the egg yolks. Cream well and stir in the vinegar.

Put the bowl in a saucepan containing warm water and place over low heat. The water should heat gradually, but never come to the boiling point. Stir the mixture until it begins to thicken. Add the remaining butter in small pieces, stirring continuously. When all the butter has been added and the sauce has the consistency of whipped cream, add the cayenne, chopped tarragon and chervil. Taste the sauce and add a little more salt if necessary.

# Beat

To beat is to blend ingredients rapidly by mixing them thoroughly and vigorously with a vertical circular motion to introduce as much air as possible into the mixture. This may be done with a slotted spoon, a wooden spoon, a fork, a wire whisk, a rotary beater or an electric beater. It is best when beating by hand to use the lower arm and wrist muscles because beating from the shoulder is tiring.

The main purposes for beating ingredients are to mix and blend them, to lighten and increase their volume or to

*For Béarnaise Sauce, strain the vinegar mixture, cream the butter and beat the egg yolks.*

*Over warm water, stir the mixture until it thickens. Then stir in the butter, in small pieces.*

*When the mixture is smooth, remove the bowl from the heat and add the cayenne, tarragon and chervil.*

stiffen and thicken them. Batter, for example, is beaten so that all the ingredients are mixed and blended together into a smooth liquid. Egg whites are beaten to increase their volume, incorporate as much air as possible and make them stiff. Cream is beaten to increase its volume and to thicken and lighten it. Raw meat is beaten with a mallet or rolling pin to break down its fibres and make it tender.

# Beater

There is a wide variety of kitchen utensils which are used to incorporate air into eggs, butter, cream, liquids and semi-

liquids to make them light. The utensils most commonly used to beat eggs, cream and light batters are rotary beaters, forks and wire whisks. For thicker mixtures, wooden spoons are easier to use, and electric beaters can be employed in all instances, except when only very light beating is required.

# Beaujolais

A red, light wine from southern Burgundy, Beaujolais is one of the most popular of French wines and is produced in large quantities. Beaujolais is a 'young' wine and should be drunk within two to three years of its production. Vintage Beaujolais is usually no more than six years old, as opposed to other vintage wines, which can be over 50 years old.

The rigid French 'appellation contrôlée, or controlled place-name, laws apply to the Beaujolais area and only wines from the finer vineyards merit official designation of quality. The best are the nine village-named growths: Moulin-à-Vent, Côte de Brouilly, Juliénas, Fleurie, Brouilly, Morgon, Chénas, St.-Amour and Chiroubles. Next in quality come Beaujolais Villages and the wines labelled Beaujolais which are linked by a hyphen to one of 36 areas of origin. These are followed by Beaujolais Supérieur and, last of all, Beaujolais.

Beaujolais goes well with beef or lamb, bouillabaisse, steaks and pâtés.

# Beaune

A town in Burgundy, Beaune gives its name to the Côte de Beaune, or slopes of Beaune, from which come the finest white wines of the BURGUNDY area. The Hospices de Beaune is a charity hospital which owns some of the finest vineyards in Burgundy. At the annual auction of the hospital's wines, international buyers assess the quality of the year's burgundies.

# Béchamel Sauce

WHITE SAUCE

*A basic white sauce, Béchamel (bay-shah-mell) was named after, and is reputed to have been introduced by, Louis de Béchamel, Marquis de Nointel, who was steward of the household at the court of Louis XIV.*

*To make a good béchamel sauce, it is necessary to use slightly more butter than flour and the creamiest of milk. Béchamel sauce may be used as a base for other sauces and mushrooms, tomatoes, cheese, shrimps, or whatever flavouring is required by the recipe, may be added. When served without additional flavouring, the sauce can be enriched with the addition of a little cream, an egg yolk, or both. When making béchamel sauce, use an enamelled or coated pan if possible, because aluminium tends to slightly discolour it.*

ABOUT 15 FLUID OUNCES

15 fl. oz. [1⅞ cups] creamy milk
1 bay leaf
6 peppercorns
1 blade mace
⅛ teaspoon grated nutmeg
1¼ oz. [2¼ tablespoons] butter
1 oz. [4 tablespoons] flour
½ teaspoon salt
¼ teaspoon white pepper

Put the milk with the bay leaf, peppercorns, mace and nutmeg in a small saucepan over low heat. Warm the milk for 10 minutes, but do not let it boil. Strain the milk into a small bowl and set it aside to cool.

Melt the butter in a medium-sized saucepan over moderate heat. Remove the pan from the heat and stir in the flour. When the flour and butter are well mixed, add the milk, a little at a time, stirring constantly with a wooden spoon.

When all the milk has been added, mix in the salt and pepper and return the pan to the heat. Bring the mixture slowly to the boil, stirring continuously. Boil for 2 minutes. Taste the sauce and add more salt and pepper if necessary.

## Bêche-de-Mer

A marine animal which is also called sea cucumber, sea slug and trepang, bêche-de-mer (besh d'mair) is the French adaptation of the Portuguese name *bicho da mar*, meaning 'sea worm'.

Although not often eaten in the West, bêche-de-mer soup is sometimes served in Chinese restaurants. The soup is sold in cans in some specialized shops.

## Beech Nuts

Small edible beech nuts are the fruit of the beech tree. Oil extracted from these nuts is used in France for cooking.

## Beef

Beef, the meat of the young ox or bullock, can be more variable in quality than other meats and the price will fluctuate according to availability. Obviously, the prime, tender cuts are always more expensive because there are fewer of them on the whole carcass. The tougher cuts, which are cheaper, are equally nutritious and, if they are cooked cor-

rectly, provide delicious, dishes.

Beef (and other meats) contain a high proportion of protein and are valuable sources of iron and Vitamins B1 and B2. Beef is ideal for would be slimmers as the carbohydrate content is nil.

When buying beef, look for meat with a fresh red colour that has a brownish tinge. If the colour is too bright it means that the meat has not been sufficiently aged and will be tough and lacking in flavour. The meat should be marbled with fat. This will make the meat moist and tender when it is cooked. The fat should be a creamy colour.

The amount of meat you buy depends on family requirements, but an approximate guide is 4-6 oz. of boned meat or, 6-8 oz. of meat with bone per person.

The United States, Ireland, Argentina and Russia are among the largest producers of beef. Connoisseurs, however, consider Scotch beef the best. The cuts pictured here are British cuts.

ROASTING

This term describes the cooking of meat by radiated heat—in olden days meat was hung on to a spit and roasted over coals or wood. Nowadays roasting is generally done in the oven, and is the best method of cooking the prime cuts.

*Suitable Cuts*

Ribs (Top, Fore and Back) Sirloin, Top Rump, Whole Fillet.

*Preparation*

Preheat oven to hot 425°F (Gas Mark 7, 220°C). Place a little cooking fat in a roasting pan and heat in the oven. Place meat in the hot fat then turn over to seal all sides. After cooking for 15 minutes reduce temperature to moderate 350°F (Gas Mark 4, 180°C).

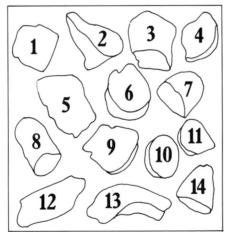

| | |
|---|---|
| *1 Neck* | *2 Foreribs* |
| *3 Sirloin* | *4 Rump steak* |
| *5 Chuck* | *6 Back ribs* |
| *7 Topside* | |
| *8 Rolled boned brisket* | |
| *9 Top rib* | *10 Top rump* |
| *11 Silverside* | *12 Shin* |
| *13 Flank* | *14 Leg* |

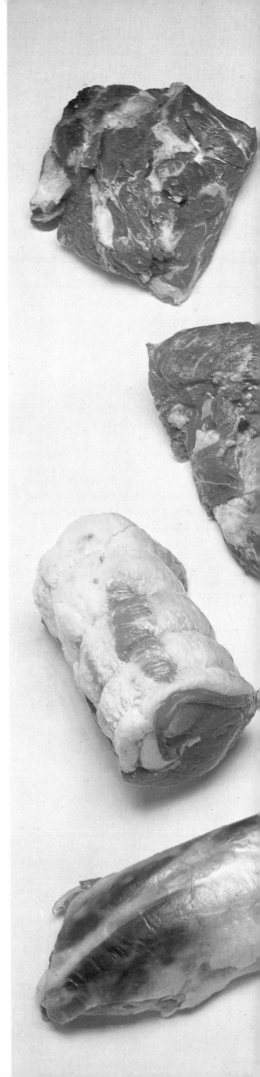

*Cooking Time*

Rare: 15 minutes to the pound and 15 minutes over (Meat thermometer temperature 140°F).

Medium: 25 minutes to the pound and 25 minutes over (Meat thermometer temperature 160°F).

Boned and rolled beef: 30 minutes to the pound and 30 minutes over (Meat thermometer temperature 175°F).

After cooking leave the meat in a warm place for 10 minutes. This makes it easier to carve.

BRAISING OR POT ROASTING

Braising is a mixture of roasting and stewing. The meat is cooked on a bed of vegetables with a little liquid, in an oven-proof casserole with a tight fitting lid. The moisture produced while cooking makes this an ideal way of cooking the medium cuts of beef. Pot roasting is similar, the only difference being the meat is cooked in a saucepan on top of the stove and then if liked transferred to an ovenproof dish and browned in the oven.

*Suitable Cuts*

Brisket, Silverside, Thick Flank, Topside.

*Preparation*

Preheat oven to moderate 350°F (Gas Mark 4, 180°C).

Fry both sides of the meat in hot fat for 2 minutes to seal in the juices. Place on a bed of fried vegetables (or according to recipe). Cover the casserole with a tight fitting lid.

*Cooking Time*

40 minutes to the pound for thinner cuts. 45 minutes to the pound for thicker, or stuffed, cuts.

STEWING OR CASSEROLING

This long slow method of cooking at a low temperature in the oven or on top of the stove makes coarser cuts of meat deliciously rich and tender.

*Suitable Cuts*

Chuck (also called Shoulder or Blade Bone), Leg, Neck, Oxtail, Shin, Skirt, Thick Flank, Salted Brisket or Silverside.

*Preparation*

Preheat oven to cool 300°F (Gas Mark 2, 150°C), or cook on top of the stove over low heat. Cut meat into pieces and continue according to recipe, or leave whole as in the case of salted meat.

*Cooking Time*

Depends on thickness and size of pieces of meat. But most stews require at least 2½ hours.

FRYING OR GRILLING [BROILING]

These are the best ways of cooking pieces of the prime cuts. The grill should be glowing red or the frying-pan very hot, as the meat should be cooked as quickly as possible.

*Suitable Cuts*

Fillet (comes from the undercut of the sirloin), Entrecôte (steak cut from the upper part of the sirloin), Minced [Ground] Beef (made into hamburgers) Rump.

*Preparation*

Add a little butter and oil to the grill or frying-pan and pre-heat.

Sprinkle meat with ground pepper (or according to recipe).

Grill or fry for 4 to 8 minutes on both sides depending on thickness and how you like steak cooked.

Rare: about 3—4 minutes each side.

Medium: about 5—6 minutes each side.

Well Done: about 7-8 minutes each side.

## Beef and Bean Casserole

*This tasty and filling casserole takes a long time to make, but it is not difficult to prepare. It is suitable for a family lunch or an informal dinner party. Serve with fresh green salad and crusty French bread.*

6 SERVINGS

1 lb. dried black-eyed beans
2½ pints [6¼ cups] cold water
1 teaspoon salt
½ teaspoon black pepper
1 lb. pork sausages
1 tablespoon pork fat or cooking oil
2 large onions, finely chopped
2 garlic cloves, crushed
2 lb. stewing beef, cut into 1-inch cubes
½ teaspoon dried savory
1 bay leaf
¼ teaspoon dried marjoram
4 large tomatoes, blanched, peeled and sliced
6 fl. oz. [¾ cup] beef stock or red wine

Put the dried beans in a large bowl and pour over enough water to cover them completely. Leave to stand for 12 hours or overnight.

Drain off the water and put the beans in a large saucepan. Add the cold water and half the black pepper. Bring to the boil, reduce the heat and simmer for 1½ hours, or until the beans are tender. Drain the beans through a sieve and reserve 12 fluid ounces [1½ cups] of the liquid the beans were cooked in.

Preheat the oven to cool 300°F (Gas Mark 2, 150°C).

Slice the sausages into 1-inch lengths. Melt the pork fat, or heat the cooking oil, in a large frying-pan over moderate heat. Put in the sausage slices and fry them for 15 minutes, or until they are evenly browned. With a slotted spoon, remove the sausage pieces from the frying-pan. Drain them on kitchen paper towels and set aside.

Pour off all but 3 tablespoons of fat from the frying-pan. Add the chopped onions and the garlic and fry, stirring occasionally, for 5 minutes, or until the onions are soft but not brown. With a slotted spoon, remove the onions from the pan and set aside.

Raise the heat. Add the beef cubes to the pan, adding more fat if necessary, and brown them quickly on all sides.

Remove from the pan with a slotted spoon and put the cubes in a large, oven-proof casserole. Add the onions and garlic, savory, bay leaf, marjoram, tomatoes and the beef stock or red wine. Stir in the salt and the pepper. Cover the casserole and place it in the oven. Bake for 2 hours.

Take the casserole from the oven and add the beans, sausage pieces and the 12 fluid ounces [1½ cups] of liquid in which the beans cooked. Return the casserole to the oven and, stirring occasionally, bake for 1 hour more, or until tender.

## Beef Braised in Soy Sauce

*This Chinese dish can be made with an inexpensive cut of beef, preferably chuck. Serve it with rice or noodles.*

4 SERVINGS

10 fl. oz. [1¼ cups] water
3 tablespoons soy sauce
5 tablespoons Chinese rice wine, or pale dry sherry
2½ teaspoons sugar
2½ teaspoons salt
2½ tablespoons vegetable oil
2 lb. lean, boneless beef, cut into 1-inch cubes

Combine the water, soy sauce, wine or sherry, sugar and salt in a medium-sized mixing bowl. Set aside.

Heat a 10-inch, heavy frying-pan over high heat. Pour in 1½ tablespoons of oil and heat for 30 seconds but do not let the oil smoke. Add half the meat to the pan and, stirring constantly, fry quickly for 2 minutes, or until the pieces are lightly browned on all sides. With a slotted spoon, remove the cubes.

Add the remaining oil to the pan and brown the rest of the meat. Return the browned meat cubes to the pan. Add the soy sauce mixture and mix well.

Bring to a boil over high heat, cover the pan. Reduce the heat to very low. Simmer for 1½ hours, stirring occasionally.

*This Beef and Bean Casserole is a hearty, unusual stew to serve for a winter dinner.*

*An economical way of using leftover beef, Beef with Cabbage is served hot with a tomato and onion sauce.*

## Beef Brazil

BEEF IN COFFEE AND WINE SAUCE

*Cooked in an unusual coffee and wine sauce, Beef Brazil makes a delicious main dish for dinner. It may be served with plain, boiled rice.*

6 SERVINGS

2 fl. oz. [¼ cup] cooking oil
3 lb. chuck or stewing steak, trimmed of fat and cut into 1-inch cubes
1 garlic clove, crushed
4 medium-sized onions, sliced
1 oz. [4 tablespoons] flour
8 fl. oz. [1 cup] dry red wine
2 teaspoons salt
½ teaspoon freshly ground black pepper
¼ teaspoon dried rosemary
¼ teaspoon dried oregano
8 fl. oz. [1 cup] black coffee

Preheat the oven to 300°F (Gas Mark 2, 150°C).

Heat the oil in a large, heavy frying-pan, over moderate heat. Add the beef cubes and brown all over. Transfer the meat, using a slotted spoon, to an oven-proof casserole. Put the garlic and onions in the frying-pan, lower the heat and allow to cook for 10 minutes or until the onions are soft but not brown.

With a wooden spoon, stir the flour into the onion mixture in the frying-pan. Cook for 1 minute, stirring continuously. Still stirring, gradually add the wine. Add the salt, pepper, rosemary, oregano and coffee. Continue to stir the mixture until it boils.

Pour the sauce over the meat in the casserole, cover and cook, stirring occasionally, in the oven for 2-2½ hours or until the meat is tender when pierced with the point of a sharp knife.

## Beef with Cabbage

*This is an economical and tasty way to use leftover roast or boiled beef. It may be served for a family lunch or dinner with buttered, boiled, or creamed potatoes.*

4 SERVINGS

8 thick slices cold, cooked beef
2 teaspoons salt
freshly ground black pepper
1 firm, white cabbage, about 2 lb. with the outside leaves removed and washed
1 tablespoon butter
1 tablespoon beef dripping
1 medium-sized onion, chopped
1¼ teaspoons flour
8 fl. oz. [1 cup] beef stock
2 tomatoes, blanched, peeled and finely chopped
2 tablespoons chopped parsley

Trim all fat from the beef slices and discard. Sprinkle them with ½ teaspoon of salt and 3 grindings of pepper.

Fill a large saucepan with water, add ½ teaspoon of salt and bring the water to the boil over high heat.

Cut the cabbage into quarters, and cut out the hard centre stalk. Add the cabbage pieces to the pan of boiling water and boil for 7 to 8 minutes or until the cabbage is tender but still crisp. Drain the cabbage thoroughly in a colander and then cut into strips.

Melt the butter in a medium-sized saucepan over moderate heat. Mix in ½ teaspoon of salt and 3 grindings of pepper. Add the cabbage, reduce the heat to very low and cook for 4 to 5 minutes, stirring occasionally. Remove the saucepan from the heat and set aside in a warm place.

Melt the beef dripping in a large frying-pan over high heat. When the fat is lightly smoking, put in the slices of beef and fry them a few at a time on both sides for 1½ minutes.

Remove the beef slices from the frying-pan. Set the beef aside on a warmed plate and keep hot.

Lower the heat to moderate, put the chopped onion in the frying-pan and cook gently for 5 minutes until brown. With a wooden spoon, mix in the flour and cook for 1 minute. Gradually stir in the beef stock. Add the tomatoes, the remaining ½ teaspoon of salt, 4 grindings of pepper and the parsley. Stir continuously until the sauce comes to the boil. Lower the heat and simmer for 1 minute.

Put the cabbage in a warmed serving dish and arrange the beef slices on top of it. Pour the sauce over the beef slices. Serve at once.

## Beef with Capers

*Sliced, cooked beef covered with a piquant caper sauce makes a pleasant lunch dish and is a good way to use leftover meat. Serve it with boiled potatoes and carrots.*

4 SERVINGS

1½ lb. roasted or boiled beef, at room temperature
1½ oz. [3 tablespoons] butter
1½ oz. [6 tablespoons] flour
1 pint [2½ cups] milk
1 tablespoon vinegar
2 tablespoons capers, drained
1 onion, finely sliced
1 teaspoon sugar
1 teaspoon salt
½ teaspoon freshly ground black pepper

Cut the beef into thin slices and arrange on a warm serving dish.

Melt the butter in a medium-sized saucepan over moderate heat. Using a wooden spoon blend in the flour and cook for 1 minute. Remove from the heat and stir in the milk gradually. Return to the heat, bring to the boil, still stirring, and simmer for 1 minute.

Add the vinegar, capers, onion, sugar, salt and pepper and stir to mix. Bring the sauce just to the boil, pour it over the beef slices and serve.

## Beef Casserole

*A simple but satisfying dish to serve at lunch or dinner, Beef Casserole may be accompanied by lightly buttered rice boiled with a bay leaf, or creamed potatoes and a root vegetable.*

4 SERVINGS

  4 tablespoons cooking oil
  2 lb. stewing beef cut into 1-inch cubes
  4 tablespoons brandy (optional)
 16 small onions, peeled
  8 small carrots, scraped
  8 small white turnips, peeled
  6 celery stalks, cut into 1-inch pieces
  4 oz. mushrooms, washed
  1 teaspoon paprika
  1 tablespoon tomato purée
  2 tablespoons flour
  1 pint [2½ cups] beef stock, or stock made with a beef stock cube
  4 fl. oz. [½ cup] red wine
  1 bay leaf
  1 teaspoon salt
  ½ teaspoon freshly ground black pepper

Put 2 tablespoons oil in a large, flame-proof casserole over moderate heat. When the oil is hot, add the beef cubes a few at a time and brown them well on all sides. If you are using the brandy, put it in a metal ladle and warm it over a flame, set light to it and add it flaming to the meat. When the brandy is no longer burning remove the meat from the casserole and set aside on a plate.

Add the rest of the oil to the casserole and, when hot, put in the onions, carrots, turnips and celery, and sauté, stirring occasionally, until the vegetables are brown. Add the mushrooms and cook for 2 minutes.

Remove the casserole from the heat and stir in the paprika, purée and the flour. Stirring continuously, add the stock, wine and bay leaf. Return the pan to the heat and bring to the boil. Add the salt and pepper.

Return the meat to the casserole, cover and simmer over low heat for 1½ to 2 hours, or until the meat is tender. Serve hot.

## Beef and Cheese Roll

*Served with a green vegetable and buttered noodles, this is a tasty and easy-to-prepare main dish for a family lunch or supper. The tomato sauce is served separately and may be made a day or two in advance, stored in the refrigerator in a covered jar, and re-heated before serving.*

4 SERVINGS

  3 thick slices white bread, crusts removed
  4 tablespoons milk
  1½ lb. minced [ground] beef
  2 eggs, lightly beaten
  2 teaspoons dry mustard
  1 teaspoon salt
  ⅛ teaspoon black pepper
  ½ teaspoon dried basil
  1 onion, finely chopped
  2 tablespoons finely chopped parsley
  1 tablespoon flour
  8 oz. mozzarella cheese, thinly sliced
  2 tablespoons melted butter
SAUCE
  1 lb. ripe tomatoes
  1½ oz. [3 tablespoons] butter
  2 onions, finely chopped
  1 garlic clove, crushed
  1 teaspoon dried thyme
  ⅛ teaspoon salt
  2 fl. oz. [⅛ cup] red wine (optional)
  ⅛ teaspoon black pepper

Put the bread into a large bowl and pour the milk over it. Gently squeeze the bread and pour off the excess milk. Add

*Easy to prepare, Beef and Cheese Roll, served with a tomato and wine sauce, is a tasty supper dish.*

the meat, eggs, mustard, salt, pepper, basil, onion and parsley. With your hands knead the ingredients together until they are thoroughly blended.

Lightly dust a piece of waxed paper or aluminium foil with the flour. Put the meat mixture on it. With floured hands, press the meat into a thin rectangle. Cover lightly with aluminium foil and place the meat in the refrigerator for 1 hour, or until it is thoroughly chilled.

Preheat the oven to moderate 350°F (Gas Mark 4, 180°C).

When the meat is cold, cover the top of it evenly with the sliced cheese.

Roll the meat, beginning at a narrow end, using the paper to lift it.

Place the beef roll carefully on to a shallow baking tin, with the joined edges underneath. Brush the meat with the melted butter. Bake in the oven for 50 minutes. Serve hot.

To make the tomato sauce, blanch the tomatoes by putting them into a large bowl and pouring boiling water over them. Drain, peel and quarter them.

Melt the butter in a medium-sized saucepan over moderate heat. Add the onions and garlic and sauté until the onions are soft but not brown.

Add the tomatoes, thyme, salt, red wine and pepper and reduce the heat to low. Cook the sauce for 45 minutes, stirring it occasionally. Serve the sauce hot in a warmed sauce boat.

## Beef with Chick-Peas

*An unusual beef stew with a delicate lemon flavour, Beef with Chick-Peas is ideal for a winter lunch or supper. Serve it with a green vegetable.*

4 SERVINGS

4 oz. [½ cup] dried chick-peas, or
  14 oz. canned chick-peas, drained
2 tablespoons vegetable oil
1½ lb. stewing beef, cut into 1-inch
  cubes
10 fl. oz. [1¼ cups] beef stock
6 tablespoons tomato paste
1 lemon, cut into very thin slices
  and seeds removed
1 teaspoon dried tarragon
1½ tablespoons finely chopped
  parsley
⅛ teaspoon salt
¼ teaspoon black pepper

*Low Cal*

If you are using dried chick-peas, soak them in cold water overnight.

Drain the chick-peas and put them in a medium-sized saucepan. Cover with water and bring to a boil over medium heat. When the water is boiling, reduce the heat to low and simmer the chick-peas for 2 hours.

Drain and set aside.

Preheat the oven to moderate 350 F (Gas Mark 4, 180°C).

Heat the oil in a large, heavy casserole over high heat. Add the meat and brown thoroughly on all sides. Add the beef stock and the tomato paste to the casserole and stir it well. Reduce the heat to moderate.

Add the lemon slices to the casserole. Stir in the chick-peas, tarragon, parsley, salt and pepper.

Cover the casserole and cook in the oven for 1½ hours or until the meat is tender when pierced with a fork. Serve hot.

---

*Beef with mushrooms, parsley and onion dumplings and sour cream is a substantial and satisfying main dish.*

## Beef with Dumplings

*This beef stew with mushrooms, dumplings and sour cream is a substantial and satisfying main dish. Serve it with a green vegetable or a fresh green salad and French bread.*

4 SERVINGS

4 tablespoons flour
1 teaspoon salt
¼ teaspoon black pepper
2 lb. stewing steak, trimmed of fat
  and cut into 1-inch cubes
1 oz. [2 tablespoons] butter
1 tablespoon vegetable oil
1 large onion, finely diced
2 tablespoons brandy, warmed
  (optional)
1 bay leaf
2 pints [5 cups] homemade beef
  stock or stock made with 2 beef
  stock cubes
6 oz. small whole mushrooms, or
  large mushrooms, quartered
5 fl. oz. [⅝ cup] sour cream

DUMPLINGS

½ lb. [4 cups] breadcrumbs made from day-old white bread

4 tablespoons water

3 eggs, lightly beaten

¼ teaspoon salt

⅛ teaspoon black pepper

1½ tablespoons chopped fresh parsley

1 medium-sized onion, finely chopped

½ teaspoon ground mace

Preheat the oven to warm 325°F (Gas Mark 3, 170°C).

Mix the flour, salt and pepper together on a large plate. Roll the beef cubes in the flour mixture until they are lightly coated on all sides.

Heat the butter and oil in a heavy frying-pan. Add the onion and cook over moderate heat, stirring occasionally, for about 5 minutes, or until it is translucent. With a slotted spoon, remove the onion and set aside on a plate.

Add the beef cubes to the pan a few at a time. Brown them well, adding more butter and oil if necessary. Remove the beef cubes as they brown and place them in a large ovenproof casserole.

If you are using the brandy, put it in a metal ladle. Set it alight and pour it, still burning, over the beef cubes in the casserole. When the brandy has stopped burning, add the onion to the casserole with a bay leaf and the hot stock.

Cover the casserole and place in the oven to cook for 2 hours.

While the meat is cooking, make the dumplings. Put the breadcrumbs into a large mixing bowl. Add the water, a little at a time, and toss lightly with a fork. The breadcrumbs should be just moistened, not soggy. Still using the fork, lightly mix in the eggs. Add the salt, the pepper, the parsley, chopped onion and mace.

With floured hands, pat and roll the mixture into walnut-sized dumplings. Add the dumplings to the casserole, with the mushrooms, cover again and cook for another 30 minutes.

Spoon the sour cream over the top just before serving.

## Beef Loaf

*Very easy to make, this cold meat loaf is ideal to serve for a picnic, in sandwiches or with salads for a summer lunch or supper. Wrapped in aluminium foil and kept in the refrigerator, this meat loaf will keep for 3 to 4 days.*

*This cold Beef Loaf, which is easy to make, is ideal for picnics or a summer lunch or supper.*

6 TO 8 SERVINGS

3 lb. lean beef, minced [ground]

4 slices bacon, rind removed and cut into small pieces

1 teaspoon dried thyme

2 teaspoons salt

½ teaspoon freshly ground black pepper

1 garlic clove, crushed

4 tablespoons red wine

1 tablespoon wine vinegar

1 teaspoon French mustard

1 tablespoon vegetable oil

Put the beef, bacon, thyme, salt, pepper, garlic, wine, vinegar and mustard in a large bowl and mix them well. Put the bowl into the refrigerator, cover and leave for at least 2 hours.

Preheat the oven to warm 325°F (Gas Mark 3, 170°C).

Using a pastry brush, grease a 2-pound loaf tin with the vegetable oil. Put the meat mixture into the tin.

Put the filled loaf tin into a large baking pan and half-fill the pan with water. Place the pan in the centre of the oven and cook the meat loaf for 1½ hours. After 1 hour, cover the loaf tin with foil to prevent the meat from becoming too dry.

Remove the meat loaf from the oven and leave it to cool for at least one hour. Unmould it by running a knife around the edges of the tin and turning it out on to a plate.

Wrap the cool meat loaf in aluminium foil and chill in the refrigerator for at least 6 hours before serving.

## Beef and Madeira Casserole

*An elegant beef casserole, this dish is ideal to serve for a dinner party. Boiled new potatoes and broccoli or spinach may accompany this dish.*

6 SERVINGS

2½ oz. [⅝ cup] flour

½ teaspoon salt

½ teaspoon black pepper

2 lb. beef fillet or lean beef sirloin, cut into thin strips

1½ oz. [3 tablespoons] butter

1 tablespoon vegetable oil

1 large onion, finely chopped

3 shallots, finely chopped

½ lb. button mushrooms, sliced

16 fl. oz. [2 cups] beef stock

½ lb. tomatoes, blanched, peeled, seeded and finely chopped

4 fl. oz. [½ cup] Madeira

4 fl. oz. [½ cup] sour cream

Preheat the oven to moderate 350°F (Gas Mark 4, 180°C).

In a large bowl, mix the flour with the salt and ¼ teaspoon pepper. Toss the beef strips in the flour mixture to cover completely and shake off any excess seasoned flour.

Heat the butter and oil in a large, heavy frying-pan over high heat. Add the beef strips and cook for 3 minutes, shaking the pan to brown the meat on all sides. Using a slotted spoon, transfer the beef to a medium-sized ovenproof casserole.

Lower the heat and add the chopped onion and shallots to the frying-pan. Stirring occasionally, sauté them for 5 minutes. Add the mushrooms to the pan and cook for 3 minutes more.

Remove the frying-pan from the heat and spoon the mushroom mixture over the beef in the casserole. Add the beef stock, tomatoes and Madeira to the casserole. Add the remaining pepper and, if necessary, add more salt.

Cover the casserole and cook in the oven for 45 minutes.

To serve, spoon the beef and gravy on to warmed plates. Hand individual portions of sour cream for each person.

## Beef Marjoram Ring

*A variation of a meat loaf, the centre of this Beef Marjoram Ring may be filled with peas or sautéed mushrooms.*

4 SERVINGS

2 lb. minced [ground] beef
2 oz. [1 cup] fresh breadcrumbs
½ teaspoon freshly ground black pepper
3 teaspoons dried marjoram
1½ teaspoons salt
3 tablespoons chopped parsley
2 small eggs, lightly beaten
1 oz. [2 tablespoons] butter
1 onion, finely chopped
SAUCE
3 tablespoons vegetable oil
1 small onion, finely chopped
1 carrot, scraped and chopped
1 small celery stalk, finely chopped
1 tablespoon flour
1 pint [2½ cups] beef stock or stock made with a beef stock cube
2 teaspoons tomato purée
bouquet garni, consisting of 2 parsley sprigs, 1 thyme sprig and 1 bay leaf tied together
3 fl. oz. [⅜ cup] Madeira

Preheat the oven to moderate 350°F (Gas Mark 4, 180°C). Lightly oil a large ring mould.

In a large bowl, combine the beef, breadcrumbs, marjoram, salt, pepper, parsley and eggs together, mixing until they are well blended.

In a frying-pan, melt the butter over high heat. Add the onion, cook until it is soft, then stir into the beef mixture. Pack the mixture into the mould and bake in the oven for 2 hours.

While the meat loaf is baking, prepare the sauce. Heat the oil in a small saucepan.

Add the onion, carrot and celery and cook over low heat until the vegetables are tender and lightly coloured.

Add the flour and, stirring with a wooden spoon, continue cooking until the mixture is quite brown. Remove the pan from the heat and add the stock gradually, stirring continuously. Add the tomato purée and the bouquet garni. Cover the pan, return to the heat and simmer for 30 minutes.

Strain the sauce through a fine sieve, pressing the vegetables with the back of a wooden spoon. Rinse the pan and pour the sauce back into it.

Return the pan to the heat and bring the sauce to the boil. Add the Madeira and stir to mix. Remove from the heat and keep warm.

When the meat loaf is cooked, let it stand on a rack for 5 minutes. Run a knife around the edges and turn it out on to a warm serving dish. Fill the centre with peas or sautéed mushrooms. Serve the sauce separately.

## Beef with Olives

*Succulent and delicious, Beef with Olives is cooked on top of the stove in a frying-pan. The cooking time depends entirely on how you like your beef done. For rare beef, cook the meat for 30 minutes. For medium-rare, extend the cooking time by 15 minutes, making the overall cooking time 45 minutes. For medium well-done, cook the meat for 1 hour. Serve the beef with creamed potatoes and a crisp green salad.*

6 SERVINGS

12 oz. green olives, stoned
1 tablespoon butter
1 tablespoon olive oil
3 lb. sirloin steak,
½ teaspoon salt
⅛ teaspoon black pepper

If the olives are very salty, place them in a small bowl and cover them with boiling water. Leave them for 5 minutes, drain and set aside.

Heat the butter and oil in a large frying-pan. When the mixture is very hot, add the meat. Lower the heat to moderate and brown the meat for 7 minutes on each side. The meat should lie fat side down for the rest of the cooking. Add the olives, salt and pepper. Cover the pan with a lid or with aluminium foil, lower the heat and cook for 15 minutes if you want the meat to be rare. If longer cooking is required, add the olives only for the last 15 minutes of cooking. Cut the steak into thick diagonal slices and serve immediately.

## Beef Roll

*A cold, glazed galantine, this beef roll is attractive to look at and very tasty. It may be accompanied by various salads for a summer lunch or buffet supper. It also makes delicious sandwiches.*

6 SERVINGS

2 lb. beef, minced [ground]
½ lb. bacon, chopped or cut into very small pieces
1 onion, finely chopped
12 oz. [6 cups] fresh breadcrumbs
1 tablespoon chopped parsley
1 teaspoon dried basil
1 teaspoon ground allspice
2 teaspoons French mustard
3 teaspoons salt
½ teaspoon black pepper
2 eggs, lightly beaten
4 fl. oz. [½ cup] cider
4 oz. stuffed olives, cut in slices
6 pints [7½ pints] water
2 carrots, cut in halves
2 small turnips, cut in halves
1 celery stalk, cut in pieces
1 small onion, cut in half
bouquet garni, consisting of 4 parsley sprigs, 1 thyme spray and a small bay leaf tied together
MEAT GLAZE
½ oz. gelatine
10 fl. oz. [1¼ cups] beef stock
¼ teaspoon white pepper

In a large bowl, mix the beef, bacon, onion, breadcrumbs, parsley, basil, allspice, mustard, 1 teaspoon of salt and the pepper together. Add the eggs and enough cider to make the mixture hold together. Mix thoroughly, using your hands. Carefully stir in the olives.

On a wet board, shape the meat mixture into a roll. Fold a sheet of greaseproof or waxed paper in half and place the roll in the centre. Fold the paper round the meat and tie it at the ends. Dip a clean cloth in hot water and wring it out. Place the meat roll on the cloth, fold the cloth firmly round the meat and sew it, or tie it, in place.

Put the water in a large pan and add the carrots, turnips, celery, small onion, bouquet garni and the remaining 2 teaspoons of salt. Bring the water to the boil. Put the meat roll in the water, cover, reduce the heat to low and simmer for 2 hours.

Lift the meat roll out carefully. When it is cool enough to handle, pull the cloth tightly round the roll to make a neat, smooth shape. Refrigerate for at least 12 hours.

Remove the cloth and paper and place the meat roll on a serving dish.

To make the glaze, put the gelatine in a quarter of the stock, in a small pan over low heat, stirring with a wooden spoon until liquid is clear. Add the remaining stock and add the pepper.

Cool the stock-and-gelatine mixture in the refrigerator until it begins to thicken. Brush it over the meat roll, coating it at least 3 times. Serve the galantine cold, cut into thin slices.

## Beef in Sour Cream Sauce

*This spicy beef dish, an adaptation of a German recipe, is traditionally eaten with dumplings. It is, however, equally good served with noodles.*

4 SERVINGS

4 tablespoons flour
1 teaspoon salt
½ teaspoon freshly ground black pepper
2 lb. chuck steak, trimmed of fat and cut into cubes
2 oz. [¼ cup] butter
1 onion, chopped
2 garlic cloves, crushed

3 teaspoons paprika
1 teaspoon ground allspice
1 bay leaf
½ teaspoon ground cloves
16 fl. oz. [2 cups] beef stock
8 fl. oz. [1 cup] sour cream
1 tablespoon lemon juice
2 tablespoons Marsala

Mix the flour, salt and pepper on a plate. Roll the beef cubes in the flour mixture to coat them all over. Shake off the excess flour and reserve.

In a large frying-pan, heat the butter over moderate heat. When the foam subsides, add the beef cubes and brown them evenly on all sides. With a slotted spoon, transfer the cubes to a plate.

Add the onion and garlic to the pan and cook them until they are soft but not brown. Add the paprika, allspice, bay leaf and cloves and mix well until all the ingredients have blended. Pour in the beef stock and, stirring constantly, bring the mixture to the boil.

Return the beef cubes to the pan and cover. Reduce the heat to low and simmer for 2 hours, or until the meat is tender when pierced with a knife.

*A delicious, succulent, dinner party dish, Beef with Olives is cooked on top of the stove in a frying-pan and takes very little time to prepare.*

Transfer the meat to a plate and cover it with aluminium foil to keep it warm. Strain the pan liquids into a measuring jug, reserving 10 fluid ounces [1¼ cups] for the sauce. Discard any extra cooking liquid.

Put the reserved liquid into a medium-sized saucepan and bring it to the boil over moderate heat. Reduce the heat to low and simmer gently for a few minutes.

Mix the sour cream, lemon juice and the excess flour in a medium-sized bowl. Stirring continuously, add the simmering liquid, a little at a time, to the sour cream mixture. Mix well and pour back into the pan. Cook gently to thicken the sauce, but do not let it boil. Stir in the Marsala..Return the beef cubes to the saucepan, stir to mix. Allow the meat to heat thoroughly, but do not let the sauce boil.

Pour into a warmed dish and serve immediately.

151

## Beef with Spiced Lemon and Caper Sauce

*This is an unusual and easy-to-make beef dish which may be served with mashed or boiled potatoes and buttered peas.*

4 SERVINGS

2 lb. stewing beef, cut into 1½-inch pieces
2 teaspoons salt
2 teaspoons freshly ground black pepper
1 oz. [2 tablespoons] butter
1 garlic clove, crushed
3 large onions, thinly sliced
1 bay leaf
¼ teaspoon ground cloves
¼ teaspoon ground ginger
1 pint [2½ cups] beef stock or stock made with a beef stock cube
3 tablespoons fresh breadcrumbs, made from 1 thick slice black or pumpernickel bread
2 teaspoons capers, drained
2 tablespoons lemon juice
grated rind of ½ lemon

Rub the beef pieces with the salt and pepper. In a large, heavy saucepan, melt the butter over moderate heat. When the foam subsides, add the beef pieces to the pan, a few at a time, and brown them evenly on all sides. With a slotted spoon, transfer the beef pieces from the pan to a warmed plate.

Add the crushed garlic and onion slices to the pan and cook them for 7 minutes, or until they are soft but not brown. Stir in the bay leaf, cloves and ginger and mix until all the ingredients are thoroughly blended. Pour in the beef stock and, stirring continuously, bring the mixture to the boil over high heat.

Return the beef pieces to the pan and cover. Reduce the heat to low and simmer for 2 hours, or until the meat is tender when pierced with the point of a sharp knife.

With a slotted spoon, transfer the meat to a warmed serving dish and cover it with foil.

Remove and discard the bay leaf. Stir in the breadcrumbs, capers, lemon juice and lemon rind and bring the liquid to a boil over high heat. If there seems to be too much gravy, boil rapidly for 3 or 4 minutes, stirring continuously, to reduce it.

Otherwise, lower the heat and simmer gently, uncovered for 1 minute. Taste and add more seasoning if required.

Pour the sauce over the meat and serve immediately.

## Beefsteak and Kidney Pudding

*A traditional English meat pudding, Beef-steak and Kidney Pudding is a perfect main dish for a winter's meal. It should be brought to the table steaming hot with the basin wrapped in a white napkin. Served straight from the bowl, it may be accompanied by mashed potatoes and peas.*

6 SERVINGS

DOUGH
1 lb. [4 cups] self-raising flour
¼ teaspoon salt
8 oz. [1 cup] suet, shredded
10 fl. oz. [1¼ cups] water

FILLING
1½ lb. chuck steak, cut into ½-inch cubes
½ lb. ox kidney, cut into small pieces
2 tablespoons flour
¼ teaspoon salt
⅛ teaspoon black pepper
2 teaspoons chopped mixed herbs

Sift the flour and salt together into a large mixing bowl. Rub in the suet with your fingertips. Mix in the water and make a soft dough. Using your hands, knead the dough, lightly, on a floured board until smooth and elastic.

With a floured rolling pin roll out the dough to a large circle about ½-inch thick. Cut a triangle (about one-third of the diameter) out of the circle and reserve it. Line a 2½- to 3-pint pudding basin with the large piece of dough, dampen the edges from where the triangle was cut and bring them together. Press the dough to the shape of the basin and trim the top edges.

Fill a large saucepan with water and bring to the boil over moderate heat.

Using a large plate or a wooden board, roll the beef and kidney pieces in a mixture of the flour, salt, pepper and the mixed herbs. Coat all the pieces on all sides.

Put the meat into the lined basin and fill this up to two-thirds with cold water. Lightly knead the reserved piece and the trimmings of dough together and roll out to a circle large enough to cover the basin. Dampen the edges of the dough and place on top of the meat. Press the edges of the dough together to seal. Cover with lightly greased aluminium foil or a cloth, large enough to contain a 2-inch pleat across the centre. Tie a piece of string under the rim of the basin.

Put the basin into a steamer over the boiling water, cover with a lid and steam for 3 hours. Add more water when necessary. Before serving, remove the foil or cloth.

*For a Beefsteak and Kidney Pudding, cut a triangle out of the dough circle.*

*Coat the beef and kidney pieces with flour, salt, pepper and herbs.*

*Cover the bowl with aluminium foil and secure it with string.*

*Tie a piece of string over the top of the basin to form a handle.*

Line the basin with the pastry, bringing the cut edges together.

Lightly press the dough to the shape of the basin. Trim the edges.

Put the meat in the lined basin and fill it two-thirds full with water.

Place a circle of dough over the basin and press it into place.

## Beef Stew—I

*An old-fashioned, rich, meaty stew, this dish will improve in flavour if it is kept in the refrigerator for 24 hours and then reheated before serving. A filling main course for a winter dinner, it may be served with rice or thick rounds of crusty, country-style bread.*

4 SERVINGS

5 oz. [1¼ cups] sifted flour
1 teaspoon salt
⅛ teaspoon black pepper
2 lb. chuck steak, cut into 1-inch cubes
2 oz. [¼ cup] beef dripping
4 large onions, sliced
    boiling water
1 turnip, peeled and cut into cubes
12 medium-sized carrots, scraped and cut into quarters lengthways
4 celery stalks with leaves, cut into 2-inch pieces
12 small onions, peeled
12 very small, new potatoes, scrubbed and left whole
8 fl. oz. [1 cup] red wine
2 tablespoons chopped parsley

Put the flour, salt and pepper into a medium-sized bowl. Dip the meat cubes into the flour mixture, thoroughly coating them all over.

Melt the dripping in a large casserole over moderate heat. Add half the sliced onions and fry, stirring occasionally, for 10 minutes, or until they are browned. Remove the onions with a slotted spoon and set aside.

Increase the heat, put the meat cubes into the casserole, a few at a time, and brown them quickly on all sides, removing those that are browned before adding more.

When all the beef cubes have been browned, return them and the browned onions to the casserole. Pour in sufficient boiling water to cover the meat and onions by half an inch.

Add the remaining sliced onions, the turnip, half the carrots and the celery, stir, lower the heat, cover the casserole and simmer for 1 hour.

Add the remaining carrots, the small onions and the potatoes, stir, cover and simmer for a further 30 minutes.

Add the wine and stir to mix. Taste the stew and add more salt and pepper if necessary. If there is not enough gravy, add a little water and cook for a few minutes more.

If the gravy is too thin, make a *beurre manié* by blending 1 tablespoon butter with 2 tablespoons flour. Form the paste into tiny balls and stir these into the stew one at a time, shaking the pan to make each one dissolve.

Add the parsley to the stew, bring to a simmer, remove from the heat and cool before placing in the refrigerator for 24 hours. Reheat by bringing the stew slowly to the boil and serve hot.

## Beef Stew—II

*Marinated in wine and herbs and cooked with spices, this beef stew makes a tasty, one-dish main course.*

4 SERVINGS

2 lb. stewing steak, cut into 1-inch cubes
1 bay leaf
1 garlic clove, crushed
1 teaspoon salt
½ teaspoon freshly ground black pepper
8 fl. oz. [1 cup] red wine
2 tablespoons vegetable oil
10 fl. oz. [1¼ cups] beef stock
2 parsley sprigs
1 celery stalk, cut into 2-inch pieces
1 thyme spray
6 cloves
½-inch piece fresh ginger, peeled and cut into thin slices
12 small potatoes, peeled
cornflour [cornstarch]
1 teaspoon brown sugar
6 oz. canned water chestnuts, drained and sliced
12 small onions, peeled

Put the meat in a large mixing bowl with the bay leaf, garlic, salt, pepper and wine. Leave to marinate in a cool place for 6 hours or overnight.

Remove the beef cubes from the marinade with a slotted spoon and drain on kitchen paper towels. Reserve the marinade.

Heat the oil over moderate heat in a large, heavy pan. Add the meat and brown the cubes on all sides. Pour in the marinade and the stock. Tie the parsley, celery, thyme, cloves and ginger in a piece of cheesecloth and add, with the potatoes and sugar, to the pan. Lower the heat, cover the pan and simmer for 1½ to 2 hours, or until the meat is tender. Add the water chestnuts and onions and cook for another 35 minutes, or until the vegetables are tender when pierced with a sharp knife.

Remove the meat and vegetables from the pan with a slotted spoon and place in a warmed serving dish. Discard the bag of herbs and spices.

Measure the gravy in the pan. To every 10 fl. oz. [1¼ cups] of gravy use 1½

teaspoons of cornflour [cornstarch]. Mix it with a little cold water in a small bowl and add it to the gravy in the pan. Raise the heat and, stirring constantly, bring the mixture to the boil. Cook for 2 minutes. Pour the thickened gravy over the meat and vegetables.

## Beef Stock

*There is really no substitute for a well-flavoured, home-made beef stock. It is an essential ingredient in many dishes, sauces and soups, and is simple to make. Although the stock takes a long time to prepare, a large quantity can be made at one time and then stored in a freezer for future use. Properly covered, with the fat unskimmed from the top, stock can also be kept in the refrigerator for about 4-5 days.*

ABOUT 3 PINTS

3¼ lb. beef shin bone, chopped
2 onions, quartered
2 carrots, roughly chopped
1 large leek, white part only, thickly sliced
2 celery stalks, thickly sliced
2 oz. [¼ cup] beef dripping
5½ pints [7 pints] water, plus 10 fl. oz. [1¼ cups]
8 whole black peppercorns
1 bouquet garni
1 tablespoon salt

Preheat the oven to 475°F (Gas Mark 9, 240°C). Put the bones and vegetables in a roasting tin, dot with dripping and roast for 45 minutes, turning occasionally.

Transfer the contents of the tin to a stockpot and pour in 5½ pints [7 pints] water. Bring the additional water to the boil in the roasting tin, scraping the base and sides. Add to the pot.

Bring to the boil, skim off the surface scum, add the peppercorns, bouquet garni and salt and simmer gently, partially covered for 3 hours or until reduced to about 3 pints [3¾ pints].

Strain the stock through a colander, then through a fine sieve into a bowl. Leave for 5 minutes, then remove fat from surface.

## Beef Stroganov

BEEF IN SOUR CREAM SAUCE

*Created for a Russian nobleman at the end of the nineteenth century, Beef Stroganov is a pleasant, simple dish to serve for dinner. Although commercial sour cream can be used in this recipe, the most satisfactory results are obtained from fresh cream which*

*is allowed to stand in a warm place for about 24 hours. Serve this dish very hot accompanied by a green vegetable and buttered noodles or a potato purée.*

4 SERVINGS

1½ to 2 lb. fillet of beef
3 oz. [⅜ cup] butter
2 medium-sized onions, thinly sliced
½ lb. button mushrooms, washed and trimmed
8 fl. oz. [1 cup] sour cream
2 teaspoons French mustard
1 teaspoon salt
½ teaspoon freshly ground black pepper

Cut the beef fillet into strips 2-inches long and ¼-inch wide. Heat 4 tablespoons butter in a large, deep frying-pan over moderate heat. Add the onions and cook gently for about 5 minutes, or until they are just brown.

Add the mushrooms and cook for 3 minutes, adding a little more butter if necessary.

With a slotted spoon, remove the onions and mushrooms from the pan. Put them on a plate and set aside. Melt the remaining butter in the frying-pan over high heat. Add the beef strips and sauté for 4 minutes, turning the meat constantly.

Add the mushrooms and onions and the salt and pepper. Mix all the ingredients well and cook over low heat for 1 minute.

In a small bowl, mix the sour cream with the mustard. Stir the sour cream, a little at a time, into the beef and vegetables. When it is well blended, raise the heat and cook for 1 minute. Do not allow the sauce to boil. Serve immediately.

## Beef Tea

*Popular in the nineteenth century as a nourishing drink for invalids, Beef Tea went out of fashion when commercially prepared meat extracts and stock cubes became widely available.*

1 lb. shin or leg of beef
1 pint [2½ cups] cold water
⅛ teaspoon salt

Low Cal

Chop the beef very finely. Place in a large jam jar or stone jar with the water.

Cover the jar and place it in a deep pan containing water. Cook over a very low heat for 8 to 10 hours or, alternatively, put it in a very cool oven, 275°F (Gas Mark 1, 140°C) for 12 hours.

Strain through a sieve, add the salt, mix well and serve hot.

## Beef and Tomato Pie

*This savoury pie may be served as a main dish, accompanied by a green salad and a vegetable. It can also be served as a first course or, cut into wedges, with drinks.*

4 SERVINGS

PASTRY

6 oz. [1½ cups] flour

⅛ teaspoon salt

1½ oz. [3 tablespoons] butter

1½ oz. [3 tablespoons] vegetable fat

2 tablespoons iced water

FILLING

1 oz. [2 tablespoons] butter

12 spring onions [scallions], chopped

1 lb. minced [ground] beef

2 large tomatoes, blanched, peeled and chopped

1 teaspoon dried sweet basil

1 teaspoon salt

½ teaspoon ground black pepper

12 fl. oz. single [1½ cups light] cream

4 eggs

Preheat the oven to moderate 350°F (Gas Mark 4, 180°C).

Lightly grease a 9-inch pie dish and dust it lightly with flour.

Sift the flour and salt into a medium-sized mixing bowl. Put in the butter and vegetable fat and cut into the flour using a table knife. With your fingertips, rub the fat into the flour until the mixture resembles fine breadcrumbs.

Add 1 tablespoon of iced water and with a knife mix it into the flour mixture. Using your hands, pat and knead the dough lightly until it is smooth and elastic, adding the remaining tablespoon of iced water if necessary. Wrap the dough in greaseproof or waxed paper and refrigerate for 20 minutes.

To prepare the filling, melt the butter in a medium-sized frying-pan over moderate heat. Sauté the spring onions [scallions] for 3 minutes. Add the beef and continue cooking, stirring occasionally, until the meat is brown.

Stir in the tomatoes, basil, salt and pepper and continue cooking for 10 more minutes. Take the pan from the heat and set aside.

Remove the dough from the refrigerator. On a floured surface, roll the pastry into a shape 2-inches larger than the pie dish. Line the pie dish with the pastry, and prick it all over with a fork. Cover the bottom of the pastry with aluminium foil, greaseproof or waxed paper and weigh down with dried beans or rice. Bake in the oven for 10 minutes. Set aside.

In a small saucepan, heat the cream until it is hot but not boiling. Break the eggs into a medium-sized mixing bowl and beat them lightly with a fork. Beating continuously, gradually pour in the hot cream. Add to the meat mixture. Mix well and pour into the pastry shell. Bake in the oven for 30 minutes. Serve hot.

*Created for a Russian nobleman, Beef Stroganov is easy to make, elegant and delicious.*

155

## Beef Wellington
FILLET OF BEEF IN PASTRY

*This elegant beef dish, called Boeuf en Croûte in France, takes a lot of preparation, but it is well worth the trouble. Served hot with Madeira sauce and accompanied by freshly cooked broccoli and grilled tomatoes, it is an ideal main course for a dinner party. It may also be served cold for a buffet dinner.*

8-12 SERVINGS

PASTRY
1½ lb. [6 cups] sifted flour
1 teaspoon salt
8 oz. [1 cup] butter, cut into tablespoon pieces and chilled
8 oz. [1 cup] vegetable fat, cut into tablespoon pieces and chilled
1 egg, lightly beaten
4 fl. oz. iced water

FILLING
1 fillet of beef or 1 contrefillet, about 3 lb., with excess fat removed
1 tablespoon brandy
½ teaspoon salt
¼ teaspoon black pepper
6 slices streaky bacon

8 oz. pâté de foie gras
1 egg, lightly beaten

SAUCE
3 oz. [⅜ cup] butter
6 shallots, finely chopped
1 pint [2½ cups] beef stock
5 fl. oz. [⅝ cup] plus 4 tablespoons Madeira

Preheat the oven to very hot 450°F (Gas Mark 8, 230°C).

Sift the flour and salt into a medium-sized mixing bowl. Add the butter, fat, egg and water. With a table knife mix to a firm dough, which should be lumpy.

On a floured surface, roll out the dough into an oblong shape. Fold it in three and turn it so that the open edges face you. Roll again into an oblong shape and proceed as before. Repeat this once again to make three folds and turns in all. Wrap the dough in greaseproof or waxed paper and chill in the refrigerator.

Rub the fillet of beef all over with the brandy and season it with the salt and black pepper. Cover the top of the meat with the bacon slices. Place the meat on a rack in a roasting tin and bake it in the oven for 15 minutes if you want the meat rare and 5 minutes longer for medium.

Take the meat out of the oven and remove and discard the bacon. Leave the beef to cool. When the beef has cooled to room temperature, spread the pâté over the top and sides. Lower the oven to hot 425°F (Gas Mark 7, 220°C).

On a floured board, roll the dough out into a rectangle about 18-inches long, 12-inches wide and about ¼-inch thick. Place the meat top side down on the pastry with the long sides of the meat parallel to the long sides of the pastry. Wrap the meat in the pastry to make a neat parcel, trimming off the excess pastry from the short ends. Seal the joins in the pastry with a little beaten egg and press with your fingertips to seal them. Be careful not to wrap the meat too tightly because the pastry will shrink slightly during baking.

Put the pastry trimmings to one side. Place the pastry-wrapped meat on a baking sheet seam side down. Use a knife to mark the top with a criss-cross pattern. Brush the top and sides with a little beaten egg.

Press the pastry trimmings into a ball, roll the pastry out and cut it into strips, circles, diamonds or leaf shapes with the appropriate pastry cutter. Decorate the

*For Beef Wellington, spread the pâté over the top and sides of the cooked and cooled beef.*

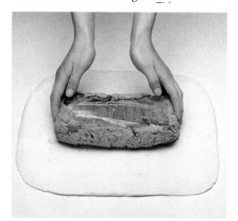

*Roll the dough into a rectangle and place the coated beef, top side down, in the centre.*

*With your hands, draw the long sides of the dough up to overlap on the beef.*

*Brush the edges of the dough with beaten egg and press them together to seal. Trim the ends.*

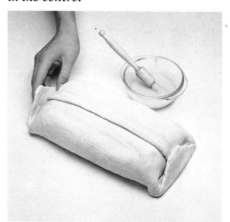

*Make an envelope fold at each end, brush the folds with beaten egg and press firmly to seal them.*

*Decorate the top with the pastry trimmings. Brush the top and sides with beaten egg.*

top of the pastry-wrapped meat with them. Brush with a little beaten egg.

Bake the meat in the oven for 30 minutes, or until the pastry is cooked.

While the meat is cooking, make the Madeira sauce. Melt 2 tablespoons butter in a medium-sized saucepan over moderate heat. Add the shallots to the pan and sauté them for 10 minutes, or until they are golden, stirring occasionally.

Pour in the stock and 5 fl. oz. [$\frac{5}{8}$ cup] of Madeira, and cook, stirring occasionally, for 30 minutes or until the sauce is reduced by half.

Strain the sauce through a sieve into a bowl. Pour it back into the saucepan and bring it to a boil.

Turn off the heat and, with a wooden spoon, stir in the remaining butter. Continue to stir until the butter has melted, then stir in the remaining Madeira. Pour the hot sauce into a warmed sauceboat and serve with the meat.

When the meat is finished cooking, turn the heat off and leave the meat to rest in the oven for 15 minutes before serving. To serve, carve the meat with a very sharp knife to minimize the pastry flaking.

## Beer

A brewed and fermented beverage made from malted barley or other starchy cereals, beer is flavoured with hops, the tiny blossoms of the hop vine. Malt beverages such as LAGER, STOUT, ALE and PORTER are classified as beer. Brewing and beer are as old as recorded history and were known to many ancient civilizations.

In general, beer contains between three and seven percent alcohol. The particular type of yeast used as the fermenting agent in the brewing process is what makes the difference between beers.

Every country that produces beer provides a variety of types and flavours. Denmark, for example, is famous for its lager and Ireland for stout.

Beer may be served any time. Its characteristic sharp tang complements highly flavoured or spicy dishes and such foods as hamburger, steak, corned beef and cabbage, Irish stew, sausage, cold meats, all pork dishes, fried dishes and grilled [broiled] lobster and oysters. All the sharper cheeses go well with beer or ale.

Beer is also used as an ingredient in many recipes, notably the Belgian dish, CARBONNADES FLAMANDES.

## Beer Soup

*Unusual and creamy, this German Beer Soup may be served with croûtons of fried bread or with slices of French bread.*

4 SERVINGS

1½ pints [3¾ cups] lager or light beer
2 tablespoons sugar
4 egg yolks
4 tablespoons sour cream
½ teaspoon ground cinnamon
½ teaspoon salt
⅛ teaspoon black pepper

Put the lager, or beer, and sugar into a large saucepan over moderate heat. Stir with a wooden spoon until the sugar has dissolved and then bring to the boil. Remove the saucepan from the heat.

Put the egg yolks into a small bowl and beat them lightly with a fork or a whisk. Beating continuously, add the sour cream a tablespoon at a time.

Put 4 tablespoons of the hot lager into the egg-and-sour-cream mixture and stir well.

Beating continuously, pour the contents of the bowl into the remaining lager. Sprinkle in the cinnamon, salt and

black pepper and stir to mix.

Return the saucepan to a very low heat and, stirring constantly, cook for a few minutes until the soup thickens. Do not allow it to boil.

Pour the soup into warmed bowls or a tureen and serve hot.

## Beetroot [Beets]

There are four main varieties of beetroot, which is the thick, fleshy root of a plant of the genus Beta. The white beetroot is the source of one-third of the world's sugar production. The red, bulbous, garden beetroot is cooked and served as a vegetable and is also used in salads. Another variety of beetroot is grown for its leaves, which are cooked and served as a green vegetable. Mangel-wurzer, another type of beetroot, is used as a food for livestock. In the United States, a beetroot is called a beet.

*An unusual contrast of colours and flavours, Beetroot and Orange Salad goes well with almost any cold meat.*

## Beetroot and Apple Salad

*This unusual salad of raw, grated beetroot and apple, with a piquant horseradish dressing, may be served with other salads for a vegetarian meal or as an accompaniment to cold roast meat.*

4 SERVINGS

3 raw medium-sized beetroots
3 medium-sized cooking apples
2 oz. [⅓ cup] sultanas or raisins
1 tablespoon horseradish sauce
3 tablespoons vegetable oil
1½ tablespoons wine vinegar
1 teaspoon sugar
½ teaspoon salt
½ teaspoon freshly ground black pepper

Peel the beetroots and coarsely grate them into a salad bowl. Core the apples and coarsely grate them into the salad bowl. Mix in the sultanas.

Make the dressing by mixing all the remaining ingredients in a small bowl. Pour the dressing over the salad, toss lightly and serve.

## Beetroot, Boiled

Small beetroots have a better flavour than very large ones. To boil beetroots, wash them well in cold water to remove the soil. Be careful not to damage the skin and the roots or, when boiling, the beetroots will 'bleed' and lose their colour.

Trim off the leaves but do not cut off the beard or top roots. If the skin or a root is cut, seal it by singeing quickly over a flame.

Put the beetroots in a large saucepan of boiling salted water, cover and simmer for 1 to 4 hours, according to size, until tender. To test that the beetroots are cooked, do not prod with a fork as this will cause 'bleeding'. Take a root out of the water and press it gently with your fingers. If the skin rubs off, the beetroot is cooked.

When the beetroots are tender, drain them well and peel by rubbing off the skin and roots. Slice off the top.

## Beetroot with Cream Sauce

*Beetroot served in a cream sauce makes a good accompaniment to roast chicken and grilled [broiled] fish.*

4 SERVINGS

1 oz. [2 tablespoons] butter
1 oz. [4 tablespoons] flour
8 fl. oz. [1 cup] chicken stock
1 small onion, finely chopped
½ teaspoon dried dill
½ teaspoon salt
¼ teaspoon white pepper
4 fl. oz. single [½ cup light] cream
6 medium-sized beetroots, cooked, peeled and sliced
1 tablespoon chopped parsley

Melt the butter in a saucepan over low heat. With a wooden spoon, stir in the flour and cook for 1 minute. Remove the pan from the heat and slowly pour in the stock, stirring continuously.

When all the stock has been added and the sauce is smooth, return the pan to the heat. Stirring continuously, bring the sauce to the boil and cook for 3 minutes, or until the sauce is smooth and has thickened. Add the onion, dill, salt and pepper and cook for 5 minutes.

Add the cream and, stirring constantly, simmer the sauce for 3 minutes. Gently mix in the beetroot slices. Make sure that all the slices are coated with the sauce. Cook over low heat for 3 minutes to heat thoroughly. Pour the beetroots and sauce into a warmed vegetable dish and sprinkle with chopped parsley.

Serve hot.

# Beetroot and Onion Salad

*This salad makes a refreshing and tasty accompaniment to cold meats, chicken or fish.*

4 SERVINGS

6 medium-sized beetroots, cooked and drained
2 tablespoons cider vinegar
5 tablespoons olive oil
2 cloves
1 teaspoon sugar
¼ teaspoon salt
¼ teaspoon black pepper
1 large onion, very thinly sliced and separated into rings

Cool the beetroots, trim them and slip off the skins with a paring knife. With a sharp knife, cut the beetroots into thin slices and put them in a salad bowl.

Mix the vinegar, oil, cloves, sugar, salt and pepper in a cup.

Pour the mixture over the beetroots. Cover the bowl with aluminium foil or plastic wrap and place it in the refrigerator to chill for 1 hour.

Remove the bowl from the refrigerator, uncover it and mix in the onion rings.

Toss the salad well and remove the cloves before serving.

# Beetroot and Orange Salad

*This is a delicious salad of contrasting flavours, textures and colours.*

4 SERVINGS

6 medium-sized beetroots, cooked
2 large oranges
2 bunches watercress
DRESSING
4 tablespoons olive oil
1½ tablespoons wine vinegar
1 teaspoon prepared mustard
¼ teaspoon dried tarragon
½ teaspoon salt
½ teaspoon sugar

Peel and slice the beetroots into rounds. Grate the rind of 1 orange and set aside. Peel the oranges, carefully removing the white pith and slice them into rounds.

Wash the watercress and cut off the stalks. Arrange the watercress on a shallow serving dish.

Arrange the beetroot and orange slices alternately, overlapping, on the bed of watercress.

Mix all the ingredients for the dressing in a cup and add the reserved grated orange rind.

Spoon the dressing over the beetroot and orange slices just before serving.

# Beetroot in Orange Sauce

*This dish must be served as soon as the beetroots have been mixed into the sauce, otherwise they will bleed and dilute the sauce, spoiling its colour and consistency.*

4 SERVINGS

1 lb. cooked beetroot, peeled
1½ oz. [3 tablespoons] butter
1 oz. [4 tablespoons] flour
1 tablespoon brown sugar
10 fl. oz. [1¼ cups] orange juice
1 tablespoon grated orange rind
juice of ½ lemon
½ teaspoon salt

Cut the beetroots into small cubes and set aside.

Melt the butter in a small saucepan over moderate heat. Stir in the flour and mix to a smooth paste with a wooden spoon. Remove the pan from the heat and stir in the sugar.

Pour in the orange juice gradually, stirring all the time. When all the orange juice has been added return the pan to the heat.

Add the grated orange rind, lemon juice and salt and, stirring continuously, cook the sauce until it is thick. Taste the sauce and add more sugar, salt or lemon juice if necessary.

Add the beetroot cubes to the sauce, cook for a minute or two to heat and serve immediately.

*A marvellous accompaniment to cold meat, Beetroot Pickles will keep for many weeks in the refrigerator.*

# Beetroot Pickles

*Beetroot pickles make a good accompaniment to cold meats and other salads. Kept in the refrigerator in tightly covered jars, the pickles will keep for many weeks.*

ABOUT 3 PINTS

6 medium-sized beetroots
cold water
12 fl. oz. [1½ cups] wine vinegar
1½ tablespoons dry mustard
½ teaspoon salt
9 oz. [1⅛ cups] sugar
2 onions, sliced
2 teaspoons dill seeds

Boil the beetroots until they are tender. Drain and set aside, reserving 10 fluid ounces [1¼ cups] of the liquid. When the beetroots are cool, slice off the tops and bottoms. Then, using your fingers, slip off the skins. Slice the beetroots and set aside.

In a medium-sized saucepan bring the vinegar and reserved cooking liquid to the boil over moderate heat. Add the mustard, salt and sugar. Stir to mix, and bring to the boil again. Remove the saucepan from the heat and set aside.

Arrange the beetroot slices and onions

in layers in clean, screw-top jars. Add the dill seeds. Cover with the hot vinegar mixture. Tightly screw on the tops of the jars. Cool and place in the refrigerator. Allow the beetroot to stand for a few days before using. Serve very cold.

## Beetroot Piquante

*An accompaniment to cold meats, chicken, veal and ham pie or cottage pie, Beetroot Piquante is served hot. The vinegar, sugar and seasoning give the beetroot a slightly sharp flavour which contrasts well with bland meats.*

4 SERVINGS

3 medium-sized beetroots, cooked and drained
5 teaspoons vinegar
2 teaspoons sugar
1 teaspoon salt
½ teaspoon black pepper
1 tablespoon butter

Cool the beetroots, trim them and slip off the skins. Using a sharp knife, chop the beetroot into small pieces.

In a medium-sized saucepan, combine the beetroot cubes, vinegar, sugar, salt and pepper together. Warm the mixture over moderate heat, stirring continuously, until the beetroot pieces are very hot.

Remove the saucepan from the heat and, with a wooden spoon, stir in the butter a little at a time. Taste and add more seasoning if needed. Transfer to a warm serving dish.
Serve immediately.

## Beetroot in Sour Cream

   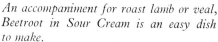

*An accompaniment for roast lamb or veal, Beetroot in Sour Cream is an easy dish to make.*

4 SERVINGS

6 beetroots, cooked, drained, peeled and sliced
4 fl. oz. [½ cup] sour cream
1 tablespoon horseradish sauce
2 teaspoons grated onion
¼ teaspoon salt
½ teaspoon black pepper
1 tablespoon chopped chives
1 teaspoon fresh dill

Put the sliced beetroot, sour cream, horseradish, grated onion, salt and black pepper in the top of a double boiler, or in a bowl over simmering water. Stirring occasionally, heat the beetroot mixture over the water on moderate heat until it is hot.

Turn the vegetable out into a warmed serving dish, garnish with the chopped chives and dill, and serve immediately.

## Beignet

Beignet (*bayn-yay*) is the French word for any piece of food which is dipped in a batter and fried in deep fat. Beignets should be light and are sometimes lighter than fritters, their English equivalent.

## Beignets d'Ananas

PINEAPPLE FRITTERS

*An easy-to-make dessert, Beignets d'Ananas (bayn-yay dah-nah-nah) is best made with fresh pineapple, although well-drained, canned pineapple slices may be substituted.*

6 SERVINGS

1 small pineapple
2 tablespoons sugar
2 tablespoons kirsch or rum
oil, for deep frying
2 tablespoons vanilla-flavoured sugar

BATTER

4 oz. [1 cup] flour
1 egg
1 egg yolk
1 tablespoon oil
5 fl. oz. [⅝ cup] milk
2 egg whites

To prepare the pineapple, cut off the crown. Slice across into 8 even slices. Cut the rind and eyes from each slice. Cut each slice in half and remove the core from the centre.

Place the slices in a bowl and sprinkle with the sugar and kirsch or rum. Leave in a cool place to macerate.

Sift the flour into a mixing bowl. Make a well in the centre and add the egg, egg yolk and oil, slowly incorporating the flour. Gradually add the milk and mix until smooth. Cover and chill for 1 hour.

Whisk the egg whites until stiff and fold into the batter.

Heat the fat in a deep-fat fryer to 375°F (190°C), or until a cube of bread turns golden brown in 40 seconds. Using a skewer, or a long-handled fork, dip the pineapple slices into the batter to coat thoroughly. Carefully drop the coated slices one by one into the hot fat.

Fry the pineapple slices on both sides, turning with a slotted spoon, until they are golden brown. Drain on absorbent paper for 1 minute and keep warm while frying the remainder. Sprinkle them with vanilla-flavoured sugar and serve hot, with cream, if desired.

## Beignets au Fromage

CHEESE FRITTERS

*Cubes of Gruyère cheese, dipped in a beer batter, deep fried and served piping hot, Beignets au Fromage (bayn-yay oh froh-mahj) is a delicious French hors d'oeuvre to serve with drinks. These beignets are also excellent cold.*

ABOUT 40 BEIGNETS

4 oz. [1 cup] flour
½ teaspoon dry mustard
¼ teaspoon salt
1 egg, lightly beaten
1 tablespoon vegetable oil
8 fl. oz. [1 cup] beer
1 egg white, stiffly beaten
1 lb. Gruyère cheese
vegetable oil for deep frying

Sift half of the flour, the mustard and salt into a medium-sized bowl. Make a well in the centre of the flour and pour in the beaten egg and the oil. With a wire whisk, beat the egg and oil, slowly incorporating the flour. Pour in the beer, a little at a time, and mix to a smooth batter. Cover and set the batter aside to rest for 1 hour.

Fold the stiffly beaten egg white into the batter. Cut the cheese into small cubes. Put the remaining amount of flour on to a large plate. Roll the cheese cubes in the flour and then dip them into the batter.

Heat the oil in a deep frying pan over high heat to 375°F on a fat thermometer or until a cube of bread becomes golden brown in 40 seconds. Drop the cheese cubes, a few at a time, into the pan and fry until they are brown. Remove the beignets with a slotted spoon and drain on kitchen paper towels.

## Beignets Soufflés

PUFFY FRITTERS

*Light, golden fritters, deep fried in oil, Beignets Soufflés (bayn-yay soo-flay) look like puffy doughnuts. Dust with sugar and serve hot with jam sauce or syrup.*

ABOUT 25 FRITTERS

8 fl. oz. [1 cup] water
3 oz. [⅜ cup] butter
4 oz. [1 cup] flour
3 eggs
1 tablespoon sugar
¼ teaspoon vanilla essence
vegetable oil for deep frying
raspberry jam or golden [light corn] syrup
juice of ½ lemon
4 tablespoons castor sugar

*Beignets Soufflés, crisp, golden fritters dusted with sugar, are a delicious hot dessert.*

Pour the water into a medium-sized saucepan, add the butter and bring to the boil over moderate heat. Take the saucepan off the heat and mix in the flour all at once, beating continuously with a wooden spoon until the batter reaches the consistency of creamed potatoes. Set aside for 45 minutes, or until the batter is cool.

When the batter is cool, drop in the eggs one at a time, beating them in with a kitchen fork. Add the sugar and vanilla essence, beating continuously until the batter is smooth.

Put a heavy, deep frying pan over low heat and fill it one-third with the vegetable oil. Do not allow the oil to get too hot.

Using a tablespoon, drop spoonfuls of batter into the hot, but not smoking, oil. Fry the beignets a few at a time. Slowly increase the heat and deep fry, turning

them over occasionally with a fork, or palette knife, for 5 to 6 minutes, or until the beignets are puffed up and golden in colour. Remove the fritters from the oil with a slotted spoon and drain them on kitchen paper towels.

Heat the jam or syrup in a small saucepan over moderate heat. Just before it comes to the boil, add the lemon juice and pour into a sauceboat.

Heap the fritters on a napkin placed on a warmed serving dish and sprinkle them with castor sugar. Serve hot.

## Bel Paese

Soft, smooth and mild, Bel Paese is a well-known Italian cheese. It is used as a table cheese as well as a melting cheese for cooking.

## Benedictine

Probably the oldest liqueur and certainly one of the most renowned, Benedictine was first made in 1510 as a medicinal elixir by a Benedictine monk at the

Fécamp monastery in Normandy. Today the secret of Benedictine's composition is so closely guarded that only three people know the exact formula. Benedictine has a base of Cognac and is flavoured with a variety of plants and herbs. The initials D.O.M., which are virtually its trademark, stand for *Deo Optimo Maximo* (To God, Most Good, Most Great). Benedictine mixed with brandy, called B. & B., makes a drier and less sweet drink.

## Bénédictine, à la

Consisting of a BRANDADE of cod and truffles, bénédictine (*bay-nay-deek-teen*) is a classic garnish for poached fish or eggs.

## Bergamot

Sometimes called bee balm, bergamot is a highly scented, North American herb of the mint family. The leaves and flowers of bergamot are used in salads. Bergamot leaves are also a popular flavouring for iced drinks.

*A hearty Norwegian soup, Bergens Fiskesuppe is an attractive combination of fish and vegetables.*

## Bergamot Sauce

*With its delicate sage and rosemary flavour, Bergamot Sauce is ideally served with roast pork. It makes an interesting alternative to the traditional apple sauce.*

MAKES ABOUT 4 FLUID OUNCES

1 oz. [2 tablespoons] butter
2 shallots, finely chopped
1 tablespoon flour
4 fl. oz. [½ cup] white wine
juice of ½ lemon
1 tablespoon chopped bergamot
leaves
½ teaspoon salt
¼ teaspoon white pepper

In a medium-sized frying-pan, melt the butter over moderate heat. When the foam subsides, add the chopped shallots. Fry for 4 to 5 minutes, or until the shallots are soft, but not brown. Add the flour to the pan, stir with a wooden spoon and cook for 2 to 3 minutes, or until the fat and flour are blended.

Slowly add the wine and lemon juice, a little at a time, stirring constantly. When the sauce has thickened slightly, stir in the bergamot leaves, salt and pepper. Cook the sauce for 2 to 3 minutes.

Pour into a warmed sauce boat and serve at once.

## Bergens Fiskesuppe

NORWEGIAN FISH SOUP

*A speciality of Bergen, Bergens Fiskesuppe (behr-gensk* FEES-keh-SOOP-peh) *is a flavourful fish soup.*

6 SERVINGS

STOCK
1 parsnip, roughly chopped
2 carrots, scraped and
roughly chopped
1 onion, sliced
1 potato, peeled and roughly
chopped
1 teaspoon salt
6 peppercorns
1 tablespoon chopped parsley
1 bay leaf
2 celery stalks with leaves, chopped
2½ lb. fish trimmings
5 pints [6¼ pints] cold water
SOUP
2 carrots, scraped and
finely chopped
1 turnip, finely diced
2 leek white parts, finely sliced
1½ lb. cod or haddock, boned and
in one piece
3 egg yolks
⅛ teaspoon salt
⅛ teaspoon black pepper
1 tablespoon chopped parsley
6 tablespoons sour cream

(Low Cal)

In a large, heavy pot, combine all the ingredients for the stock with the cold water. Bring to the boil over high heat. Cover the pan, lower the heat and simmer

gently for 30 minutes. Strain the stock through a fine sieve into a large bowl. With the back of a wooden spoon, press the fish trimmings and vegetables in the sieve to squeeze out as much liquid as possible.

Rinse the pan and return the strained stock to it. Place it over high heat and boil rapidly, uncovered, for about 20 minutes or until the stock is reduced to about 2½ pints. Strain once again through a fine sieve.

Return the stock to the pan. Add the carrots, turnip and leeks. Place the pan over high heat and bring it to the boil. Lower the heat and simmer, uncovered, for 10 minutes. Add the fish and simmer for another 5-10 minutes. Remove the pan from the heat and, using a slotted spoon, lift out the fish and set aside on a plate.

In a medium-sized mixing bowl, whisk the egg yolks. Gradually beat in about 4 fluid ounces of the hot soup. Beating all the time with a wire whisk, slowly pour the egg mixture into the soup.

Using a fork, separate the fish into flakes and add it to the soup. Add the salt and the pepper. Reheat the soup over low heat but do not let it boil.

Sprinkle with parsley and garnish each serving with 1 tablespoon of sour cream. Serve immediately.

## Berliner Eintopf

BERLIN STEW

*A tasty and satisfying stew, Berliner Eintopf (bair-*LEE*-nehr* INE*-tohf) is an ideal way to use leftover meat.*

4 SERVINGS

1½ oz. [3 tablespoons] butter
1 large onion, diced
3 potatoes, peeled and
finely chopped
½ lb. fresh green beans, sliced into
small pieces
2 carrots, scraped and diced
½ cabbage, cut into 4 wedges
15 fl. oz. [2 cups] meat stock
1 tablespoon tomato ketchup
1 teaspoon salt
⅛ teaspoon black pepper
1 teaspoon prepared mustard
breadcrumbs made from 1 slice
of bread
1½ lb. cooked meat (beef, veal or
pork) cut into thin strips or
small cubes
2 tablespoons chopped parsley

Melt the butter over moderate heat in a large, heavy saucepan. Sauté the onion in the butter for 5 minutes, stirring occasionally. Add the potatoes, beans, carrots and cabbage and sauté for 2 minutes. Add the meat stock, ketchup, salt, pepper and prepared mustard, and stir well.

Cover the saucepan, reduce the heat and simmer the stew for 40 minutes or until the vegetables are cooked.

Stir in the breadcrumbs and meat and cook for another 5 minutes.

Put the stew in a warmed serving dish, sprinkle with parsley and serve.

## Berry Torte

*This American Berry Torte is a combination of crushed digestive biscuits [graham crackers] and cream cheese with a topping of blueberries, loganberries, blackberries or blackcurrants. The sugar must be adjusted according to the tartness of the fruit. The following recipe is for blueberries, but if you use other fruit, the quantity of water should be slightly increased.*

6 SERVINGS

3 oz. [⅜ cup] plus 1 teaspoon butter, melted
6 oz. digestive biscuits [3 cups graham crackers], crushed
8 oz. [1 cup] sugar
1½ lb. full fat cream cheese
4 eggs
1 teaspoon lemon juice
2 teaspoons cornflour [cornstarch], mixed with 1 tablespoon water
2 teaspoons grated lemon rind
12 oz. blueberries
2 tablespoons water

Preheat the oven to moderate 350°F (Gas Mark 4, 180°C). Grease an 8-inch round cake tin with a removable bottom with 1 teaspoon of butter.

In a medium-sized mixing bowl, combine the crushed biscuits, 3 ounces [⅜ cup] sugar and the melted butter with a wooden spoon. Lightly press the crumbs into the buttered pan, covering the bottom and halfway up the sides of the pan evenly.

In a medium-sized mixing bowl, beat the cream cheese with a wooden spoon or a fork until it is smooth. Gradually beat the remaining sugar, eggs, lemon juice and half the lemon rind into the cheese, until it is a thick, smooth cream.

Pour the cream cheese mixture into the lined cake tin. Bake in the oven for 35 minutes. Leave the torte to cool and then chill it in the refrigerator overnight.

In a medium-sized mixing bowl, combine the berries, water, cornflour [cornstarch] mixture and remaining lemon rind. Pour the mixture into a saucepan and cook for 2 to 3 minutes over moderate heat stirring once or twice. Remove the mixture from the heat and leave to cool.

Spread the berry mixture evenly over the torte and serve.

---

*Cream cheese in a crumb crust and topped with fresh fruit, Berry Torte is a rich dessert or tea-time offering, and may be made with any berry.*

## Besugo al Horno
BREAM BAKED WITH POTATOES

*An extremely decorative Spanish dish, Besugo al Horno (beh-zoo-goh ahl ohr-noh) makes an elegant main course for a lunch or dinner party. Serve it with a light white wine such as Pouilly-Fuissé, Alsatian Riesling, Petit Chablis or Moselle.*

4 SERVINGS

2 bream, each about 2 lb.,
   cleaned but with heads and tails
   left on
1½ teaspoons salt
1 lemon, cut into 6 sections
2 small black olives
1 oz. [½ cup] fresh breadcrumbs
2 garlic cloves, finely chopped
1 tablespoon paprika
1 tablespoon finely chopped parsley
3 medium-sized potatoes, peeled
   and cut into ¼-inch rounds
⅛ teaspoon black pepper
8 fl. oz. [1 cup] water
3 fl. oz. [⅜ cup] olive oil

Preheat the oven to moderate 350°F (Gas Mark 4, 180°C).

Wash the fish under cold, running water and dry them thoroughly with kitchen paper towels. Sprinkle 1 teaspoon of salt over the fish and, with a very sharp knife, make three parallel, crossways cuts across each fish. The cuts should be about ½ inch deep, 3 inches long and 1½ inches apart. Insert a section of lemon, skin side up, into each cut and insert an olive in the eye socket of each fish.

In a small bowl, mix together the breadcrumbs, garlic, paprika and parsley. Spread the potato rounds evenly on the bottom of a large, shallow baking tin. Sprinkle them with the rest of the salt and the pepper. Pour the water over the potatoes. Place the fish on top of the potatoes. With a pastry brush brush the fish with the olive oil.

Sprinkle the breadcrumb mixture over the fish and bake it in the centre of the oven for 30 minutes or until the flesh is creamy, the skin crisp and the potatoes cooked.

Serve immediately.

## Betel Nut
The fruit of the areca palm, the ARECA NUT is known as the betel nut by the people of Asia almost all of whom chew it.

## Beurres Composés
Beurres Composés (*bur cum-poh-zay*), or compound butters, are butters into which various flavourings have been beaten. The flavouring is either crushed, beaten, mashed, purée in a blender, or pounded in a mortar and then added to well-creamed butter. The mixture is then, in some cases, passed through a sieve. It is usually chilled so that it hardens and may be cut into fancy shapes.

These savoury butters are used to flavour sauces and grilled fish or meat. They are also used to baste meat or fish during cooking, for filling sandwiches, hard-boiled eggs and as a spread for canapés.

## Beurre d'Ail
GARLIC BUTTER

*Use Beurre d'Ail (bur die) on grilled fish, steaks, lamb chops and canapés and to enrich sauces. Although the following recipe suggests the use of a pestle and mortar, you can crush the garlic in a garlic press and then mix it into well-creamed butter. The result, however, will not be as good, either in taste or texture.*

2 cloves garlic, unpeeled
2 oz. [¼ cup] butter

Drop the garlic into a small pan of boiling water. Return to the boil over high heat. Remove the pan from the heat and drain the garlic. Rinse the garlic in cold water and peel the cloves.

In a mortar, pound the garlic to a smooth paste. Add the butter, a little at a time, and continue pounding until the garlic and butter are completely mixed and smooth.

Put the mixture through a fine sieve, taste it and add a little salt if necessary.

Put the garlic butter in a small bowl, cover and chill.

## Beurre Bercy
BUTTER WITH SHALLOTS AND WINE

*An accompaniment to grilled meat and fish, Beurre Bercy (bur bair-see) may be served either spread on the meat or fish or separately. Ask your butcher to split a marrow bone in half and remove the marrow in one piece.*

3 oz. beef marrow
2 tablespoons finely chopped
   shallots
6 fl. oz. [¾ cup] white wine
3 oz. [⅜ cup] butter
2 teaspoons finely chopped parsley
1 teaspoon lemon juice
½ teaspoon salt

Dip a knife into hot water and finely dice the marrow. Drop the diced marrow into a small pan of boiling, salted water. Simmer for 2 minutes, drain and set aside.

Put the shallots and wine in a small frying-pan and bring the mixture to a boil over high heat. Lower the heat to moderate and cook, uncovered, until the liquid has reduced to about one-quarter. Set aside to cool.

In a small bowl, cream the butter with a wooden spoon until it is soft and fluffy. Mix it, a spoonful at a time, into the cool wine mixture. Beat well before adding the marrow, parsley, lemon juice and salt. Mix, cover and chill until the mixture hardens.

## Beurre au Citron
HOT LEMON-BUTTER SAUCE

*A hot butter sauce, Beurre au Citron (bur oh see-trawn) is an excellent accompaniment for boiled or grilled fish, asparagus and broccoli. This sauce should be served as soon as it has been made because hot butter sauces tend to turn oily and lose their creamy consistency when reheated. If you have to reheat this sauce, place it in a bowl, in another bowl of water which is just warm enough to prevent the butter from congealing. If the sauce does congeal it can be used in the same way as a cold butter mixture.*

2 fl. oz. [¼ cup] lemon juice
¼ teaspoon salt
⅛ teaspoon white pepper
6 oz. [¾ cup] chilled butter, cut into
   tablespoon pieces
3 tablespoons hot vegetable stock
   or hot water

In a small saucepan boil the lemon juice, salt and pepper over moderate heat until the juice is reduced to one-quarter.

Remove the saucepan from the heat and, using a wire whisk, beat in 1 piece of butter. When the butter is absorbed add another piece and continue whisking until the butter is absorbed. Return the pan to a very low heat and, whisking continuously, add the rest of the butter piece by piece. By the time the last piece of butter has been whisked in, the sauce should be thick and creamy. Remove the saucepan from the heat.

---

*A Spanish recipe, Besugo al Horno, bream baked with potatoes, is an economical and attractive main dish for a lunch or dinner party.*

Just before serving, whisk in the hot stock or water a teaspoon at a time. Taste the sauce and add more salt and pepper if necessary. Serve in a sauceboat.

## Beurre au Citron
COLD LEMON BUTTER

*Beurre au Citron (bur oh see-trawn) is a cold lemon butter which is used to garnish cold hors d'oeuvre. The term may also refer to a hot lemon butter sauce.*

6 oz. [¾ cup] butter
  rind of 1 lemon, finely grated
¼ teaspoon salt
¼ teaspoon white pepper

In a small bowl, beat the butter with a wooden spoon until it is well creamed. Beat in the lemon rind, salt and pepper. Push the mixture through a fine sieve. Cover and chill.

## Beurre de Crevettes à Froid
COLD SHRIMP BUTTER

*A flavouring for fish soups and sauces, Beurre de Crevettes à Froid (bur d' kreh-vet ah fwah) is also used as a garnish for hors d'oeuvre and cold fish.*

4 oz. cooked shrimps, peeled
4 oz. [½ cup] butter
1 tablespoon lemon juice
½ teaspoon salt

Place the shrimps in a mortar and pound well until they are finely crushed.

Beat the butter in a small mixing bowl until it is quite soft. Mix the pounded shrimps into the butter. Add the lemon juice and salt.

Push the mixture through a fine sieve and chill.

Alternatively, the shrimps, butter, lemon juice and salt can be put into a blender and blended to a smooth paste.

## Beurre de Crustacés
SHELLFISH BUTTER

*A delicate, well-flavoured pink-coloured butter, Beurre de Crustacés (bur d' crew-stah-say) is used to flavour and enrich fish sauces and soups, to stuff hard-boiled eggs, for canapés and as a sandwich spread. Shellfish butter is traditionally made in a large mortar, the shells of the shellfish pounded with the meat and the*

*butter to a smooth paste. The mixture is then pushed through a fine sieve. Although the result is a beautifully smooth and delicious paste, it takes a long time to make and the process is tedious. Extremely good results can be achieved, however, by making the shellfish butter in an electric blender.*

4 oz. whole, cooked shrimps,
  unpeeled or 8 oz. cooked shellfish
  surplus, such as legs, shells and
  eggs of various shellfish
4 oz. [½ cup] butter
½ teaspoon salt
¼ teaspoon white pepper

Chop the shrimps or the surplus shellfish into pieces and put half into an electric blender.

Melt the butter in a small saucepan over moderate heat. Pour half the butter over the shrimps and blend at high speed. When the mixture is well blended, turn it into a saucepan.

Blend the remaining shellfish and melted butter in the same way and add to the saucepan.

Place the saucepan over moderate heat and warm the mixture. Blend the mixture in the blender again and, if necessary, a third time.

Press the mixture, with the back of a wooden spoon, through a fine sieve into a bowl. Beat the sieved mixture well. Season with the salt and pepper and chill until the mixture hardens.

## Beurre d'Estragon
TARRAGON BUTTER

*Beurre d'Estragon (bur dess-trah-gawn) may be served as an accompaniment to grilled meats and fish, or used to enrich a sauce or soup.*

4 oz. [½ cup] butter
1 tablespoon lemon juice
2 to 3 tablespoons finely chopped
  fresh tarragon
¼ teaspoon salt
⅛ teaspoon white pepper

Cream the butter with a wooden spoon in a small mixing bowl until it is light and creamy. Drop by drop, beat the lemon juice into the butter. Then beat in the tarragon, salt and pepper.

Chill until firm.

## Beurre Manié
A French culinary term, Beurre Manié *(bur mahn-yay)* refers to a paste mixture

of equal parts of flour and butter which is one of the simplest and most satisfactory methods of thickening sauces, gravies and soups.

To make beurre manié, in a saucer blend 2 tablespoons butter and 4 of flour together with a wooden spoon. With your fingertips, form the mixture into small balls and, one by one, whisk them into the hot liquid to be thickened with a wire whisk. Bring the liquid to simmering point, still stirring, and simmer for 1 to 2 minutes to completely absorb the butter. If the liquid needs additional thickening, add more beurre manié.

## Beurre Marchand de Vins
SHALLOT BUTTER WITH RED WINE

*Beurre Marchand de Vins (bur mahr-shawn d' van) may be served with steaks, hamburgers or liver or used to enrich a brown sauce.*

2 tablespoons finely chopped
  shallots
3 fl. oz. [⅜ cup] red wine
2 tablespoons brown stock
½ teaspoon salt
¼ teaspoon white pepper
4 oz. [½ cup] butter
1 tablespoon chopped parsley
  juice of ¼ lemon

In a small saucepan, simmer the shallots, wine, stock, salt and pepper over moderate heat until the liquid has been reduced by half. Let the liquid cool.

Cream the butter in a small mixing bowl until it is light and creamy. Beat the butter, a tablespoon at a time, into the wine mixture. Mix in the parsley and the lemon juice. Taste the mixture and add more salt, pepper and lemon juice if necessary.

Chill the mixture before using it.

## Beurre de Moutarde
MUSTARD BUTTER

*Beurre de Moutarde (bur d' moo-tard) may be served with kidneys, liver, steaks or grilled fish. It may also be used to enrich a sauce.*

4 oz. [½ cup] butter
1 tablespoon prepared French
  mustard
¼ teaspoon salt
⅛ teaspoon white pepper
2 tablespoons fresh chopped
  parsley or fresh mixed herbs

In a small mixing bowl, cream the butter with a wooden spoon, until it is light and creamy. Beat the mustard, a teaspoon at a time, into the butter. Beat in the salt and pepper and parsley, or mixed herbs. Chill to allow the butter to harden before using it.

## Beurre Nantais
WHITE BUTTER SAUCE

*Warm, thick and creamy, Beurre Nantais (bur NAWN-tay) is traditionally served with pike, although it is equally delicious served with any boiled, baked or grilled fish. This sauce should be served as soon as it has been made because it tends to become oily and to lose its creamy consistency if it is reheated. If, however, you do have to reheat this sauce, place it in a bowl, in a bowl of water which is just warm enough to prevent the butter from congealing. If the sauce does congeal, it can be used in the same way as a cold butter mixture.*

3 fl. oz. [⅜ cup] white wine vinegar
3 fl. oz. [⅜ cup] dry white wine or lemon juice
1 tablespoon finely chopped shallots
¼ teaspoon salt
¼ teaspoon white pepper
12 oz. [1½ cups] chilled butter, cut into 24 pieces
lemon juice if necessary

In a medium-sized saucepan, boil the vinegar, wine or lemon juice, shallots, salt and pepper over moderate heat until the liquid is reduced to 1 tablespoon.

Remove the saucepan from the heat and, using a wire whisk, beat in 1 piece of butter. When the butter is absorbed, add another piece and continue whisking until it is absorbed.

Return the pan to a very low heat and, whisking continuously, add the rest of the butter, piece by piece. By the time the last piece of butter has been whisked in, the sauce should be thick and creamy. Remove the saucepan from the heat.

Taste and, if necessary, beat in additional seasoning and lemon juice. Transfer the sauce to a warmed bowl and serve at once.

---

*Beurres Composés, savoury compound butters, are used to flavour sauces, grilled fish and meat and as spreads. Beurre au Citron, Beurre de Crevettes à Froid, Beurre de Moutarde and Buerre à l'Oeuf are a few.*

## Beurre Noir
BROWN BUTTER SAUCE

*Despite its name, Beurre Noir (bur nwahr) should never be black. To avoid it looking black, the butter should first be clarified. It may be served with eggs, boiled or sautéed fish, vegetables, chicken breasts or calf's brains.*

6 oz. [¾ cup] butter
3 tablespoons chopped parsley
4 tablespoons wine vinegar or lemon juice
¼ teaspoon salt
¼ teaspoon black pepper

To clarify the butter, cut it into small pieces and place in a saucepan over moderately low heat. When the butter has melted, skim off the foam and pour the clear, remaining butter into a bowl. Discard the milky residue at the bottom of the pan. Rinse out the pan and strain the butter back into it.

Place the pan over moderate heat. The butter will foam and sputter for a few seconds and when it has stopped it will begin to brown. When the butter has turned a golden nut-brown, remove the pan from the heat and stir in the parsley. Pour the mixture into a bowl.

Pour the vinegar or lemon juice into the same saucepan and boil it over moderately high heat until it has reduced to 1 tablespoon. Stir the liquid into the browned butter. Add the salt and pepper to the mixture.

Place the bowl over hot water until ready to serve.

## Beurre à l'Oeuf
EGG YOLK BUTTER

*Beurre à l'Oeuf (bur ah lerf) may be used as a sandwich spread, for canapés, and to stuff hard-boiled eggs.*

4 oz. [½ cup] butter
4 egg yolks, hard-boiled and sieved
¼ teaspoon salt
¼ teaspoon white pepper
1 to 2 tablespoons chopped fresh chives

In a small bowl, beat the butter well with a wooden spoon until it is light and creamy.

Beat the sieved egg yolks into the butter and season with the salt and pepper and chives.

Chill the mixture until it hardens before using it.

## Beverage

A liquid refreshment of varying stimulation, the term 'beverage' covers the spectrum from soft drinks to liqueurs, from tea to wine, from infusions of herbs to beer, from coffee to whisky.

## Bharta

CURRIED AUBERGINE PUREE

*A spicy purée of aubergines, Bharta (BAR-tah) is a vegetable dish which is usually served as part of a North Indian meal. It is easy to make and very tasty.*

6 SERVINGS

2 lb. aubergines [eggplants]
1 lb. tomatoes, blanched, peeled and cut into pieces or 14 oz. canned peeled tomatoes, drained
2 teaspoons ground coriander
1 teaspoon ground cumin
1 teaspoon turmeric
2 tablespoons chopped coriander leaves
5 tablespoons clarified butter or vegetable oil
1 onion, finely chopped
2 garlic cloves, crushed
1½-inch piece fresh ginger, peeled and finely chopped
1 green chilli, finely chopped (optional)
1 teaspoon salt
juice of ½ lemon

*Low Cal*

Preheat the oven to moderate 350°F (Gas Mark 4, 180°C).

Wash, dry and cut the aubergines in half lengthways. Make 2 or 3 gashes in the pulp of each aubergine half. Place the aubergine halves pulp-side up in a baking dish. Cover with aluminium foil and bake in the oven for 1 hour.

When the aubergines are cool enough to handle, scoop the pulp from the skin with a spoon. Put the pulp into a medium-sized mixing bowl and discard the skins. Mash the pulp with a fork. Mix in the tomatoes, coriander, cumin, turmeric and 1 tablespoon of chopped coriander leaves. Stir to mix and set aside.

Heat the clarified butter, or vegetable oil, in a large frying-pan over high heat. Add the onion, lower the heat and, stirring frequently, fry for 8 minutes or until the onion is soft and translucent, but not brown. Add the garlic, ginger and chilli (if you are using it) and fry for another 5 minutes, still stirring.

Add the aubergine mixture and cook, stirring frequently, until the liquid has evaporated and the mixture is thick. Taste the mixture and add the salt if necessary. Put the bharta in a heated serving dish, squeeze the lemon juice over the top, sprinkle with the remaining chopped coriander leaves and serve.

## Bicarbonate of Soda

Also known as BAKING SODA and sodium bicarbonate, bicarbonate of soda is an ingredient in BAKING POWDER. Bicarbonate of soda is also used by itself as a raising agent in recipes involving sour milk or some acid factor like molasses, honey and spice, or where a darkening effect is desired, as in gingerbread and chocolate cake.

Bicarbonate of soda can be used to remove sour smells from stoves, refrigerators and cooking utensils.

## Bife à Portuguêsa

PORTUGUESE STEAK

*Portuguese dishes tend to be highly seasoned and this recipe for fillet steaks in red wine is no exception. If you prefer, you can use rump steak instead of fillet. Although less tender, it usually has more flavour. Bife à Portuguêsa (beef ah por-too-GAY-zah) is traditionally served with Batatas à Portuguêsa, arranged in a ring around the meat.*

4 SERVINGS

4 large garlic cloves, peeled, 2 crushed and 2 cut in half
1 tablespoon tomato purée
1 tablespoon red-wine vinegar
1 teaspoon salt
¼ teaspoon black pepper
4 fillet steaks, about 1-inch thick
2 oz. [¼ cup] butter
1 teaspoon thyme
2 large bay leaves
4 thin slices lean smoked ham (preferably prosciuto)
2 fl. oz. dry red wine
1 teaspoon lemon juice
1 lemon, cut into 6 slices

In a small bowl, mix the crushed garlic, tomato purée, vinegar, salt and pepper together. Coat the steaks with the garlic mixture, cover them and set them aside for 30 minutes.

In a large, heavy frying-pan, melt the butter over moderate heat. When the foam subsides, add the garlic halves, the thyme and the bay leaves to the pan. Cook them for 2 minutes, stirring continuously. Remove the garlic and the bay leaves and discard.

Add the steaks to the pan and fry over moderate heat for about 4 minutes on each side. Turn the steaks at 1 minute intervals, so that they brown quickly and evenly. The steaks should be brown on the outside, but pink in the centre.

Transfer the steaks to a heated serving dish and keep hot.

Roll up the ham slices and add them to the same frying-pan. Turning them frequently fry them over high heat for 2 minutes. Place a ham roll on each steak.

Carefully pour away almost all the fat from the pan. Add the wine and lemon juice to the remaining fat. Bring to the boil over high heat. Stir well and simmer gently for 1 minute.

Remove the sauce from the heat and pour over the steaks. Garnish with lemon slices. Serve at once.

# Biff à la Lindström

SWEDISH HAMBURGERS

*Most people think of smörgåsbord and meatballs when they think of Swedish food. But the cuisine of Sweden also includes hamburgers. They are, however, hamburgers with a difference, as this recipe for Biff à la Lindström (BEEF ah lah leend-STREWM) shows, and they may be served topped with fried eggs.*

4 SERVINGS

1½ oz. [3 tablespoons] butter
1 onion, finely chopped
2 lb. lean minced [ground] beef
1 small egg
1 tablespoon capers, drained and finely chopped
½ teaspoon paprika
1 teaspoon salt
¼ teaspoon black pepper
2 teaspoons white vinegar
2 tablespoons double [heavy] cream
3 tablespoons very finely chopped beetroot [beet]
1½ tablespoons vegetable oil

In a small pan, melt 1 tablespoon of butter over moderate heat. When the foam subsides, add the onion and fry it for 5 minutes, or until it is soft.

Put the onion in a large mixing bowl. Add the meat, egg, capers, paprika, salt pepper and vinegar. Mix well together with your hands. Moisten with the cream, stir in the chopped beetroot and shape the mixture into 4 large, round patties.

In a large, deep frying-pan gently heat the remaining butter and the oil. When the butter foam subsides, add the patties. Cook over moderate heat for 7 minutes on each side, or until they are deep brown on the outside.

Remove the hamburgers from the pan, drain well on kitchen paper towels, place them on a warmed serving dish and serve at once.

# Bifteck Haché au Vin Rouge

MINCED [GROUND] BEEF IN RED WINE SAUCE

*Hamburgers are thought to be traditionally American, but when served with a red wine sauce, they become unmistakably French. Bifteck Haché au Vin Rouge (beef-teck ah-shay oh van rooj) is easy to make (you can prepare the hamburgers beforehand and keep them in the refrigerator) and just the answer for a light lunch or supper. Serve with a green salad or grilled [broiled] tomatoes.*

4 SERVINGS

3 oz. [⅜ cup] butter, softened
1 large onion, finely chopped
2 lb. lean minced [ground] beef
1 egg, beaten
1 teaspoon salt
½ teaspoon black pepper
½ teaspoon dried oregano
¼ teaspoon dried marjoram
2 oz. [½ cup] flour
1 tablespoon oil
5 fl. oz. [⅝ cup] red wine

In a large frying-pan melt one-third of the butter over moderate heat. Add the onion and fry for 8 minutes or until soft but not brown.

Remove the onion from the pan with a slotted spoon and place in a large mixing bowl. Add the beef, another third of the butter, the egg, salt, pepper, oregano and marjoram to the onion and mix together with your hands. Taste and add more salt and pepper if necessary.

Form the meat mixture into patties approximately ¾-inch thick. Sprinkle the flour on a board and roll the patties lightly in it, coating them on all sides. Shake off the excess flour.

Put half the remaining butter and the oil in a frying-pan and place over moderately high heat. When the butter foam begins to subside, add the patties and fry for 3 to 4 minutes or more on each side, depending on whether you like your hamburgers rare, medium or well done. Arrange the hamburgers on a warmed serving dish and keep them hot while you prepare the sauce.

Pour the fat from the frying-pan. Add the wine to the pan and boil it rapidly over high heat until it has been reduced by half.

Cut the remaining butter into small pieces. Remove the frying-pan from the heat and briskly stir in the butter, piece by piece, letting one piece dissolve before adding the next.

When all the butter is melted, pour the sauce over the hamburgers and serve.

---

*Thick, meaty hamburgers topped with fried eggs, Biff à la Lindström is a tasty supper dish.*

## Bifteck Marchand de Vins

SAUTEED STEAK WITH RED WINE SAUCE

*This classic French dish has many variations and is served all over France. Here is the basic recipe. You may add mushrooms, bacon and tomatoes to the sauce if you wish. Bifteck Marchand de Vins (beef-teck mahr-shawn d'van) may be served with a mixed salad or a green vegetable and fried potatoes.*

6 SERVINGS

2½ lb. fillet of beef
2 tablespoons butter
1 tablespoon vegetable oil
SAUCE
2 tablespoons flour
1½ oz. [3 tablespoons] butter
1 tablespoon vegetable oil
2 tablespoons finely chopped
    shallots
1 garlic clove, crushed
10 fl. oz. [1¼ cups] red wine
10 fl. oz. [1¼ cups] beef stock
1 bay leaf
⅛ teaspoon thyme
1 teaspoon salt
⅛ teaspoon black pepper

Trim any excess fat from the beef and cut the meat into pieces about 2 inches

*Sautéed fillet steak in a herb-flavoured red wine sauce, Bifteck Marchand de Vins is a classic French dish.*

square and ½ inch thick. Dry well on kitchen paper towels.

Melt the butter and oil in a large frying-pan over moderate heat. Add the pieces of beef and fry for 2 to 3 minutes on each side, so that the outside is browned but the inside is still pink.

Remove the meat from the pan with tongs. Place in a warmed serving casserole and keep hot while you make the sauce.

In a small mixing bowl, make a beurre manié or flour-butter paste by creaming together the flour and 1 tablespoon of butter with a wooden spoon. Set aside.

In a large frying-pan, melt the remaining butter and the oil over moderate heat. When the foam subsides, add the chopped shallots and garlic and fry, stirring constantly, for 5 minutes, or until the shallot is soft.

Add the wine, beef stock, bay leaf, thyme, salt and the black pepper to the pan. Simmer over moderate heat until the sauce is reduced by half.

Remove the pan from the heat and, using a wire whisk, stir in the beurre manié a teaspoonful at a time, letting each

piece dissolve before adding the next.

When the paste is completely absorbed, return the pan to the heat and simmer for 1 minute over moderate heat, whisking gently. Remove the bay leaf. Pour the sauce over the meat and serve at once.

## Bifteck Sauté Bercy

SAUTEED STEAK WITH SHALLOT AND WINE SAUCE

*Cooked in a frying-pan and served with a sauce of white wine and shallots, Bifteck Sauté Bercy (beef-teck soh-tay bair-see) is a delicious way to serve steak. The steaks should be between ¾ to 1-inch thick and should weigh no less than 8 ounces each. The cooking time for medium-rare steaks is from 3 to 4 minutes on each side. A simple test is that when a little red juice oozes on the surface, the steak is done to medium-rare. Serve with steamed broccoli and sauté potatoes.*

4 SERVINGS

4 fillet steaks
1 teaspoon salt
1 teaspoon freshly ground black
    pepper
1½ oz. [3 tablespoons] butter
1 tablespoon oil

SAUCE

3 oz. [$\frac{3}{8}$ cup] plus 1 tablespoon
butter, softened
3 shallots, finely chopped
5 fl. oz. [$\frac{5}{8}$ cup] dry white wine
$\frac{1}{4}$ teaspoon salt
$\frac{1}{4}$ teaspoon black pepper
2 tablespoons chopped parsley

Trim the steaks of any excess fat and wipe them dry with kitchen paper towels. Season the steaks with the salt and pepper

Heat the butter and oil in a large frying-pan over moderately high heat. When the butter is hot and the foam begins to subside, add the steaks and sauté them for 3 to 4 minutes on each side.

Remove the steaks from the frying-pan and put them on a hot plate. Cover and keep them hot while you make the sauce.

Pour the fat out of the frying-pan. Add 1 tablespoon butter to the pan and melt it over moderate heat. Add the shallots and fry them for 1 minute. Pour in the wine and, stirring, boil rapidly until it is reduced to half. Take the pan off the heat and beat in the remaining butter a little at a time. When all the butter has been absorbed and the sauce thickened, add the salt, pepper and parsley.

Spoon the sauce over the steaks and serve immediately.

## Bifteck Sauté au Beurre

STEAK SAUTEED IN BUTTER

*Tender fillet steak sautéed in butter and covered with a wine sauce, Bifteck Sauté au Beurre (beef-teck soh-tay oh bur) is traditionally accompanied by sautéed mushrooms, tomatoes and sautéed or baked potatoes.*

4 SERVINGS

4 steaks, fillet or entrecôte, about
$\frac{1}{2}$ lb. each, cut $\frac{3}{4}$ to 1-inch thick,
trimmed of excess fat
1 teaspoon salt
$\frac{1}{2}$ teaspoon freshly ground black
pepper
3 oz. [$\frac{3}{8}$ cup] butter
1 tablespoon oil
5 fl. oz. [$\frac{5}{8}$ cup] red wine

Dry the steaks thoroughly with kitchen paper towels. Season each one with the salt and pepper.

Melt half of the butter and the oil in a large, heavy frying-pan over high heat. When the butter is hot and the foam begins to subside, put the steaks in the pan and sauté them for 4 minutes. If the fat begins to burn, reduce the heat.

Turn the steaks over and sauté them on the other side for another 4 minutes. The steaks are medium-rare when a little red juice begins to ooze from them.

If you prefer the steaks well-done, saute them for 1 to 2 more minutes on each side.

Transfer the steaks to a hot plate and cover with another hot plate to keep warm while you prepare the sauce.

Pour out the fat from the frying-pan. Add the wine to the pan and over a high heat, stirring continuously, boil for 2 minutes, or until the liquid is reduced by half. Remove the pan from the heat and stir in the remaining butter adding a small piece at a time. When the butter is completely absorbed, pour the sauce over the steaks and serve.

## Bien me sabe de coco

VENEZUELAN SPONGE CAKE

*A Venezuelan recipe, Bien me sabe de coco (bine may sah-bay day koh-koh), a light sponge cake with a coconut topping, may be served as a dessert for a lunch or dinner party or for a special tea.*

8 SERVINGS

CAKE

$\frac{1}{2}$ tablespoon butter
4 egg whites
$3\frac{1}{2}$ oz. [$\frac{3}{8}$ cup plus 1 tablespoon]
granulated sugar
4 egg yolks
4 tablespoons sweet white wine
4 oz. [1 cup] flour
$\frac{1}{2}$ teaspoon baking powder

COCONUT TOPPING

5 fl. oz. [$\frac{5}{8}$ cup] coconut milk made
with 1-inch slice of coconut
cream dissolved in boiling water
3 oz. [$\frac{3}{8}$ cup] castor sugar
3 egg yolks
7 fl. oz. [$\frac{7}{8}$ cup] sweet white wine
$\frac{1}{4}$ teaspoon cinnamon

Preheat the oven to moderate 340°F (Gas Mark 4, 180°C). Grease the inside of a shallow, 9-inch deep round cake tin with the butter.

In a large mixing bowl, beat the egg whites with a wire whisk, or rotary beater, until they form soft peaks. Beating continuously, gradually add the granulated sugar. Continue beating until the egg whites are stiff.

In another bowl, beat the egg yolks and the wine together with a wire whisk, or rotary beater, until the yolks have become thick and pale and the batter holds the shapes of a ribbon when the whisk is lifted.

Pour the egg-yolk mixture over the

beaten egg whites and, with a metal spoon, lightly cut and fold the egg yolks into the beaten whites. When the egg yolks have been thoroughly incorporated, sift the flour and baking powder on top of the mixture and continue to fold until all the flour and baking powder have been incorporated. This step should be done quickly and lightly or the cake will be heavy.

Pour the cake batter into the cake tin and bake in the centre of the oven for 25 minutes, or until a skewer comes out clean when inserted into the cake. Remove the cake from the oven and turn it out on to a cake rack to cool.

Put 5 fluid ounces [$\frac{5}{8}$ cup] of coconut milk and the sugar into a medium-sized saucepan and, over moderate heat, cook, stirring continuously, until the syrup reaches a temperature of 230°F on a sugar thermometer, or a small amount dropped into iced water hardens immediately into a thread. Remove the pan from the heat.

In a large bowl, beat the 3 egg yolks with a wire whisk, or rotary beater, until they are thick and pale. Beating continuously, add the hot coconut milk syrup and continue beating until thick. Set aside to cool.

Pour the wine into a bowl and stir in the cinnamon. Place the cooled cake on a serving plate and pour the cinnamon and wine mixture evenly over it. When the cake has absorbed the wine, cover it with the coconut cream. Chill the cake in the refrigerator for at least $\frac{1}{2}$ hour before serving.

If liked the cake base may be made the day before and stored in an airtight tin.

## Bigarade

The French name for the bitter, sour or Seville orange, this is a quite separate variety from the sweet orange. Although the fruit has more pips and a more sour juice than those of sweet oranges, the rind and blossoms are much more fragrant.

The traditional wedding orange-blossom is from the bitter orange tree, and was originally believed to be an aphrodisiac. The flowers are also used to make orange-flower water. The aromatic oils of the bigarade are used to make Dutch bitters, and are the base for orange-flavoured liqueurs such as curaçao, triple sec and Grand Marnier.

Marmalade was first made from barrels of bigarade oranges preserved in seawater which washed ashore off the Scottish coast of Dundee. Rather than waste the fruit, the thrifty Scots preserved the rinds in sugar. The best marmalade is still made from Seville oranges, but if they are unobtainable, half sweet oranges and half grapefruit can be used in the same way to produce a bitter – sweet marmalade.

## Bilberry

The bilberry is the dark-blue berry of a dwarf bush that grows wild in Europe, Asia and America. The tart, sweet bilberry is called a blueberry in the United States. Bilberries are used in jams, syrups, liqueurs and pies.

Bilberries are known as blueberries in Scotland and in parts of Britain they are called whortleberries.

## Bind

To bind is a culinary term which means to moisten a mixture with enough egg, cream, sauce or other liquid to hold it together.

## Bircher Muesli

*Created by Dr. Max Bircher-Benner of Switzerland as a complete meal, Bircher Muesli (beer-ker mews-lee) is a delicious and wholesome fruit and oatmeal dish. Although it was not originally intended as a breakfast food, it is usually served as such today. It may, however, also be served as a dessert. The following recipe is for an apple muesli, which is the best for texture and flavour, but other fruit, such as pineapple, banana or berries, may be substituted if desired. If the muesli is being served as a dessert, the following recipe will make 2 servings.*

1 BREAKFAST SERVING

1 tablespoon oatmeal, soaked
   overnight in 2 tablespoons of milk
   juice of 1 lemon
   juice of 1 orange
1 large tart apple
1 tablespoon honey
1½ tablespoons double [heavy] cream
1 tablespoon chopped nuts
1 tablespoon raisins

Put the soaked oatmeal in a small serving bowl. Mix in the lemon juice and the orange juice. Grate the whole apple, including the peel and core, into the bowl. Mix it quickly into the juice to prevent the apple from discolouring. Stir in the honey and cream. Sprinkle the top with the nuts and raisins and serve.

## Bird's Nest

The nests of the salangane, a type of swallow or swift, are particularly enjoyed by the Chinese. The salangane makes its nest in the coastal grottoes of China and the East Indies, building it with its own thick, glutinous saliva, rich in protein. Salangane nests are added to soup, where they impart a rich and spicy flavour.

## Bird's Nest Soup

*Probably the best known of all Chinese dishes, Bird's Nest Soup is one of the tastiest and most expensive of Oriental dishes. The edible birds' nests are available at most Chinese food stores.*

4 SERVINGS

4 birds' nests
2½ pints [6¼ cups] chicken stock
1 teaspoon salt
½ teaspoon white pepper
4 oz. [½ cup] cooked
   chicken, finely shredded
4 slices ham, finely chopped
¼ teaspoon monosodium glutamate

*(Low Cal)*

Soak the birds' nests for 12 hours in warm water in a medium-sized bowl, changing the water once or twice. Remove any protruding feathers from the nest with tweezers.

Bring the chicken stock to the boil over high heat in a large saucepan. Add the salt and pepper and drop the birds' nests into the boiling stock. Reduce the heat to low, cover the pan and simmer for 20 minutes.

Stir in the chicken, ham and monosodium glutamate. Continue simmering for 1 minute, then remove the pan from the heat. Pour the soup into a heated tureen and serve at once.

## Birnbrot

PEAR BREAD

*The Swiss are famous for their cakes and pastries. Birnbrot (beern-broht), a pear tea bread, is usually accompanied by steaming cups of hot chocolate. If dried*

*pears are not available, you can use canned or fresh pears, well drained and diced.*

ONE LARGE LOAF

BREAD
2 oz. [¼ cup] plus 1 teaspoon sugar
5 fl. oz. [⅝ cup] lukewarm milk
1 tablespoon dried yeast
10 oz. [2½ cups] flour
⅛ teaspoon salt
2 oz. [¼ cup] plus 1 tablespoon
   butter
1 egg, lightly beaten
   beaten egg and milk for glaze
FILLING
8 fl. oz. [1 cup] water
8 oz. [1⅓ cups] dried pears, coarsely
   chopped
4 oz. [⅔ cup] stoned, dried prunes,
   coarsely chopped
2½ oz. [½ cup] seedless raisins
   juice of ½ lemon
2 oz. [½ cup] walnuts, chopped
2 tablespoons sugar
2 tablespoons kirsch
   grated rind of 1 lemon
¼ teaspoon ground cinnamon
¼ teaspoon ground nutmeg
1½ tablespoons dry red wine

In a small bowl, dissolve 1 teaspoon of sugar in the lukewarm milk. Sprinkle the yeast on the milk and stir to mix. Let the mixture stand in a warm, draught-free place for about 10 minutes, or until the yeast bubbles up and the mixture almost doubles in bulk.

Sift the flour, salt and the remaining sugar into a large, warm mixing bowl. Rub 2 ounces [¼ cup] butter into the flour mixture with your fingertips. Make a well in the middle of the flour mixture and pour in the yeast and the lightly beaten egg. Stir to mix with a wooden spoon. Then, using your hands, lightly knead and pat the dough into a ball.

Turn the dough out on to a lightly floured surface and knead for 10 minutes, sprinkling the surface with a little extra flour when necessary to prevent the dough from sticking.

Shape the dough into a ball and place it in a large, greased bowl. Cover the bowl with a cloth and place it in a warm, draught-free place for 45 minutes or until the dough doubles in bulk.

While the dough is rising, prepare the filling. In a small saucepan bring the water to the boil. Add the pears, prunes, raisins and lemon juice to the water and, stirring frequently, simmer over low heat for 10 minutes, or until the fruit is tender and can be mashed easily with the back of a spoon.

Drain the fruit thoroughly. Purée it in a blender or rub it through a strainer with the back of a spoon. Stir the walnuts, sugar, kirsch, grated lemon rind, cinnamon and nutmeg into the fruit purée.

When the ingredients are well mixed, stir in the wine a little at a time. The purée should be very thick, so add the wine with caution.

Using a pastry brush, evenly coat a large baking sheet or Swiss-roll tin with the remaining tablespoon of butter.

Lightly dust a piece of greaseproof or waxed paper, which is about 18-inches square, with flour. Punch the dough to get rid of air pockets. Transfer it to the paper. Knead the dough lightly and roll it into a square about $\frac{1}{4}$-inch thick.

With a palette knife, spread the filling over the dough, covering it smoothly to within 1 inch of its edges. Fold the edges over the filling and roll the dough like a Swiss [jelly] roll using the paper to lift the dough.

---

*A favourite Swiss bread, Birnbrot is filled with a rich mixture of kirsch, red wine, dried fruit, nuts and spices.*

Transfer the roll to the buttered baking sheet and lightly prick the outside surface all over with a fork. Put the roll in a warm place to rise for about 1 hour.

Preheat the oven to fairly hot 400°F (Gas Mark 6, 200°C).

Brush the top, sides and ends of the bread with the egg-and-milk mixture. Bake in the middle of the oven for 10 minutes, then turn the oven down to moderate 350°F (Gas Mark 4, 180°C), and bake for a further 50 minutes, or until the crust of the bread is golden and crisp.

Transfer the bread to a wire cake rack to cool. Serve at room temperature.

## Birnensuppe
PEAR SOUP

*Fruit soups are popular in Germany and Scandinavia. Birnensuppe* (BIRN-en-zoop-peh) *is a refreshing, easy to prepare first course for a summer meal.*

4 SERVINGS

2 lb. firm dessert pears, peeled, cored and diced
1 pint [2½ cups] water
½ teaspoon aniseed or ⅛ teaspoon crushed anise
2-inch piece cinnamon
3 oz. [⅜ cup] sugar
2 oz. [⅓ cup] seedless raisins
5 fl. oz. [⅝ cup] medium sweet sherry or Madeira

Put the pears into a medium-sized pan and cover them with water. Add the aniseed and cinnamon and gently poach the pears over low heat for about 40 minutes, or until they are tender.

Place a strainer over a large bowl and force the softened pears through it with the back of a wooden spoon. Add sugar to taste. Chill the soup in the refrigerator for 3 hours.

Put the raisins in a medium-sized bowl and cover them with the sherry or Madeira. When the soup has chilled, stir in the raisins and liquid and serve in small chilled bowls.

# Biryani

SPICED RICE WITH LAMB

*A North Indian dish of Moghul origin, Biryani (bir-yah-nee) is a fragrant mixture of meat, spices, nuts and saffron rice. The traditional meat in a Biryani is lamb, but today prawns, chicken or other meats are also used by Indian cooks. It is a main dish, the quantity of lamb being double that of the rice, and so it may be served alone with a yogurt salad or as a part of a much larger and elaborate Indian meal, consisting of other meat and vegetable dishes with chutneys and pickles.*

6 SERVINGS

8 tablespoons clarified butter or cooking oil
2 garlic cloves, crushed
1-inch piece fresh ginger, peeled and finely chopped
¼ teaspoon cayenne pepper
1½ teaspoons cumin seeds
2 lb. lean lamb, boned and cut into 1 inch cubes
4-inch piece cinnamon
10 cloves
8 peppercorns
1 teaspoon cardamom seeds
10 fl. oz. [1¼ cups] yogurt
2 teaspoons salt

1 lb. [2⅔ cups] basmati rice, washed, soaked in cold water for 30 minutes and drained
½ teaspoon saffron threads soaked in 2 tablespoons boiling water for 10 minutes
2 onions, thinly sliced
1½ oz. [⅜ cup] almonds, blanched and slivered
1½ oz. [⅜ cup] pistachio nuts
2 oz. [⅓ cup] sultanas or raisins

*A fragrant Indian dish of lamb, spices, nuts and saffron rice, Biryani is served with a yogurt salad.*

In a large pan, heat 4 tablespoons clarified butter, or cooking oil, over moderate heat.

Add the garlic, ginger, cayenne pepper and cumin seeds to the pan. Fry for 3 minutes. Raise the heat, add the lamb cubes and fry well for 10 or 15 minutes, or until the meat is browned lightly on all sides. Stir in the cinnamon, cloves, peppercorns, cardamom, yogurt and 1 teaspoon of salt. Mix well and add 5 fluid ounces [⅝ cup] of water. Bring the mixture to the boil. Lower the heat, cover the saucepan and simmer for 35 minutes or until the lamb is tender.

In a large saucepan, bring 3 pints of water to the boil. Add the remaining salt and pour in the drained rice. Boil briskly for 1½ minutes. Take the pan off the heat, drain the rice thoroughly and set aside.

Preheat the oven to moderate 350°F (Gas Mark 4, 180°C).

Pour 1 tablespoon of clarified butter or oil into a large ovenproof casserole dish. Put one-third of the parboiled rice in the bottom of the casserole. Sprinkle one-third of the saffron water over it. With a slotted spoon, remove one-third of the lamb cubes from the saucepan and put them over the rice. Put in another third part of the rice sprinkled with saffron water.

Remove all the remaining meat cubes from the pan with a slotted spoon and put them on top. Finish with a last layer of the remaining rice. Pour all the liquid left in the saucepan in which the lamb was cooked carefully over the rice and meat. Sprinkle the remaining saffron water over the top layer of rice. Cover the casserole well, using aluminium foil to seal it. Place the casserole in the oven and cook for 20 to 30 minutes, or more until the rice is cooked and has absorbed all the liquid.

In a small frying-pan, heat 3 tablespoons of clarified butter or oil over high heat. Add the onions, lower the heat to moderate and, stirring frequently, fry for 10 minutes, or until they are golden brown. With a slotted spoon, remove the onions and set aside on kitchen paper towels to drain.

Add the almonds, pistachio nuts and sultanas to the pan, adding more clarified butter or oil if necessary. Fry them for 3 minutes, or until the nuts are lightly browned. Remove the nuts and sultanas with a slotted spoon and set aside on a plate.

Pile the rice and lamb attractively on a large heated serving dish and sprinkle the top with the nuts, sultanas and onions.

Serve immediately with a chilled yogurt salad.

# Biscuit

The word 'biscuit' is derived from the Old French 'béscuit' which means 'twice-cooked'. 'Biscuit' originally described small, flat, flour cakes which were baked twice to ensure their crispness. The term now covers a great variety of confectionery, both sweet and savoury.

Home-made biscuits are usually made from a firm dough of fat, flour, sugar and various flavourings which is rolled or cut into small, flat portions and baked until crisp.

In the United States, the biscuit is a soft, small, unsweetened cake, made from leavened dough, which resembles a scone.

# Biscuit Crust

SWEET PASTRY

*This is a sweet rich shortcrust pastry suitable for fruit or jam tarts, flans or pies. If the sugar is omitted, this pastry may be used for savoury flans and pies.*

TWO 8-INCH TARTS

5 oz. [⅝ cup] plus 1 tablespoon butter
8 oz. [2 cups] self-raising flour
1 tablespoon flour
⅛ teaspoon salt
1 tablespoon castor sugar
1 egg, beaten and mixed with 1 tablespoon cold water

Preheat the oven to fairly hot 400°F (Gas Mark 6, 200°C). Prepare two 8-inch flan tins by greasing them with 1 tablespoon of butter and dusting them with 1 tablespoon of flour. Set aside.

Sift the self-raising flour and the salt into a medium-sized mixing bowl. Cut the butter into the flour with a table knife. With your fingertips, rub the butter into the flour until the mixture resembles fine breadcrumbs. Mix in the sugar. Make a well in the centre of the flour mixture and pour in the beaten egg and water. Mix quickly with the knife and then with your fingers to make a firm dough.

Put the dough on a floured board and knead lightly until smooth.

Form the pastry into a ball. Cover it and chill for 20 minutes.

Divide the pastry into two equal portions. Roll one portion out on a floured board into a circle about ¼-inch thick and 2-inches larger than the flan tin. Using your rolling pin, lift the pastry on to the tin and press it down well to fit the bottom and sides of the tin. Roll over the top of the tin with a rolling pin to cut off the surplus pastry. The edge of the

pastry may be left plain or pinched with your fingers to flute the edges. Line the other flan tin in the same way.

Bake blind or fill the pastry shells with the desired filling and bake in the oven for 30 to 40 minutes.

# Biscuit fin au Beurre

FRENCH SPONGE CAKE

*One of the easier French cakes to make, Biscuit fin au Beurre (bees-kwee fan oh bur) is a fine, light sponge cake which may be served plain, dusted with icing [confectioners'] sugar or split into two layers, filled with a buttercream and iced.*

ONE 10-INCH CAKE

2 oz. [¼ cup] plus ½ tablespoon butter, melted
3 oz. [¾ cup] plus 2½ tablespoons flour
4 eggs, separated
4 oz. [½ cup] castor sugar
1 teaspoon vanilla essence

Preheat the oven to moderate 350°F (Gas Mark 4, 180°C). Lightly grease a round cake tin, 10-inches in diameter and 2-inches deep, with ½ tablespoon butter. Sprinkle the tin with flour, knocking out any excess. Set aside.

In a medium-sized mixing bowl, beat the egg yolks and sugar together with a wooden spoon until the mixture is pale yellow and thick.

In another mixing bowl, whip the egg whites with a wire whisk or rotary beater until they stand in firm peaks.

Using a metal spoon, fold the egg whites into the egg-yolk-and-sugar mixture, sifting the flour in at the same time. Then quickly mix in the butter and vanilla essence.

Turn the mixture into the cake tin. Bake for 35 to 40 minutes, or until the cake has risen and is lightly browned.

Remove the cake from the oven and leave it in the tin for 6 to 8 minutes.

Run a knife around the edge of the tin and reverse the cake on to a wire cake rack, giving the tin a light tap on the bottom.

If the cake is not to be iced, immediately turn it over so that the puffed side is uppermost. Leave to cool for about 1 hour before icing or serving.

# Bishop

A hot or mulled wine which is popular in northern European countries, Bishop, or Bischof, is usually made with a basis of wine and flavoured with orange, cinnamon, cloves and anise.

## Bishop's Bread

*An interesting and unusual fruitcake, Bishop's Bread is made without butter and has a sponge-like texture. It may be served plain or sliced and spread with butter.*

ONE 9-INCH CAKE

1 teaspoon butter
5 oz. [1¼ cups] plus 1 tablespoon flour
4 eggs
4 oz. [½ cup] castor sugar
¼ teaspoon salt
2 oz. [⅓ cup] candied peel, chopped
2 oz. [⅓ cup] glacé cherries, chopped
3 oz. [¾ cup] shredded almonds
2½ oz. [⅓ cup] chocolate bits

Preheat the oven to moderate 350°F (Gas Mark 4, 180°C). Grease a 9-inch cake tin with the butter. Lightly coat the cake tin with 1 tablespoon of flour.

In a medium-sized mixing bowl, beat the eggs and sugar together with a wire whisk until the mixture is pale yellow and makes a ribbon trail on itself when the whisk is lifted. With a metal spoon, fold in 4 ounces [1 cup] of flour.

In a small bowl, combine the remaining flour with the salt, candied peel, cherries, almonds and chocolate bits. Fold the fruit-and-flour mixture into the egg mixture. Pour into the tin. Bake for 40 to 45 minutes, or until a skewer inserted into the cake comes out clean.

Remove the cake from the oven and turn out on to a wire cake rack.

## Bismarck Herring

A pickled and spiced herring, Bismarck Herring is served as an hors d'oeuvre with brown bread and butter.

## Bisque d'Homard

LOBSTER BISQUE

*A bisque is a thick shellfish soup, generally made from a purée of lobster or crayfish. Bisque d'Homard (beesk doh-mahr) is a rich, delicious lobster soup.*

4 TO 6 SERVINGS

2 x 1½ lb. lobsters
3½ oz. [⅜ cup plus 1 tablespoon] unsalted butter
2 celery stalks, finely chopped
1 carrot, scraped and finely chopped
2 shallots, finely chopped
⅛ teaspoon thyme
⅛ teaspoon cayenne pepper
⅛ teaspoon white pepper
⅛ teaspoon salt
3 tablespoons brandy
8 fl. oz. [1 cup] dry white wine
1 pint [2½ cups] fish stock
1 tablespoon sherry
1 pint [2½ cups] milk
2 oz. [½ cup] flour
4 tablespoons double [heavy] cream

If you buy live lobsters, insert a sharp knife between the body and tail of each lobster to sever the spinal cord. (This will kill the lobster.) Place the lobster on its back and split it open to the end of its tail. Spread the body open and remove the small sac at the back of the head and the coral (red roe) if there is any. Discard the sac, but reserve the coral.

Melt 1½ ounces [3 tablespoons] of

*Rich and creamy Bisque d'Homard is a perfect start for a formal dinner party.*

butter in a deep pan over moderate heat. When the foam subsides, add the celery, carrot, shallots, thyme, cayenne pepper, white pepper and salt. Cook for 8 minutes, stirring constantly with a wooden spoon, until the vegetables are soft but not brown.

Add the lobsters to the vegetables in the pan. Cook over high heat for 2 to 3 minutes, turning them frequently with a large spoon.

Heat 2 tablespoons of brandy in a ladle. Set the brandy alight and pour into the saucepan. When the flames have died out, add the wine and stock. Cover and simmer over low heat for 20 minutes.

Remove the lobsters from the pan and place them on a plate. When they are cool, remove the meat from the shells. Cut the meat up very finely, add the sherry and coral to the meat, mix well and set aside.

Pour the contents of the pan through a sieve. Return the liquid to the pan. Mash the vegetables through the sieve with the back of a wooden spoon into the pan. Set aside.

Crush the shells in a blender or mortar and pestle. Add the crushed shells to the stock and wine in the saucepan and simmer over low heat for 25 minutes. Strain the stock through a sieve and set it aside.

In a small saucepan, scald the milk (bring to just under boiling point). Take off the heat and set aside.

In a large saucepan, melt the remaining butter over moderate heat. Add the flour and stir to mix with a wooden spoon. Remove the pan from the heat and mix in the hot milk, a little at a time, stirring continuously, until the mixture is smooth.

Return the pan to the heat, and, still stirring, bring the mixture to the boil.

Add the stock and puréed vegetables to the sauce in the pan. Cover and simmer for 30 minutes.

Raise the heat and, when the soup is bubbling vigorously, add the cream. Stir to mix and add the lobster meat mixture and the remaining brandy. Taste the soup and add more salt and pepper if necessary.

This soup may be reheated but it must not be boiled again, because this will impair its delicate flavour.

## Bistecca alla Fiorentina

GRILLED [BROILED] MARINATED STEAK

*Bistecca alla Fiorentina* (bee-STEKH-kah AHL-lah fee-oh-ren-TEE-nah) *is a traditional Italian dish. It may be served with a salad or green vegetable.*

*Bistecca alla Pizzaiola is a colourful Neapolitan dish of steak with a tomato, garlic and olive sauce.*

---

4 SERVINGS

2 lb. T-bone, sirloin or round steak, cut 1-inch thick
1 teaspoon salt
1 teaspoon freshly ground black pepper
3 tablespoons olive oil
3 tablespoons red wine vinegar
1 bay leaf
1 teaspoon thyme
2 garlic cloves, crushed
1 teaspoon dried oregano
2 tablespoons chopped parsley
5 fl. oz. [⅝ cup] dry red wine

Place the steak in a long, shallow dish. Mix the olive oil, vinegar, bay leaf, thyme, garlic, oregano, parsley and wine in a small bowl. Pour the marinade over the steak. Cover and leave at room temperature for 5 hours or in the refrigerator for 8 hours. Turn the steak and baste every hour or so.

Preheat the grill [broiler] to its highest temperature.

Remove the steak from the dish and discard the marinade. Pat the steak dry with kitchen paper towels because the meat will not brown if it is too damp. Sprinkle the pepper on to the steak.

Grill [broil] the steak for about 4 minutes on each side or longer depending on whether you like your steak rare, medium or well-done.

Transfer the steak to a heated serving dish, sprinkle with salt and serve.

## Bistecca alla Pizzaiola

PAN-GRILLED STEAK WITH TOMATOES AND GARLIC

*A famous Neapolitan dish, Bistecca alla Pizzaiola* (bee-STEHK-kah AHL-lah peedz-eye-YOH-lah) *is a tasty way of cooking rump or porterhouse steak.*

4 SERVINGS

6 tablespoons olive oil
1½ lb. fresh tomatoes, blanched, peeled and coarsely chopped
1¾ teaspoons salt
½ teaspoon black pepper
1 teaspoon dried oregano
1 teaspoon dried basil
2 garlic cloves, crushed
4 oz. green olives, stoned and quartered
4 rump or porterhouse steaks, not less than ½ lb. each

In a medium-sized pan, heat half the oil over moderate heat. Add the tomatoes, ¾ teaspoon of salt, ¼ teaspoon of black pepper, the oregano, basil, garlic and olives to the pan. Cover the pan and simmer the sauce gently for 15 minutes, stirring occasionally.

Dry the steaks with kitchen paper towels and rub them with the remaining salt and pepper.

Heat the remaining oil in a large frying-pan over moderate heat until it is very hot. Add the steaks to the pan and brown them for 2 to 3 minutes on each side.

Spread the sauce over each steak, cover the pan and cook for a further 5 minutes. Serve immediately.

177

## Bitkis

MEAT PATTIES IN TOMATO SAUCE

*An ideal main dish to serve for a family lunch or supper, Bitkis are economical and easy to prepare. This Russian dish may be accompanied by buttered noodles and a green vegetable.*

4 SERVINGS

SAUCE

1 oz. [2 tablespoons] butter
1 oz. [4 tablespoons] flour
15 fl. oz. [1⅞ cups] beef stock
1 lb. tomatoes, blanched, peeled and chopped or 14 oz. canned tomatoes
    bouquet garni, consisting of 4 parsley sprigs, 1 thyme spray and 1 small bay leaf tied together
⅛ teaspoon black pepper
½ teaspoon salt
5 fl. oz. [⅝ cup] sour cream

BEEF PATTIES

1½ lb. lean, minced [ground] beef
1 onion, finely chopped
1 tablespoon chopped parsley
3 x ½-inch slices bread, cut into small pieces
3 fl. oz. [⅜ cup] water
1 egg yolk
½ teaspoon salt
¼ teaspoon black pepper
4 tablespoons vegetable oil

To make the sauce, melt half of the butter in a medium-sized, heavy saucepan over moderate heat. With a wooden spoon, stir in the flour. Stirring continuously, cook the flour-and-butter mixture for 3 minutes. Still stirring, gradually add the stock and cook the sauce for 5 minutes or until it is smooth and thick.

Add the tomatoes, bouquet garni, black pepper and salt. Stir well. Cover the saucepan and reduce the heat to very low. Simmer the sauce for 40 minutes stirring occasionally.

Remove the bouquet garni and, with the back of a wooden spoon, force the sauce through a sieve into a bowl. Stir in the remaining butter and the sour cream and place the sauce to one side.

Preheat the oven to moderate 350°F (Gas Mark 4, 180°C).

Put the beef, chopped onion and parsley in a medium-sized bowl. Put the bread in another bowl and pour on the cold water. With your hands, squeeze out as much water as possible from the bread. Add the dampened bread to the beef mixture.

Put the ingredients through a mincer [grinder]. Return them to the bowl. Mix in the egg yolk, ½ teaspoon of salt and the black pepper. With floured hands, shape the beef mixture into 8 slightly flattened patties.

Heat the vegetable oil in a heavy frying-pan over moderate heat. Fry the beef patties for 3 minutes, or until they are brown, then turn them over and fry them for a further 3 minutes, adding more vegetable oil if necessary. With a slotted spoon, transfer the beef cakes to an ovenproof dish or casserole and cover them with the tomato sauce. Bake in the oven for 20 minutes. Serve immediately.

## Bitokes

HAMBURGERS WITH CREAM SAUCE

*Hamburgers are, of course, delicious on their own, but served with a smooth cream sauce, as in this Russian recipe for Bitokes* (bee-tohk), *they become a little more special.*

4 SERVINGS

2 oz. [¼ cup] butter, softened
1 medium-sized onion, chopped
1½ lb. minced [ground] beef
½ teaspoon salt
¼ teaspoon black pepper
¼ teaspoon thyme
2 eggs
8 oz. [2⅔ cups] dry breadcrumbs
1 tablespoon vegetable oil

SAUCE

2 fl. oz. [¼ cup] beef stock
4 fl. oz. single cream [½ cup light cream]
⅛ teaspoon grated nutmeg
½ teaspoon lemon juice
¼ teaspoon salt
¼ teaspoon freshly ground black pepper
1 tablespoon butter

Melt 2 tablespoons butter in a small frying-pan over moderate heat. Add the onion to the butter and fry for about 5 minutes, or until it is soft and translucent. Remove the onion from the pan with a slotted spoon and place in a large mixing bowl.

Add the beef, 2 tablespoons of the butter, the salt, pepper, thyme and 1 egg to the onion in the mixing bowl. Using your hands, mix the ingredients together until they are completely blended. Taste and correct the seasoning if necessary.

Form the meat into patties about ¾-inch thick. Beat the remaining egg and dip each patty into it. Coat the patties with the breadcrumbs.

Put the remaining butter and the oil in a large frying-pan and heat over moderately high heat. When the butter foam subsides, fry the patties for 2 to 3 minutes or longer on each side, depending on whether you like your hamburgers rare, medium or well-done. Remove the hamburgers from the pan and transfer them to a warmed serving dish. Keep hot while you make the sauce.

Pour the fat from the frying-pan. Add the stock to the pan and boil it rapidly over high heat, until it has been reduced by half.

Add the cream to the stock. Boil rapidly for 1 to 2 minutes, or until it has thickened slightly. Season with the nutmeg, lemon juice, salt and pepper.

Remove the pan from the heat. Stir in the tablespoon butter. When the butter is completely absorbed, spoon the sauce over the hamburgers and serve.

## Bitters

Bitters are highly scented and flavoured mixtures of varying alcoholic strength. Aromatic bitters are used as apéritifs and digestifs. Flavouring bitters are used to add flavour to various drinks, such as cocktails. Most bitters of repute are made from formulae which are kept closely guarded secrets. Bitters are the result both of infusion and distillation processes applied to aromatic plants, seeds, herbs, barks, roots, and fruits, all carefully blended on a spirit base. Bitters are usually sold under the name of the substance that has been used to give the predominant flavour, such as orange or peach bitters. The best known bitter is probably ANGOSTURA.

## Black Bean Casserole

*This bean casserole makes an unusual and tasty accompaniment to barbecued spareribs or baked ham. If you do not want to soak the beans overnight, you can boil them for* 4 *minutes and soak them for only* 2 *hours.*

4 SERVINGS

1 lb. dried black beans
1 large onion, chopped
2 garlic cloves, crushed
3 celery stalks, diced
1 carrot, diced
    bouquet garni, consisting of 1 parsley sprig, 1 thyme spray and 1 small bay leaf tied together
1 teaspoon salt
¼ teaspoon black pepper
1½ oz. [3 tablespoons] butter
6 fl. oz. [¾ cup] dark rum
5 fl. oz. [⅝ cup] yoghurt

Put the beans in a bowl, cover them with water and soak them overnight.

*Black beans, rum, celery, carrot, onion and sour cream combine to make this unusual casserole.*

Drain the beans and put them in a saucepan. Cover them with 2½ pints [6¼ cups] of cold water. Add the onion, garlic, celery, carrot, bouquet garni, salt and black pepper.

Bring the beans and vegetables to a boil over moderately high heat. Reduce the heat to low, cover and simmer for 2 hours, or until the beans are almost tender. Discard the bouquet garni.

Preheat the oven to moderate 350°F (Gas Mark 4, 180°C).

Put the beans and all the liquid in a large bean pot or ovenproof casserole. Blend in the butter and half of the rum. Cover the casserole and bake in the oven for 2 hours or until the beans are completely tender. Stir in the remaining rum, top with the yoghurt and serve immediately.

## Black Bean Soup

*A meal in itself, Black Bean Soup is thick and filling and a good dish to serve in mid-winter.*

8 SERVINGS

1 lb. black-eye beans
1 medium-sized onion, finely chopped
2 celery stalks, coarsely chopped
1 bay leaf
1 small bacon [pork] hock
4 pints [5 pints] cold water
¼ teaspoon black pepper
salt, if necessary
4 hard-boiled eggs, coarsely chopped
2 tablespoons red wine vinegar
2 tablespoons chopped parsley
1 lemon, cut into wedges

*(Low Cal)*

Put the beans in a colander and wash them under cold, running water. When the water runs clear, drain the beans and put them in a large saucepan or flameproof casserole.

Add the onion, celery, bay leaf and bacon hock. Pour in the water and bring to a boil over high heat. Remove the scum as it rises to the surface. When the scum stops rising, reduce the heat to low and simmer for 3 hours, or until the beans are soft.

Remove the bacon hock, reserving the meat for another meal or sandwiches, and discard the bone. Remove and discard the bay leaf. Purée the soup in a blender or rub it through a strainer with the back of a wooden spoon.

Pour the puréed soup back into the pan. If it is too thick, add a little water. Taste the soup and add the black pepper and, if necessary, a little salt.

Return the pan to moderate heat and bring the soup to a simmer. Stir in the eggs and vinegar. Pour the soup into a warmed tureen. Sprinkle with the chopped parsley. Serve with the lemon wedges.

## Blackberry

Blackberries are the fruit of a bush which grows wild in hedgerows and woods. They are cultivated all over the temperate zone of the Northern Hemisphere and also known as brambles.

The round berries, about $\frac{1}{2}$-$\frac{3}{4}$ inch in diameter, should be shiny purple-black in colour, soft and juicy and easily pulled off the stem. To prepare the fruit, discard any stems and leaves, rotten or under-ripe berries and wash and dry well. Whether picked fresh or bought in punnets, they should be cooked or eaten the same day, as they spoil rapidly.

The season for picking blackberries is late summer, but they can be fozen or cooked and enjoyed all the year round. Open-freeze for the best results, then pack in polythese bags or containers. Alternatively, dry pack the fruit, layering with sugar in rigid containers, leaving a $\frac{1}{2}$-inch headspace. Frozen on their own, blackberries are best stored for 6 months,

however, if frozen with sugar, puréed or stored in a medium syrup they will keep for up to a year.

Blackberries are also made into wines, spirits and liqueurs, particularly in Europe.

They make delicious hot or cold desserts as well as preserves. Cooked purée is the basis for fools, mousses, ice-creams, sorbets [sherbet] and sauces.

## Blackberry and Apple Pie

*Made with shortcrust pastry, this traditional single crust, English fruit pie may be served with fresh double [heavy] cream or custard sauce.*

6 SERVINGS

6 oz. [1½ cups] **flour**
1 tablespoon castor [superfine] **sugar**
3 oz. [6 tablespoons] **butter, cut into small pieces**
2 tablespoons iced water
**lightly whipped sweetened cream, to serve**

FILLING

1 lb. **blackberries**
¾ lb. **cooking apples, peeled, cored and sliced**
4 oz. castor [½ cup superfine] **sugar**
2 tablespoons **water**

For the pastry, put the flour and sugar into a bowl. Rub in the butter until it resembles breadcrumbs, then stir in the water to make a firm dough. Knead into a ball, cover and chill for 20 minutes.

Preheat the oven to fairly hot 400°F (Gas Mark 6, 200°C) and place a shelf above centre.

Meanwhile, layer the blackberries, apple slices and 7 tablespoons of sugar in a 1½-pint pie dish, forming the filling into a dome in the centre. Gradually pour in the water.

Roll out pastry on a lightly floured surface to a circle 2 inches larger than the pie dish. Cut a strip around the edge and press it on to the rim of the dish. Dampen the rim of the pastry and cover with the pastry lid sealing the edges well. Trim off the extra pastry and flute around edge.

Lightly brush the top of the pie with water and sprinkle with the remaining sugar.

Bake for about 30 minutes or until golden brown. Serve hot or cold with lightly whipped sweetened cream, double [heavy] cream or custard sauce.

## Blackberry Bounce

*A refreshing and delicious drink, Blackberry Bounce may be served hot or cold.*

2½ PINTS

2 pints [5 cups] **cooked, strained blackberry juice**
8 oz. [1 cup] **sugar**
10 fl. oz. [1¼ cups] **brandy**

Pour the blackberry juice into a large saucepan and add the sugar. Stir with a wooden spoon and cook over low heat until the sugar is dissolved. Raise the heat and bring to the boil. Boil for 5 minutes, stirring occasionally. Skim off any scum that rises to the surface of the juice.

Allow to cool for 10 minutes and stir in the brandy. Serve hot or cold.

## Blackberry Fool

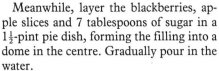 

*This simple summer dessert is a particular favourite with children.*

4 SERVINGS

1 lb. **blackberries**
2 fl. oz. [¼ cup] **water**
4 oz. [½ cup] **sugar**
10 fl. oz. **double cream [1¼ cups heavy cream], chilled**

Put the blackberries, water and sugar in a medium-sized saucepan. Cover the saucepan and stew the blackberries over low heat for 30 minutes or until pulpy.

With the back of a wooden spoon, rub the blackberries through a strainer into a bowl. Leave to cool.

*Made with shortcrust pastry, **Blackberry and Apple Pie** is a traditional English summer dessert.*

*Rum-flavoured chocolate and a creamy vanilla custard, Black Bottom Parfait is a mouth-watering dessert.*

Put the chilled cream into a bowl and beat it with a wire whisk until it begins to thicken and stiffen.

Fold the blackberries into the cream. Pour the blackberry fool into individual dessert glasses or one serving bowl. Put in the refrigerator to chill for at least 1 hour before serving.

## Black Bottom Parfait

*'Black bottom' describes a dessert which literally has just that: chocolate custard at the bottom of the dessert, topped with a delicious vanilla or contrasting custard. These two-tiered chocolate and vanilla parfaits make a mouth-watering dessert for a lunch or dinner party. They are easy to make and very attractive.*

4 SERVINGS

- 2 teaspoons cornflour [cornstarch]
- 14 fl. oz. [1¾ cups] milk
- 5 oz. [5 squares] plain dessert chocolate, broken into small pieces
- 2 tablespoons dark rum
- 3 egg yolks
- 3½ oz. [7 tablespoons superfine] sugar
- 1 teaspoon vanilla essence
- ⅓ oz. powdered gelatin
- 4 tablespoons cold water
- 5 fl. oz. [⅝ cup] thick [heavy] cream, whipped
- 2 egg whites
- ¼ teaspoon salt
- ¼ teaspoon cream of tartar chocolate caraque for decoration

Put the cornflour [cornstarch] and milk in a saucepan and bring to the boil, stirring constantly. Cook over low heat for 5 minutes, then set aside and leave to cool a little.

Melt the chocolate with the rum in a bowl set over a pan of gently simmering water.

Beat the egg yolks and 3 oz. [6 tablespoons] sugar in a small saucepan until pale and thick. Gradually stir in the cooled milk and cook, stirring, over low heat for 5 minutes, or until thickened slightly: do not overcook.

Pour half the custard into a bowl and stir in the melted chocolate and half the vanilla essence.

Spoon into 4 sundae glasss and chill.

Sprinkle the gelatine over the cold

water in a cup, leave to soften, then stand the cup in boiling water and dissolve. Stir into the remaining custard with the remaining vanilla essence. Fold in the whipped cream.

Whisk the egg whites, salt and cream of tartar in a bowl until stiff. Whisk in the remaining castor sugar.

Fold the whisked egg whites into the vanilla custard. Spoon this on top of the chocolate custard. Chill the parfaits for at least 4 hours.

Twenty minutes before serving, remove the custards from the refrigerator. Decorate with chocolate caraque and serve.

## Black Bottom Pie

*A classic from the Deep South, this delicious pie is believed to date from the turn of the century. Like Black Bottom Parfait, it takes its name from the bottom layer of smooth, dark chocolate custard but in this case it is topped with a rum-flavoured custard.*

ONE 8-INCH PIE

6 oz. made-weight shortcrust [pie crust] pastry, defrosted if frozen
3 oz. [3 squares] plain dessert chocolate, broken into pieces
4 tablespoons cold water
3 egg yolks
2 teaspoons cornflour [cornstarch]
7 tablespoons castor sugar
7 fl. oz. [⅞ cup] milk
9 fl. oz. [1⅛ cups] thick [double] cream
½ teaspoon vanilla essence
⅓ oz. powdered gelatine
4 tablespoons cold water
2 tablespoons dark rum
2 egg whites
1 tablespoon icing [confectioners'] sugar
chocolate caraque, to decorate

Preheat the oven to fairly hot 400°F (Gas Mark 6, 200°C). Roll out the pastry on a lightly floured board and gently ease it into an 8-inch round pie dish. Press down an edge around the dish, trim any excess pastry. Prick the base, line with foil and baking beans and bake blind for 10 minutes.

Reduce the oven temperature to 375°F (Gas Mark 5, 190°C), remove the foil and beans and bake for a further 5 minutes. Leave until cold.

Melt the chocolate with the cold water in a bowl set over a pan of simmering water. Allow to cool.

Whisk the egg yolks, cornflour [cornstarch] and 3 oz. [6 tablespoons] sugar in a bowl until pale and thick.

Heat the milk and 4 fl. oz. [½ cup] cream in a pan over medium heat until hot but not boiling. Gradually pour on to the egg yolk mixture, stirring constantly. Stir in the vanilla essence, return to the pan and cook over low heat, stirring, until thickened.

Mix half the custard with the melted chocolate. Pour into the pastry case, cool and chill until firm.

Sprinkle the gelatine over the cold water in a cup, leave to soften, then stand the cup in hot water until dissolved. Stir into the remaining custard with the dark rum.

Whisk the egg whites in a bowl until stiff. Whisk in the remaining castor sugar.

Fold the whisked egg whites into the rum-flavoured custard. Spread over the chocolate custard and chill for 2 hours or until firm.

Whisk the remaining cream and icing [confectioners'] sugar together until thick. Pipe or spread the cream over the pie. Decorate with chocolate caraque in the centre.

## Blackcurrant

The blackcurrant bush with its clusters of round small shiny fruit was first cultivated in Europe in the early 16th century and transplanted to the US a century later.

Long before its high Vitamin C content was analysed, the blackcurrant was pressed for its juice to soothe sore throats. Now, it is made into lozenges to dissolve in the mouth for the same purpose, and into a sweet syrup cordial, sometimes with extra Vitamin C added. The fresh juice makes a delicious summertime drink with added lemon juice to sharpen the taste, while the French liqueur, crème de cassis, is added to chilled white wine to make KIR, another refreshing drink.

When buying fresh blackcurrants, choose those which look bright and shiny. Avoid mushy or stuck together berries, checking the underlayer of the punnet for squashed fruit. Blackcurrants will keep for up to 3 days if stored in the salad compartment of the refrigerator.

Canned or bottled blackcurrants in syrup are also available; sharpen the syrup with lemon juice for cooking.

To prepare the fresh fruit, trim the blackcurrants off their stalks by running a fork through the clusters. The small tops and tails are not noticeable when the currants are cooked. When freezing, wash and dry the trimmed fruit and dry-pack layers of fruit and sugar in a rigid container with a ½-inch headspace, or lay them on a tray, open freeze and store in polythene [plastic] bags. Alternatively, stew the fruit with a little water, adding sugar to taste, cool and pack with a ½-inch headspace in rigid containers. Puréed fruit should also be frozen in this way. It will keep 3-6 months, while whole frozen fruit will keep for up to a year.

The high pectin level in this fruit makes it very good for jam making as it sets easily. Its refreshing sharp flavour makes it a wonderful topping for cheesecake and it is excellent in water ices and sorbets [sherbet]. Purée with cream to make fools, add to SUMMER PUDDING or combine with apples to make pies.

Blackcurrants are also surprisingly good in savoury dishes, particularly game recipes such as venison or duck.

## Blackcurrant Jam

*A good jam for beginners to make, Blackcurrant Jam sets very easily because of its high pectin content. But take care not to add the sugar too soon, because this can make the jam too firm.*

5 LB. JAM

2 lb. fresh blackcurrants
1½ pints [3¾ cups] water
3 lb. [6 cups] sugar, warmed

Remove the stalks from the currants and wash and drain thoroughly.

In a large pan, bring the water to the boil. Add the fruit and simmer gently, uncovered, over low heat for 50 to 60 minutes, or until the fruit is soft.

Add the warmed sugar to the pan and stir with a wooden spoon until it is dissolved. Raise the heat to high and bring to the boil. Boil rapidly for 10 minutes.

Remove a spoonful of the jam from the pan and put it on a plate. Allow it to cool and then push it with your finger. If it wrinkles and a drop of the jam will not fall off your finger, it is ready.

If the jam does not seem ready, continue boiling for another 5 minutes and test again.

When the jam is ready, remove the pan from the heat and pour the jam into clean, warm, dry jars, leaving a ½-inch space at the top of each.

Using a hot, damp cloth wipe the outsides of the jars while they are still hot. Cover the jars with small rounds of wax paper. Fasten cellophane covers over the tops of the jars with rubber bands. Label and date the jars and store them in a cool, dark, dry place.

## Blackcurrant Liqueur

Made chiefly in France, where it is known as crème de cassis, blackcurrant liqueur is sweet and dark red. For a refreshing drink add chilled soda water to a measure of the liqueur.

## Black Forest Cherry Cake

*This elegant German cake, from Swarzwald – 'Black Forest' –, takes a great deal of care and patience to make, but is well worth the extra time. Flavoured with kirsch and covered with luscious swirls of whipped cream, chocolate and cherries, Black Forest Cherry Cake is ideal for special occasions.*

8 TO 10 SERVINGS

2 oz. [½ cup] flour
2 oz. [½ cup] cocoa
a pinch of baking powder

3 oz. [6 tablespoons] **butter, plus extra for greasing**
5 **eggs**
5 oz. [$\frac{5}{8}$ cup] **castor sugar**
$\frac{1}{2}$ teaspoon **vanilla essence**
FILLING AND DECORATION
5 oz. [5 squares] **plain dessert chocolate, at room temperature**
1$\frac{1}{2}$ lb. **canned Morello cherries**
3 fl. oz. [$\frac{3}{8}$ cup] **kirsch**
1-1$\frac{1}{4}$ pints [2$\frac{1}{2}$-3 cups] **whipping cream**
4 tablespoons **sugar cherries, to decorate**

Preheat the oven to 350°F (Gas Mark 4, 180°C) and place the shelves above and below the centre. Grease 3 × 7 to 8-inch round sandwich tins and line the bases carefully with circles of non-stick paper.

Sift the flour, cocoa and baking powder on to a plate. Melt the butter and cool.

Heat a saucepan of water. Remove from heat, place the eggs, sugar and vanilla essence in a large mixing bowl over the hot water and whisk until thick and creamy. Remove bowl from over pan and continue whisking egg mixture until cool.

Using a large metal spoon, carefully

*Black Forest Cherry Cake is a kirsch flavoured chocolate cake covered with cream and chocolate curls.*

fold in half the flour mixture, then the cooled butter and the remaining flour.

Divide the mixture between the three tins and level the surfaces. Bake for 15-20 minutes or until the sponge springs back when pressed lightly with a finger. Cool in the tins for 5 minutes, then turn out on to wire racks and remove the paper. Leave until cold.

Meanwhile, prepare the filling and decoration. Use a grater or vegetable peeler to shave the chocolate into curls. Cover loosely and chill.

Drain the cherries and mix 3 fl. oz. [⅜ cup] of the juice with the kirsch.

Whisk the cream and sugar until the mixture is thick and will hold its shape.

Place one sponge layer on a plate, sprinkle with one-third of the cherry juice and kirsch, spread generously with cream and top with half the cherries. Put the second sponge on top with another one-third of juice, cream and rest of cherries. Top with the third sponge layer, sprinkled with the remaining juice.

Spread the sides and top with cream and coat the sides with the chocolate curls. Pipe the remaining cream decoratively on top of the cake and decorate with the fresh or maraschino cherries arranged in a circle with some more chocolate curls in the centre. Chill for 1 hour before serving.

In Germany, 7 fl. oz. [⅞ cup] kirsch would be used to soak the cake and the cherry juice omitted.

## Black Pepper Cookies

*Black pepper gives a subtle spicy taste to these sweet biscuits (cookies). Serve them as a dessert with coffee or a mid-afternoon snack.*

ABOUT 36 COOKIES

5 oz. [⅝ cup] butter, softened, plus extra for greasing
¾ teaspoon freshly ground black pepper
¾ teaspoon ground cinnamon
¼ teaspoon ground cloves
1½ teaspoons vanilla essence [extract]
7 oz. castor [⅞ cup superfine] sugar
1 egg, lightly beaten
5 oz. [1¼ cups] self-raising flour
¼ teaspoon salt
3 oz. [6 tablespoons] cocoa powder

Preheat the oven to fairly hot 375°F (Gas Mark 5, 190°C). Grease a large baking sheet.

To make the biscuits place the butter, pepper, cinnamon, cloves and vanilla essence into a large mixing bowl and beat until smooth. Gradually beat in the sugar and then the egg until the mixture is light and creamy.

*Delicious with after-dinner coffee, Black Pepper Cookies have an excitingly spicy flavour.*

Gradually sift the flour, salt and cocoa powder over the mixture and mix to a firm dough.

With floured hands, break off small pieces of dough and roll into 1-inch balls. Place the balls on the baking sheet, spaced well apart and flatten the balls with your hand, forming flat biscuits of about ¼-inch thick.

Bake for 12 minutes in the preheated oven. Remove biscuits from baking sheet and leave on a wire rack until cold before serving.

Store the biscuits in an airtight container for up to 2 days.

## Black Pudding

Also known as blood sausage, black pudding is very popular in France and northern England. There are various ways of making black puddings, but pig's blood, finely ground trimmings of pork fat, onions and herbs are the usual ingredients. The mixture is stuffed into the gut, tied, brushed with blood, which makes it black, and boiled.

## Black Velvet

A popular drink in England, a Black Velvet is made of equal quantities of iced stout and iced champagne. The traditional way of making this drink is to pour the stout and the champagne simultaneously into a tall, cold glass. It must not be stirred and must be drunk immediately

before the bubbles fade and the taste flattens.

## Blanc de Blancs

Blanc de Blancs is the name of a champagne made exclusively from white grapes of the Champagne area, in contrast to most champagnes, which are made from both black and white grapes. Blanc de Blancs is a lighter and paler wine than other champagnes and may be, but is not always, of a higher quality than the blends.

## Blanch

This is a culinary term for a process involving the easy removal of outer skins of such foods as almonds, tomatoes and peaches by soaking in boiling water.

Blanching also means to plunge an ingredient into boiling water either to harden it, or, in the case of some green vegetables, to partially cook it.

Blanching of all vegetables is necessary before freezing.

Food is also blanched to remove too strong a taste, such as for cabbage, onions or bacon.

## Blancmange

A pudding made from milk and cornflour, Blancmange originated in France, and it is said that the secret of its preparation was lost during the French Revolu-

*Veal in a creamy white wine sauce, Blanquette de Veau is served with toast triangles.*

---

tion. It is made today essentially as a children's pudding.

## Blanquette

A white ragoût, fricassée or stew based on veal, lamb, chicken or sweetbreads, with a sauce made from the juices or gravy in which the meat has cooked, is known in French cookery as a Blanquette (blon-ket). The sauce is enriched with a mixture of egg yolks and cream and is flavoured with a bouquet garni, onion and lemon juice. A blanquette is traditionally garnished with croûtons of bread, button mushrooms and small onions cooked in a court bouillon.

## Blanquette de Veau

VEAL IN CREAM SAUCE

*Served with boiled rice and garnished with sautéed mushrooms and croûtes, Blanquette de Veau (blon-ket d' voh) is an ideal main dish to serve for a dinner party. A red Bordeaux-Médoc or rosé will best complement this dish.*

4 SERVINGS

1½ lb. veal, shoulder or breast, cut into 1½-inch cubes
2 medium-sized onions, studded with 2 cloves each
2 medium-sized carrots, scraped and cut into quarters
3 fl. oz. [⅜ cup] white wine bouquet garni, consisting of 4 parsley sprigs, 1 thyme spray and 1 small bay leaf tied together
½ teaspoon salt
⅛ teaspoon white pepper
1½ oz. [3 tablespoons] butter
6 tablespoons flour
5 fl. oz. single cream [⅝ cup light cream]
2 egg yolks
4 slices white bread, toasted and cut into triangles

Put the veal cubes in a large saucepan with enough water to cover them. Over moderate heat, bring the water to a boil and simmer the veal for 2 minutes.

Skim off the scum from the top of the liquid and reduce the heat to low. Add the onions, carrots, wine, bouquet garni, salt and pepper. Cover the saucepan and simmer over low heat for 1½ hours, or until the meat is tender when pierced with a fork.

Strain off the liquid into a bowl and reserve 1¼ pints [3⅛ cups] for the sauce.

Put a lid on the saucepan to keep the veal warm while you make the sauce.

In a heavy medium-sized saucepan melt the butter over low heat. Stir in the flour with a wooden spoon. Cook the butter-and-flour mixture for 2 minutes. Remove the pan from the heat. Stirring constantly, gradually add the reserved stock. When the stock is blended in, return the pan to moderate heat and, still stirring, bring the sauce to the boil.

Continue stirring and boil for 3 minutes until the sauce becomes thick and smooth. Remove the sauce from the heat.

In a small bowl, beat the cream and egg yolks together with a wooden spoon. Stir 4 tablespoons of the hot sauce, a spoonful at a time, into the cream-and-egg yolk mixture. When the sauce is well mixed with the cream and egg yolks, return it to the saucepan gradually, beating it with a wire whisk. Replace the saucepan on low heat and cook, stirring until the sauce just boils.

Transfer the veal to a heated serving dish and pour the sauce over it.

Garnish with the toast triangles and serve immediately.

## Blend

To blend is to mix various ingredients together until they are completely combined. For instance, flour and butter are blended together to a smooth paste before milk or stock is added to make a sauce. When the liquid is added, it, too, is stirred and cooked until the sauce is smooth and blended.

Depending on the ingredients to be blended, blending is done with a wooden spoon, fork, wire whisk, rotary beater or electric blender.

## Au Bleu

Au Bleu (oh bler) is a method used in some European countries of cooking fresh-water fish, especially trout. The freshly caught fish is quickly plunged, dead or alive, into boiling court bouillon.

## Blinis

BUCKWHEAT PANCAKES

*Blinis are a Russian and Polish dish. In Russia, they were made for the Maslenitsa festival – the carnival before weeks of fasting for Lent. Traditionally blinis are served after the zakuski – hors d'oeuvres – but before the main course with alcohol.*

10-12 BLINIS

2 oz. [½ cup] buckwheat flour
5 oz. [1¼ cups] flour
2 teaspoons easy-blend dried yeast
9 fl. oz. [1⅛ cups] lukewarm milk
2 eggs, separated
¼ teaspoon salt
1 teaspoon sugar
3 oz. [6 tablespoons] butter, melted and cooled
3 oz. [6 tablespoons] butter for frying
ACCOMPANIMENTS
7 fl. oz. [⅞ cup] sour cream, mixed with 2 tablespoons chopped fresh herbs
1 onion, finely chopped
2 hard-boiled eggs, chopped
½ lb. red or black caviar
    slices of salted or pickled herring, or smoked salmon
    lemon wedges, to garnish
    lettuce leaves, to garnish

Mix together the buckwheat flour and flour in a bowl. Stir in the yeast. Add the warm milk and mix until blended.

Cover with cling film and set aside in a warm place for 1 hour or until the batter has doubled in volume.

Stir the batter, beat in the egg yolks, salt, sugar and 2 tablespoons of the butter. Cover the bowl with cling film and set aside in a warm place for 1 hour.

Whisk the egg whites until stiff. Fold into the batter, set aside for 30 minutes.

Prepare all the accompaniments. Ar-

range on a serving dish in a circle, with the sour cream and herbs on a bed of lettuce leaves in the centre. Arrange the other ingredients around the edge and garnish with lemon. Cover with cling film and chill until ready to serve.

Heat 1 tablespoon butter in a large frying-pan. Spoon about 2 tablespoons of the batter into the pan for each blini, cooking 2 or 3 at a time. The blinis will spread to about 4 inches. Cook for 2-3 minutes, then brush with some of the remaining melted butter, turn over and cook for a further 2 minutes.

Remove from the pan and keep hot. Add more butter to the pan before cooking each batch.

When all the blinis are cooked, arrange on a heated serving dish, brush each one with melted butter and serve with the accompaniments. Each diner should help themselves to 2 or 3 blinis, spoon some sour cream on to them and then pile up with other accompaniments.

The traditional way of serving blinis is for everyone to help themselves to the accompaniments from serving platters at the table.

## Bloater

A fresh herring salted in brine, dried and lightly smoked is called a bloater. They are a speciality of the fishing port Great Yarmouth, on the Eastern coast of England. Bloaters make a tasty dish for breakfast, high tea and supper. They are usually split before cooking and are best grilled [broiled], seasoned with pepper and served with butter. Bloater paste makes a savoury sandwich filling or a spread for toast and biscuits. The cooked bloaters are made into a purée, either by mashing with a fork or blending in a liquidizer, then mixed with softened butter and seasoned with salt and pepper. Chill the paste before serving.

## Bloody Mary

*One of the first vodka based cocktails to be invented in the U.S.A., Bloody Mary is a mixture of vodka and tomato juice. Rarely drunk before World War II, it became increasingly popular after the war and is now one of the most famous of cocktails.*

1 COCKTAIL

8 to 12 ice cubes
2 teaspoons fresh lemon juice
4 fl. oz. [½ cup] tomato juice
3 fl. oz. [⅜ cup] vodka
2 drops Worcestershire sauce
2 drops Tabasco
⅛ teaspoon black pepper
    dash of celery salt (optional)

Fill a cocktail shaker with ice cubes and add the lemon juice, tomato juice, vodka, Worcestershire sauce and Tabasco sauce. Season with the black pepper. Shake the cocktail shaker vigorously. Strain the drink into the cocktail glass. Sprinkle the top with a dash of celery salt if you wish. To serve Bloody Mary 'on the rocks', prepare as directed above and strain into a whisky glass filled with 2 or 3 ice cubes.

## Blotkake

NORWEGIAN SPONGE CAKE

*A light, layered sponge cake from Norway, Blotkake (blut-kah-keh) is sandwiched with cream and topped with multerberries, the sweet, yellow berries found only in the north of Scandinavia. They are similar to raspberries in size and shape. Canned multerberries can be bought from stores specializing in Scandinavian foods, but raspberries make an excellent substitute.*

8 SERVINGS

1 teaspoon butter
6 eggs
8 oz. [1 cup] sugar
1 teaspoon vanilla essence
5 oz. [1¼ cups] self-raising flour
FILLING
15 fl. oz. double cream [1⅞ cups heavy cream]
2 oz. [¼ cup] castor sugar
1 large can multerberries, drained and dried, or 1 lb. raspberries

Preheat the oven to moderate 350°F (Gas Mark 4, 180°C). Lightly grease a loose-bottomed, round, 9-inch cake tin with the butter. Line the bottom of the tin with vegetable parchment or greaseproof or waxed paper.

Break 4 whole eggs into a large mixing bowl. Separate the yolks from the whites of the two remaining eggs. Add the yolks to the whole eggs and reserve the whites in a medium-sized mixing bowl.

Add the sugar and vanilla essence to the eggs and, using a wire whisk or rotary beater, beat until the mixture is thick and pale yellow. Lightly sift the flour into the egg-and-sugar mixture and blend in with a metal spoon.

Beat the egg whites with a wire whisk or rotary beater until they form stiff peaks. Gradually add the whites to the egg-and-flour mixture and fold them in.

*A light, layered sponge cake topped with fruit, Blotkake may be served either for tea or as a dessert.*

Turn the mixture into the cake tin. Place in the centre of the oven. After 10 minutes, lower the heat of the oven to warm, 325°F (Gas Mark 3, 170°C) and bake for a further 50 minutes, or until the cake is cooked. Test by inserting a skewer into the centre of the cake. If the skewer comes out clean, the cake is ready. After removing the cake from the oven, let it stand for 5 minutes before removing it from the tin. Place it on a wire cake rack and leave to cool.

For the filling, pour the cream and half of the sugar into a medium-sized mixing bowl. With a wire whisk, or rotary beater, whip the cream until it thickens and forms soft peaks.

When the cake is completely cooled, carefully cut it into three layers of equal depth using a long, sharp knife.

Place one layer of the cake on an attractive serving dish and, using a table knife, spread about ½ inch of whipped cream over the top. Place the second layer on top of the cream, and spread another ½ inch of whipped cream on top. Place the third layer on to the cream leaving the top of the cake plain.

Spread the remaining cream around the sides of the cake and pipe an attractive border around the top rim and the base. Completely cover the top with the fruit mixed with the remaining sugar.

## Blueberry

Blueberries are the small fruits of shrubs which are native to North America. The bilberry of Britain belongs to the same family as the blueberry. Blueberry pie is a traditional dessert in the United States, where blueberries are also eaten stewed or in puddings, jams and preserves. Blueberries are now being cultivated in Britain.

## Blueberry Crumble

*Although usually eaten as a dessert, in the United States, Blueberry Crumble is sometimes served at breakfast. A simple*

*fruit dish with a crumble topping, it can be served hot or cold with cream.*

6 SERVINGS

2 oz. [¼ cup] plus 1 teaspoon softened butter
8 oz. [2 cups] plus 1 teaspoon flour
6 oz. [¾ cup] sugar
1 egg, beaten
4 fl. oz. [½ cup] milk
2 teaspoons baking powder
½ teaspoon salt
1 lb. fresh blueberries, hulled, washed and drained
TOPPING
4 oz. [½ cup] sugar
6 tablespoons flour
½ teaspoon cinnamon
2 oz. [¼ cup] butter

Preheat the oven to fairly hot 375°F (Gas Mark 5, 190°C). Grease a 9-inch square cake tin or a soufflé dish with the teaspoon of butter and lightly dust with the teaspoon of flour. Set aside.

In a medium-sized mixing bowl, mix the sugar, remaining butter and egg together with a wooden spoon. When the ingredients are thoroughly mixed, stir in the milk.

Reserving 4 tablespoons of flour, sift the remainder with the baking powder and salt and fold them into the mixture. Lightly toss the blueberries in the reserved flour to prevent them from sinking to the bottom and then stir them into the batter. Pour into the baking tin.

To make the topping, sift the sugar, flour and cinnamon into a small bowl. Add the butter to the mixture and rub it in well with your fingertips until it resembles fine breadcrumbs.

Sprinkle the topping over the batter in the baking tin. Bake in the oven for 45 to 50 minutes, or until it is crisp and golden.

## Blueberry Muffins

*Although these fruity muffins are usually served for breakfast in the United States, they make a welcome addition to the tea table served piping hot, split and buttered.*

36 MUFFINS

4 oz. [½ cup] plus 1 tablespoon melted butter
14 oz. [3½ cups] plus 1 tablespoon flour
1½ teaspoons salt
6 oz. [¾ cup] sugar
4 teaspoons baking powder
4 eggs
10 fl. oz. [1¼ cups] milk
10 oz. fresh blueberries, hulled, washed and drained

Preheat the oven to very hot 450°F (Gas Mark 8, 230°C). Using a pastry brush, grease the muffin tins (the smaller the tins are, the better) with 1 tablespoon butter and lightly sprinkle them with 1 tablespoon of flour. Tip and rotate the tins to distribute the flour evenly and shake out the excess. Set aside.

In a medium-sized mixing bowl, sift together the flour, salt, sugar and baking powder.

In another bowl, beat the eggs with a wire whisk until they are pale yellow in colour and fall in a steady ribbon from the whisk. Add the melted butter and milk to the egg mixture and stir with a wooden spoon.

Stir the egg mixture into the flour, as quickly as possible. Do not over-mix —the ingredients should be just combined.

Toss the blueberries in a little flour to prevent them from sinking to the bottom of the muffins, and fold them into the batter.

Spoon the blueberry batter into the greased, floured muffin tins and bake for about 15 minutes, or until a skewer inserted into a muffin comes out clean. If you use very small muffin tins, they will be done in about 8 minutes.

Remove the muffins from the oven. Cool in the tins for about 4 minutes and then turn them out on to a plate and serve immediately.

## Blue Dorset

A chalk-white, crumbly cheese with a horizontal blue vein running through it, Blue Dorset gets its name from the county in southwestern England where it is made.

## Bluefish

A member of the sea bass family, the bluefish lives in tropical and temperate waters. It is bright blue in colour and about four feet long and has an average weight of six pounds. The bluefish has many names and is known as 'elf' in South Africa and 'tailor' in Australia. It is somewhat sweet-flavoured and may be prepared like bass.

## Blumenkohlsuppe

CAULIFLOWER SOUP

*A thick, creamy soup from Germany, Blumenkohlsuppe (BLOO-men-kohl-zoop-peh) is just the thing for cold evenings. Since it is a fairly filling soup, it is best followed by a light main course.*

4 SERVINGS

1 large cauliflower
1½ pints [3¾ cups] chicken stock
¼ teaspoon salt
2 oz. [¼ cup] butter
6 tablespoons flour
10 fl. oz. [1¼ cups] milk
½ teaspoon white pepper
¼ teaspoon ground mace
½ teaspoon dried chervil
1 egg yolk
2 tablespoons single [light] cream
½ teaspoon lemon juice

Trim the cauliflower by cutting away the thick stem at the base and the green leaves. Break off the flowerets, put them in a colander and rinse them in cold water. Reserve 10 small flowerets and coarsely chop the rest.

In a medium-sized pan, bring the stock, with the salt, to the boil over high heat. Put the whole flowerets in the pan and boil for about 10 minutes, or until they are tender but not soft. Remove the flowerets from the pan with a slotted spoon and set aside. Reserve the stock.

In a large pan, melt the butter over moderate heat. Add the flour to the butter, lower the heat and cook, stirring constantly, with a wooden spoon for 1 to 2 minutes. The mixture should not be allowed to brown as this will spoil the colour of the soup.

Stirring continuously with a wooden spoon, add the stock and the milk, a little at a time, to the butter-and-flour mixture. When all the liquid has been added and the mixture is smooth, raise the heat and bring it to a boil.

Reduce the heat to low and simmer for 2 to 3 minutes. Add the chopped cauliflower, pepper, mace and chervil to the pan and simmer, half-covered, for 15 minutes, or until the cauliflower is soft enough to be mashed.

Remove the pan from the heat and pour the cauliflower and all the liquid through a sieve set over a bowl. Rub the cauliflower through the sieve with a wooden spoon. Do not use a liquidizer as this will make the soup too smooth.

Return the puréed cauliflower to the saucepan. In a medium-sized bowl, beat the egg yolk and the cream with a fork. Beat in the hot purée, a tablespoon at a time, until at least 8 tablespoons of purée have been added. Pour the mixture back into the pan, whisking continuously. Add the reserved flowerets to the pan and cook over moderate heat for 2 to 3 minutes, stirring constantly. Do not let the soup boil as it will curdle.

Stir in the lemon juice, taste for seasoning and serve at once.

## Boar's Head

The Normans introduced the wild boar's head to England as a dish served with great ceremony at Christmas. The head was stuffed, boiled or roasted and decorated with laurels and served on a large platter. The wild boar, however, has been extinct in the British Isles for hundreds of years.

---

*A thick, creamy and filling cauliflower soup, Blumenkohlsuppe is just the dish for cold evenings.*

## Boerenkaas Soep
FARMERS CHEESE SOUP

*An unusual cheese and vegetable soup topped with grilled bacon, fried bread and cheese, Boerenkaas Soep (BOO-run-kass soop) from the Netherlands, is a very filling starter or main dish.*

4 SERVINGS

2 oz. [¼ cup] butter
1 large leek, finely chopped
2 large carrots, scraped and finely diced
1 large potato, peeled and finely diced
1 small cauliflower, trimmed, washed and separated into flowerets
2 celery stalks with their leaves, finely diced
1½ pints [3¾ cups] chicken stock
8 lean bacon slices
4 large slices white bread, cut about ½-inch thick and trimmed of crusts
4 oz. Edam cheese, finely sliced

In a medium-sized saucepan, melt the butter over moderate heat. When the butter foam subsides, add the leek, carrots, potato, cauliflower and celery to the pan and fry for 10 minutes, stirring frequently. Add the stock to the vegetables and bring the liquid to the boil over high heat.

Partly cover the saucepan and reduce the heat to low. Simmer the vegetables for about 20 minutes, or until they are tender but not soft.

While the vegetables are cooking, fry the bacon in a medium-sized frying-pan over moderate heat for about 3 minutes on each side or until the bacon is brown and crisp around the edges. With tongs remove the bacon from the pan and place it on kitchen paper towels to drain.

Add the slices of bread to the bacon fat in the pan and fry them for about 2 minutes on each side or until crisp and brown. With tongs remove the bread from the pan and place it on kitchen paper towels to drain.

Preheat the grill [broiler] to high.

Pour the soup into a medium-sized flameproof soup tureen. Cover the surface of the soup with a layer of the bacon slices, a layer of the fried bread and then a layer of the sliced cheese.

Place the tureen under the grill [broiler] and cook for 5 minutes, or until the cheese melts and begins to brown. (If your soup tureen will not fit under the grill, turn the soup into individual heat-proof soup bowls, each topped with the bacon, fried bread and cheese, and slide them under the grill.) Serve at once.

## Bobotie
SPICY MINCED [GROUND] BEEF PIE

*A South African dish, Bobotie (boh-boo-tee) is baked minced [ground] meat, with herbs and curry powder. It is quick and easy to make and very tasty. It may be served with rice and a mixed salad.*

4 SERVINGS

2½ tablespoons butter
1 tablespoon vegetable oil
2 medium-sized onions, coarsely chopped
1 garlic clove, finely chopped
1½ tablespoons curry powder
2 oz. [½ cup] shredded almonds
4 oz. [⅔ cup] sultanas or raisins
1 teaspoon mixed herbs
juice of ½ lemon
1 teaspoon salt
1 tablespoon sugar
1 tablespoon wine vinegar
⅛ teaspoon black pepper
2 lb. lean minced [ground] beef
3 thick slices white bread
10 fl. oz. [1¼ cups] milk
2 eggs, lightly beaten

Preheat the oven to moderate 350°F (Gas Mark 4, 180°C). Grease a large, deep pie dish with ½ tablespoon butter.

In a small frying-pan, melt the remain-

*Baked minced [ground] beef with herbs and curry powder, Bobotie is an economical supper dish.*

ing butter and oil. When the foam subsides, add the onions and garlic to the pan and fry, over moderate heat, for about 10 minutes, or until the onions are lightly browned.

Remove the onions and garlic from the pan and place them in a large mixing bowl. Sprinkle the curry powder over the onions and add the almonds, sultanas, mixed herbs, lemon juice, salt, sugar, vinegar, pepper and meat. Mix well with a wooden spoon.

Soak the bread in the milk. Squeeze the milk from the bread and mash the bread into the meat mixture together with 1 beaten egg. Turn the mixture into the buttered pie dish and press it down with the back of a spoon.

If necessary add a little extra milk to the milk squeezed from the bread to make up 6 fluid ounces [¾ cup].

Beat the remaining egg into the milk with a whisk. Pour the milk-and-egg mixture over the meat in the pie dish. Stand the pie dish in a pan of water and bake for about 1 hour, or until the top of the Bobotie is light golden brown and firm to the touch.

# Boeuf Bouilli à la Diable
DEVILLED BOILED BEEF

*An unusual way of using leftover, cold boiled beef, Boeuf Bouilli à la Diable, (berf bwee-yee ah la dee-ahbl), takes only a few minutes to prepare. The thick slices of beef are spread with mustard, dipped in breadcrumbs and grilled [broiled] until golden brown. Served with sautéed potatoes and a green vegetable, this dish makes a satisfying main course.*

4 SERVINGS

2 lb. cold boiled beef, cut into ½-inch thick slices
2 tablespoons thick prepared mustard
1 tablespoon melted butter
4 oz. [1⅓ cups] fine white breadcrumbs

Preheat the grill [broiler] to moderate.

Thickly spread one side of each slice of beef with the mustard. Lightly sprinkle over the melted butter.

Spread the breadcrumbs on a plate and, holding the slices by one edge, dip the meat into the breadcrumbs.

Place the slices of meat under the grill [broiler] and cook for 5 to 6 minutes on each side, or until both sides are golden. Reduce the heat if the breadcrumbs begin to burn.

Remove the slices of beef from the heat and arrange on a warmed serving plate. Serve at once.

# Boeuf Bouilli Froid à la Parisienne
COLD BOILED BEEF

*An attractive and tempting way to serve cold beef, Boeuf Bouilli Froid à la Parisienne (berf bwee-yee fwahd ah lah pah-reeze-yen) is accompanied by a variety of cold vegetables in season and decorated with onion rings. The dish is then sprinkled with vinaigrette dressing.*

6 SERVINGS

2 lb. cold boiled beef, cut into thin slices
3 medium-sized cold boiled potatoes, thinly sliced
1 lb. cold, cooked French beans
2 hard-boiled eggs, thinly sliced
1 small onion, thinly sliced and pushed out into rings
1 bunch watercress
DRESSING
2 tablespoons wine vinegar
6 tablespoons olive oil
¼ teaspoon salt
⅛ teaspoon black pepper
½ teaspoon prepared mustard
½ teaspoon dried tarragon
¼ teaspoon dried basil
1 garlic clove, crushed

Arrange the beef slices overlapping each other on a long dish in one straight row. Arrange the cold, cooked vegetables and eggs in alternate order around the beef.

Decorate the meat with the onion rings. Put a sprig of watercress in the centre of each onion ring.

To make the vinaigrette dressing, put all the ingredients into a screw-top bottle. Shake vigorously until they are well mixed. Pour 6 to 8 tablespoons of the dressing, according to taste, over the vegetables surrounding the meat. Serve at once.

*Boeuf Bouilli Froid à la Parisienne, garnished with cold vegetables, is an attractive and tempting way to serve cold beef.*

# Boeuf Bourgeoise
### BEEF WITH CHICKEN LIVER SAUCE

*Slivers of beef covered with a chicken liver sauce, Boeuf Bourgeoise (berf boor-jwaz) is an elegant main dish for a dinner party. It may be served with courgettes [zucchini] or broccoli sautéed in butter and boiled new potatoes.*

4 TO 6 SERVINGS

2 oz. [¼ cup] butter
8 oz. chicken livers
1 bay leaf
¼ teaspoon dried thyme
1 teaspoon salt
½ teaspoon freshly ground black
   pepper
1 truffle, very finely chopped
   (optional)
2 lb. fillet or entrecôte steak, cut
   into thin strips across the grain
2 fl. oz. [¼ cup] brandy, warmed

Melt 2 tablespoons butter in a large, heavy frying-pan over moderate heat. Add the chicken livers, bay leaf, thyme, ½ teaspoon of salt and ¼ teaspoon of black pepper and sauté quickly, stirring occasionally, for 7 minutes, or until the chicken livers are just cooked.

Remove and discard the bay leaf. Put the chicken livers and the chopped truffle (if you are using it) in an electric blender and blend at high speed for 2 minutes, or rub the chicken livers through a sieve into a bowl with the back of a spoon and stir in the chopped truffle. Set aside.

Sprinkle the beef strips with the remaining salt and pepper. Put the remaining butter in the frying-pan and melt it over high heat. Quickly brown the beef strips in the butter, stirring constantly, for 1 minute. Remove the frying-pan from the heat. Put the warmed brandy in a ladle, set it alight and pour it flaming over the meat. Allow the flames to die out.

With a slotted spoon, remove the beef strips from the frying-pan. Put them on a warmed serving dish and keep hot.

Add the puréed chicken livers to the juices in the pan, and stir to mix. If the sauce is too thick, dilute it with a little brandy, beef stock or red wine. Taste the sauce and add more salt and pepper if necessary. Heat the sauce thoroughly over moderate heat. Pour it over the beef strips.

Serve immediately.

---

*One of the most famous of all French dishes, Boeuf Bourguignonne is a delicious beef stew with red wine, bacon, onions and mushrooms.*

# Boeuf Bourguignonne
### BEEF STEWED IN RED WINE WITH BACON, ONIONS AND MUSHROOMS

*One of the most famous French beef dishes, Boeuf Bourguignonne (berf boor-gheen-yon) is excellent to serve as a main dish for a dinner party. It should be made a day in advance and reheated before serving, as the flavour is enhanced by keeping the stew in the refrigerator for 24 hours. Accompany this dish with boiled, new potatoes, buttered noodles or steamed rice. A young, fairly full-bodied red wine, such as Beaujolais, Côtes du Rhône, Burgundy or St. Emilion, will complement this dish well.*

6 SERVINGS

6 oz. streaky bacon, in one piece
2½ pints [6¼ cups] water
1 tablespoon olive oil
3 lb. lean, stewing steak, cut into
   2-inch cubes and dried on kitchen
   paper towels
1 carrot, sliced
1 onion, sliced
1 teaspoon salt
¼ teaspoon freshly ground
   black pepper
4 tablespoons flour
1¼ pints [3⅛ cups] red wine, Mâcon
   or Burgundy
16 fl. oz. [2 cups] beef stock
1 tablespoon tomato paste
3 garlic cloves, crushed
½ teaspoon thyme
1 bay leaf
2 tablespoons chopped parsley
ONIONS
1½ tablespoons butter
1 tablespoon vegetable oil
18 small onions
5 fl. oz. [⅝ cup] home-made beef
   stock or red wine
   bouquet garni, consisting of 2
   parsley sprigs, 1 thyme spray and
   1 small bay leaf tied together
¼ teaspoon salt
¼ teaspoon white pepper
MUSHROOMS
2 tablespoons butter
2 teaspoons oil
1 lb. mushrooms, quartered

With a sharp knife, cut off the bacon rind and reserve it. Cut the bacon into strips ¼-inch thick and 1½-inches long. Place the bacon strips in a medium-sized saucepan and cover with the 2½ pints [6¼ cups] of water. Bring the water to a boil over moderate heat, then reduce the heat and simmer gently for 10 minutes. Drain off the water and dry the bacon strips on kitchen paper towels.

Preheat the oven to very hot 450°F (Gas Mark 8, 230°C).

Heat the olive oil in a large, flameproof casserole over moderate heat. Add the bacon strips to the casserole and cook them for 3 minutes, turning several times so that they brown on both sides. Remove the bacon strips from the casserole with a slotted spoon, put them on a plate and set aside.

Over moderate heat, reheat the fat in the casserole until it is very hot. Add the beef cubes a few at a time and, stirring occasionally, brown them quickly on all sides. As the cubes brown, transfer them with a slotted spoon to the plate with the bacon.

Add the sliced carrot and onion to the same fat and sauté them quickly over moderate heat for 5 minutes, stirring occasionally.

Pour away the fat and return the beef and bacon to the casserole. Stir in the salt and pepper. Sprinkle the flour over the meat cubes and toss them lightly with a wooden spoon to cover them with the flour. Place the casserole, uncovered, in the centre of the oven for 4 minutes. Toss the meat again and return the casserole to the oven for another 4 minutes.

Remove the casserole from the oven and reduce the oven temperature to warm 325°F (Gas Mark 3, 170°C).

Stir the wine, beef stock, tomato paste, garlic, thyme, bay leaf and bacon rind into the casserole, and bring to simmering point over moderate heat.

Cover the casserole and put it in the lower part of the oven. Cook for 3½ to 4 hours, or until the meat is tender when pierced with a fork. While the meat is cooking, prepare the onions and mushrooms.

To cook the onions, heat 1½ tablespoons of butter and 1 tablespoon of oil in a medium-sized, heavy frying-pan over moderate heat. Add the onions to the pan and fry them over moderate heat for 10 minutes, stirring occasionally so that they brown on all sides.

Pour in the beef stock or red wine and add the bouquet garni, salt and pepper. Taste and add more salt and pepper if necessary. Cover the pan, reduce the heat and simmer the onions for 40 minutes, or until they are tender but still retain their shape. Remove the bouquet garni and put the onions to one side.

Wipe out the frying-pan. Heat 2 tablespoons of butter and the oil in the pan over moderate heat. As soon as the foam begins to subside, add the mushrooms to the frying-pan. Toss and shake the pan for 5 minutes, or until the mushrooms are lightly browned. Set aside.

When the meat is tender, place a strainer over a large saucepan and pour the contents of the casserole into it. Rinse out the casserole and put the beef and bacon back into it. Discard the bay leaf. Add the onions and mushrooms and keep hot.

Skim any fat from the strained sauce and simmer it over moderate heat for 2 minutes. If the sauce is too thin, boil it rapidly to reduce and thicken it. Pour the sauce over the meat and vegetables. Sprinkle with chopped parsley just before serving.

## Boeuf Braisé Prince Albert

BRAISED FILLET OF BEEF STUFFED WITH PATE DE FOIE GRAS AND TRUFFLES

*This is an expensive dish suitable for an important dinner party. Surround the fillet with sliced carrots, celery or courgettes [zucchini] and potato balls. A château-bottled claret from the Médoc would be an ideal accompaniment to this dish. If you do not wish to stuff the fillet, do not slit it but cook it the same way. When the fillet is cooked, place it on a serving dish and cover the top with sautéed mushrooms.*

8 SERVINGS

VEGETABLES
6 canned truffles
4 fl. oz. [½ cup] Madeira
1½ oz. [3 tablespoons] butter
2 medium-sized carrots, finely diced
1 celery stalk, diced
1 medium-sized onion, finely diced
1 slice of ham, finely diced
¼ teaspoon salt
⅛ teaspoon black pepper
  bouquet garni, consisting of 4 parsley sprigs, 1 thyme spray and 1 small bay leaf tied together

STUFFING
1 tablespoon butter
4 shallots, finely chopped
4 oz. pâté de foie gras
1 tablespoon Madeira
1 tablespoon brandy
⅛ teaspoon dried allspice
⅛ teaspoon dried thyme
⅛ teaspoon black pepper

MEAT
3 lb. fillet of beef
½ teaspoon salt
¼ teaspoon black pepper
2 or 3 slices of bacon
2 tablespoons butter
1 tablespoon oil
1 pint [2½ cups] beef stock
1 tablespoon arrowroot
1 tablespoon Madeira

Slice the truffles in quarters. Place them in a small bowl with the juice from the can and one-quarter of the Madeira.

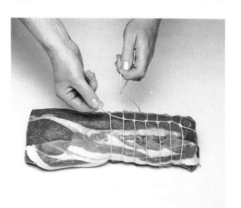

*For Boeuf Braisé Prince Albert, an elegant dinner party dish, cut a deep slit down one side of the fillet of beef. Fill the slit with the foie gras mixture and the truffles. Cover the slit with the bacon strips and tie the fillet securely with loops of string at 1-inch intervals.*

Place to one side to marinate.

To cook the vegetables, melt the butter in a small saucepan over moderate heat. Add the carrots, celery, onion, ham, salt, black pepper and bouquet garni. Cook, stirring occasionally, for 15 minutes over

moderate heat until the vegetables are quite tender but not browned. Pour in the remaining Madeira and boil the liquid down, stirring occasionally, until it has almost evaporated. Place to one side.

To make the stuffing, melt the butter in a small saucepan and fry the shallots in it over moderate heat for 6 minutes. Take the pan off the heat and add the pâté, Madeira, brandy, allspice, thyme and pepper and beat to mix with a wooden spoon. Place to one side.

To prepare the beef, with a sharp knife cut a deep slit down one side of the fillet to within ¼-inch of the two ends and to within ¼-inch of the other side.

Season the inside of the slit with the salt and pepper. Fill the slit with the pâté mixture. Insert the truffles in a line down the centre of the slit, reserving their marinade. Do not stuff the fillet slit so full that it cannot be closed. Lay the bacon strips the length of the closed slit and tie the fillet securely with loops of string at 1 inch intervals.

Preheat the oven to moderate 350°F (Gas Mark 4, 180°C).

Heat the butter and the oil over moderate heat in a large flameproof casserole. Brown the fillet lightly on both sides. Pour off the fat.

Cover the fillet with the cooked vege-tables. Pour in enough of the beef stock to come halfway up the sides of the fillet. Over moderate heat, bring the liquid to a simmer.

Lay a piece of aluminium foil over the fillet, cover the casserole and cook in the lower part of the oven for 45 minutes if you like your beef rare and for 55 minutes for medium rare. Baste the meat every 15 minutes while it cooks.

Remove the beef from the oven and remove and discard the trussing string and the bacon. Place the beef, slit side down on a warmed serving dish. Leave the meat at room temperature for 10 minutes before carving.

Skim the fat off the liquid in the casserole. Add the truffle marinade and rapidly boil down the liquid over high heat, stirring continuously until it has reduced to 15 fluid ounces [$1\frac{7}{8}$ cups].

Mix the arrowroot to a paste in a small bowl with the 1 tablespoon of Madeira and stir it into the sauce. Reduce the heat and, stirring continu-ously, simmer for 2 to 3 minutes. Taste the sauce and add more seasoning if necessary.

Spoon 3 tablespoons of the sauce on to the fillet. Serve the rest of the sauce in a warmed sauceboat. To serve, carve the fillet into $\frac{1}{2}$-inch slices.

## Boeuf à la Catalane

BEEF STEW WITH RICE, TOMATOES
AND HERBS

*A beef stew from the French-Spanish border country on the Mediterranean coast, Boeuf à la Catalane (berf ah lah kah-tah-lahn) may be served with a green salad, French bread and a young red wine, such as Beaujolais.*

6 SERVINGS

2 slices streaky bacon, diced
1 pint [2½ cups] water
2 tablespoons olive oil
3 lb. stewing steak, cut into 1-inch
   thick 2½-inch squares
2 medium-sized onions, sliced
8 oz. [1⅓ cups] long-grain rice
10 fl. oz. [1¼ cups] dry white wine
15 fl. oz. [1⅞ cups] beef stock
½ teaspoon salt
¼ teaspoon black pepper
2 garlic cloves, crushed
¼ teaspoon dried thyme
¼ teaspoon dried basil
¼ teaspoon dried oregano
⅛ teaspoon saffron
1 bay leaf
1 lb. ripe tomatoes, blanched,
   peeled, seeded and chopped
4 oz. [1 cup] Gruyère or Parmesan
   cheese, grated

Preheat the oven to warm 325°F (Gas Mark 3, 170°C).

Place the diced bacon in a medium-sized pan and cover with the water. Bring the water to a boil over moderate heat. Reduce the heat and simmer gently for 10 minutes. Drain off the water and dry the bacon on kitchen paper towels.

Heat the oil in a heavy, large frying-pan over moderate heat and add the bacon. Fry the bacon for 3 minutes, turning it several times so that it browns. Remove the bacon with a slotted spoon and put it in a large flameproof casserole.

Dry the meat on kitchen paper towels. Over moderate heat, reheat the oil in the frying-pan until it is very hot. Quickly brown the meat a few pieces at a time. Transfer the pieces of meat as they brown to the casserole with a slotted spoon.

Lower the heat to moderate, add the onions to the frying-pan and fry them lightly for 5 minutes, stirring occasionally. Remove the onions with a slotted spoon and add them to the casserole. Add the rice to the frying-pan, still using the same fat, and stir and cook for 2 to 3 minutes, or until the rice looks milky. Turn the rice into a medium-sized bowl.

Add the wine to the frying-pan, stir for 1 minute to dissolve the coagulated juices and pour the liquid into the cas-

*From the Mediterranean, Boeuf à la Catalane is a tempting one-dish meal of beef, tomatoes, cheese and rice.*

serole. Add the stock to the casserole and place it over moderate heat. Stir in the salt, pepper, garlic, thyme, basil, oregano, saffron and bay leaf. Bring the liquid to simmering point. Cover the casserole and place it in the lower part of the oven. Leave to cook for 1 hour.

Remove the casserole from the oven, stir in the tomatoes, bring to simmering point on top of the stove, cover and return the casserole to the oven for an additional 2 hours, or until the meat is tender when pierced with a fork.

Tilt the casserole and skim off the fat. Stir the rice into the casserole. Place the casserole on top of the stove and bring the liquid to simmering point over moderate heat.

Raise the oven heat to fairly hot 375°F (Gas Mark 5, 190°C).

Return the casserole to the lower part of the oven. Cook for 20 minutes, or until the rice is tender and the liquid is absorbed.

Remove the casserole from the oven, taste and add more salt and pepper if necessary. Remove the bay leaf. Stir the cheese into the hot beef mixture.

## Boeuf Chinois

BEEF WITH CHINESE MUSHROOMS
AND GREEN PEPPERS

*A simple way to serve rump steak, Boeuf Chinois (berf sheen-wah) is excellent with rice and bean sprout salad.*

4 SERVINGS

8 medium-sized dried Chinese mushrooms
1½ lb. rump steak, cut into thin strips
1 teaspoon salt
½ teaspoon freshly ground black pepper
½ teaspoon ground ginger
4 tablespoons vegetable oil
2 shallots, sliced
1 garlic clove, crushed
3 medium-sized green peppers, white pith removed, seeded and sliced
3 celery stalks, chopped
10 fl. oz. [1¼ cups] chicken stock
2 teaspoons butter
2 teaspoons cornflour [cornstarch]
4 tablespoons water
1 tablespoon soy sauce

Soak the mushrooms in warm water for 30 minutes. Drain and pat dry with kitchen paper towels. Slice and set aside.

*A beef shell filled with chopped meat and mushrooms, Boeuf à la Cuiller is a magnificent dinner party dish that is sure to impress your guests.*

Rub the beef strips with salt, pepper and ginger. In a frying-pan, heat the oil over moderate heat. Add the beef and, stirring, cook for 3 minutes on each side. Add the shallots, garlic, green peppers, celery, mushrooms and stock and bring the mixture to the boil over moderate heat. Reduce the heat to low, cover and cook for 10 minutes.

Meanwhile, in a saucepan, melt the butter over low heat. Mix in the cornflour [cornstarch] and cook for 2 minutes. Add the water and soy sauce and raise the heat to moderate. Bring to the boil, still stirring. Remove the pan from the heat and stir the thickened liquid into the beef mixture. Simmer for 5 minutes. Pour into a serving dish and serve at once.

## Boeuf à la Cuiller

CHOPPED BRAISED BEEF SERVED IN A
BEEF SHELL

*An elaborate and elegant way of serving braised beef, Boeuf à la Cuiller (berf ah lah*

kwee yair) *is an excellent main dish for a dinner party because, although it is rather complicated, it may be prepared well in advance and reheated and assembled 10 minutes before serving. Accompany this dish with buttered parsley potatoes, and, petits pois. Serve a red wine such as Côte Rôtie or Châteauneuf-du-Pape.*

8 SERVINGS

MARINADE

2 celery stalks, sliced
3 garlic cloves, crushed
2 medium-sized onions, sliced
2 carrots, scraped and sliced
2 teaspoons salt
6 black peppercorns
6 juniper berries
1 tablespoon dried thyme
2 bay leaves
grated rind of ½ orange
2 tablespoons red wine vinegar
2 pints [5 cups] red wine
2 fl. oz. [¼ cup] brandy
5 fl. oz. [⅝ cup] olive oil

MEAT

4 lb. lean piece of topside [top round] beef, cut into an even square, trimmed and tied with string
4 tablespoons vegetable oil
1 to 2 pints [2½ to 5 cups] home-made beef stock or stock made with a beef stock cube

FILLING

2 tablespoons butter

1 tablespoon vegetable oil

8 oz. mushrooms, sliced

1 small onion, finely chopped

4 slices ham, chopped

1 tablespoon Worcestershire sauce

1 tablespoon tomato purée

4 oz. [$\frac{1}{2}$ cup] butter, melted

1 egg

$\frac{1}{8}$ teaspoon salt

4 oz. [$1\frac{1}{3}$ cups] fine dry breadcrumbs

3 oz. [$\frac{3}{4}$ cup] grated Parmesan cheese

$1\frac{1}{2}$ tablespoons chopped parsley

Put all the ingredients for the marinade into a large bowl and mix them well. Put the meat in the bowl and baste it with the marinade. Cover the bowl with aluminium foil and place it in the refrigerator to marinate overnight.

Remove the meat from the marinade. Put the meat on a rack placed over a baking tin and leave it to drain for 30 minutes, reserving the marinade. Dry the meat with kitchen paper towels.

Preheat the oven to moderate 350°F (Gas Mark 4, 180°C).

Heat the oil in a large flameproof casserole over moderately high heat. When the oil is hot, put the meat in the casserole and brown it on all sides, turning frequently. When it is brown, remove it from the casserole and place it to one side.

Add the beef marinade to the casserole and boil it quickly over moderately high heat, until it is reduced by half. Remove and discard the bay leaves and peppercorns from the marinade. Return the meat to the casserole.

Add sufficient beef stock to almost cover. Heat until the liquid simmers. Skim off any fat and cover the casserole.

Put it on the lowest shelf in the oven and, turning the meat every hour, cook it for 3 hours, or until it is almost tender.

When the meat is cooked, remove it from the pan and reserve the sauce. Place the beef onto a plate and put another one on top. Place a heavy weight on top of it to keep its shape. Leave it for 1 hour. Then remove the trussing string.

When the meat is cool, trim the edges with a sharp knife. Holding the beef firmly slice out a small square cavity in the centre leaving a 1-inch thick shell.

To make the filling, chop the meat from the centre, and the leftover trimmed pieces, into small squares. Put them in a large, heavy saucepan.

Heat the butter and oil in a frying-pan over moderate heat. Add the chopped onion to the pan and cook, stirring occasionally with a wooden spoon, for 5 minutes or until the onion is soft. Add the mushrooms to the pan and cook for a further 3 minutes.

Stir the mushrooms and onion and the chopped ham into the chopped beef. Still stirring, add half of the reserved sauce with the Worcestershire sauce and tomato purée. Cover the pan and simmer gently over low heat for 10 to 15 minutes, stirring occasionally. The mixture should be fairly thick, but if it is too dry, add a little more sauce to it. Remove from the heat, cover the pan and set aside.

Preheat the oven to very hot 450°F (Gas Mark 8, 230°C).

Break the egg into a small bowl. Add the salt and beat with a fork until the mixture is fluffy. Place the beef shell in a baking tin. Using a pastry brush, cover the beef shell with the beaten egg mixture.

In a large bowl mix the breadcrumbs with the Parmesan cheese and spread a layer of the mixture over the meat, then brush the shell with the melted butter. Place the beef shell in the oven for 10 minutes.

Replace the pan containing the mushroom, ham and onion mixture over moderate heat. Stirring continuously, reheat the mixture for 3 minutes. In another pan reheat the remaining sauce until it is hot but not boiling.

Remove the browned shell from the oven and place on a large warmed platter. Spoon the filling into the cavity in the centre of the beef and garnish with the chopped parsley. Pour the sauce into a warmed sauceboat and serve separately, with the meat.

## Boeuf Daniell

BEEF WITH CORN AND TOMATOES

*A hearty winter stew, Boeuf Daniell (berf dani-ell) is best if served straight from the casserole, accompanied by a mixed salad.*

4 SERVINGS

4 tablespoons paprika pepper

2 lb. topside [top round] beef, cut in 2-inch cubes

2 oz. [$\frac{1}{4}$ cup] butter

2 medium-sized onions, chopped

2 garlic cloves, chopped

8 oz. canned tomatoes

1 teaspoon dried thyme

1 bay leaf

1 teaspoon salt

6 grindings black pepper

2 carrots, scraped and cut in rounds

7 fl. oz. [$\frac{7}{8}$ cup] dry white wine

1 lb. frozen or canned, drained corn kernels

5 fl. oz. single [$\frac{5}{8}$ cup light] cream

6 tablespoons brandy

2 tablespoons flour

Sprinkle the paprika on a large plate. Roll the beef cubes in the paprika so that they are well coated. Set them aside.

Melt the butter in a heavy, flameproof casserole over moderate heat. Add the onions and garlic, reduce the heat to low and cook them for 4 minutes. Add the meat cubes to the casserole, a few at a time, and brown them well. Mix in the tomatoes, thyme, bay leaf, salt, pepper and carrots. Cover the casserole and cook the stew over very low heat for 20 minutes.

Pour in the wine, mixing well with a large spoon. Simmer the stew, covered, for another 45 minutes. Add the corn to the casserole, cover it again and cook the stew for a further 20 minutes.

In a medium-sized mixing bowl, beat together the cream, brandy and flour with a wire whisk. Add the cream mixture to the stew, stirring with a spoon to blend. Simmer for 15 minutes and serve.

## Boeuf en Daube

BEEF STEW WITH BACON, MUSHROOMS AND RED WINE

*The secret of Boeuf en Daube (berf on dohb) an excellent French stew, lies in the marinade and long, slow cooking.*

6 SERVINGS

MARINADE

16 fl. oz. [2 cups] red or dry white wine

6 tablespoons Cognac

2 tablespoons olive oil

6 carrots, scraped and sliced

2 onions, sliced

2 garlic cloves, crushed

2 bay leaves

1 teaspoon salt

1 teaspoon black pepper

$\frac{1}{2}$ teaspoon dried sage

STEW

$3\frac{1}{2}$ lb. stewing steak, trimmed of fat and cut into 2-inch cubes

3 oz. [$\frac{3}{4}$ cup] flour

8 slices bacon, halved

$1\frac{1}{2}$ lb. tomatoes, blanched, peeled and chopped

12 oz. mushrooms, sliced

12 fl. oz. [$1\frac{1}{2}$ cups] beef stock

In a large bowl, mix all the ingredients for the marinade thoroughly. Add the meat to the marinade and stir well to ensure that all the beef cubes are coated with the marinade.

---

*Beef, corn, tomatoes and white wine combine to make Boeuf Daniell, a delicious and unusual stew.*

Cover the bowl with aluminium foil and refrigerate for 4 hours.

Preheat the oven to moderate 350°F (Gas Mark 4, 180°C).

Drain the marinade through a sieve placed over a large bowl. Reserve the liquid. Transfer the meat to a plate and set aside. Place the marinated vegetables in a small bowl.

Place the flour in a paper bag and put the drained beef cubes in it. Holding the top of the bag tightly closed, shake the bag vigorously. This will coat the beef evenly with the flour. Empty the contents of the bag into a sieve and shake the sieve to dislodge the excess flour. Place the sieve and beef to one side.

To blanch the bacon, fill a medium-sized saucepan with water and bring to the boil over high heat. Add the bacon slices to the pan and boil them for 5 minutes. Drain the bacon and pat the slices dry with kitchen paper towels.

Line a large flameproof casserole with a quarter of the bacon. Cover this with a quarter of the vegetables. Top with a layer of beef and then a layer of tomatoes and mushrooms. Continue making layers until all the ingredients have been added, ending with tomatoes and a final layer of bacon.

Pour over the beef stock and enough marinade to almost cover the contents of the casserole. Cover the casserole tightly and place it on top of the stove. Bring the liquid to the boil over moderate heat.

Place the casserole in the oven, reduce the temperature to cool, 300°F (Gas Mark 2, 150°C). Cook for 4 hours.

Remove the casserole from the oven and serve the daube immediately.

## Boeuf en Daube Martigues

BEEF STEW WITH TOMATOES

*Another version of Boeuf en Daube, this dish tastes best when the beef has been marinated for 12 hours. If this is not possible, marinate the beef for at least 6 hours. Boeuf en Daube Martigues (berf on dohb mah-teeg) may be accompanied by French bread and buttered peas.*

6 SERVINGS

MARINADE

1 medium-sized onion, sliced
1 medium-sized carrot, scraped and sliced
   grated rind of 1 orange or lemon
1 teaspoon freshly-ground black pepper
6 allspice berries, crushed
4 parsley sprigs
1 pint [2½ cups] white wine

STEW

3 lb. lean topside [top round] beef, cut into 2-inch cubes
2 tablespoons vegetable oil
5 slices bacon
2 onions, sliced
1 teaspoon flour
5 fl. oz. [⅝ cup] beef stock
1 teaspoon salt
   bouquet garni, consisting of four parsley sprigs, 1 thyme spray, and 1 small bay leaf, tied together
6 small tomatoes, blanched, peeled and sliced
12 green olives, stoned
6 canned anchovy fillets, drained and mashed

In a large bowl combine all the ingredients for the marinade. Stir well, and add the chopped beef. Spoon the marinade over the beef.

Cover the bowl with aluminium foil and place in the refrigerator for at least 6 hours or 12 hours if possible.

Preheat the oven to warm 325°F (Gas Mark 3, 170°C).

With a slotted spoon, remove the meat from the marinade and set aside. Reserve the marinade and vegetables.

Heat the oil in a large, flameproof casserole over moderate heat. Add the meat cubes, a few at a time, and fry them quickly, turning them over frequently, until they are browned on all sides. With a slotted spoon, transfer the meat to a plate. Add the bacon and onion to the casserole and fry for 10 minutes, stirring occasionally, or until they begin to brown.

Sprinkle the flour on to the onions and bacon, and stir to mix. Add the reserved marinade, stock, salt and bouquet garni to the casserole and bring to a boil over moderate heat. Return the meat to the casserole, cover and place it in the oven. Cook for 2 hours.

Stir in the tomatoes, olives and mashed anchovies. Cook for a further 2 hours or until the meat is tender when pierced with a fork. Before serving, remove the bouquet garni.

## Boeuf à la Mode

BRAISED BEEF IN RED WINE

*One of the truly classic dishes of French cuisine, Boeuf à la Mode (berf ah lah mohd) is a perfect dish for an elegant dinner party. And much of it can be prepared ahead of time. The cold version, Boeuf à la Mode en Gelée is equally famous and can provide an excellent centre-piece for a buffet. Ask your butcher if he will lard the beef with bacon.*

6 SERVINGS

5 lb. piece of beef, topside [top round] or top rump [bottom round], boned, trimmed, larded and tied
4 tablespoons vegetable oil
1½ pints [3¾ cups] beef stock
1 calf's foot, or 2 small, cracked veal knuckles

MARINADE

5 tablespoons brandy
1 pint [2½ cups] dry red wine
3 medium-sized carrots, scraped and sliced
1 medium-sized onion, finely sliced
2 garlic cloves, crushed
4 allspice berries
   bouquet garni, consisting of 3 parsley sprigs, 1 thyme spray and 1 bay leaf, tied together
1 teaspoon salt
1 teaspoon freshly ground black pepper
½ teaspoon dried basil
   grated rind of ½ orange

ONIONS AND CARROTS

2 oz. [¼ cup] butter
1 lb. small white onions, peeled
1 lb. carrots, scraped and quartered
¾ pint [1⅞ cups] beef stock
3 tomatoes, sliced
1 bunch of watercress

Mix all of the ingredients for the marinade together in a large deep bowl. Add the meat and spoon the marinade over it. Put the bowl in the refrigerator, covered, for at least 12 or preferably 24 hours, basting the meat occasionally.

Just before cooking, remove the meat from the marinade and let it drain on a rack placed over the bowl containing the remaining marinade, for 5 minutes. Pat the meat with kitchen paper towels to remove any excess liquid. Reserve the marinade.

In a large, heavy, flameproof casserole heat the vegetable oil over high heat. Add the beef and fry it until it is browned on all sides. Pour off the excess oil and add the reserved marinade, the beef stock and the calf's foot or veal knuckles. Bring the liquid to a boil, cover the casserole tightly, lower the heat to very low and simmer slowly for 3½ to 4 hours.

During the last hour of cooking, prepare the carrots and onions, Melt the butter in a large frying-pan over moderate heat. Add the onions and carrots and, turning frequently, brown them lightly all over. Transfer them to a large saucepan, add the beef stock and cook over low heat for 10 minutes, or until they are almost tender. Drain the vegetables and set aside. Discard this stock (or keep it as a base for soup).

At the end of the cooking time, remove

the meat from the casserole, strain the cooking liquid, and, as it cools, skim off the fat. Rinse the casserole dish. Return the braised meat, carrots, onions, and the strained stock to the casserole and cook, uncovered, over moderate heat for 30 minutes.

Transfer the meat and vegetables to a hot serving platter. Boil the braising liquid briskly over high heat, stirring continuously with a metal spoon until the liquid has reduced to about half. Taste for seasoning and add salt and pepper if necessary.

Serve the beef whole, or sliced, surrounded by the carrots and the onions, and garnish with tomatoes and watercress. Pour the sauce into a warmed sauceboat and serve separately.

## Boeuf à la Mode d'Arles
BEEF STEW WITH RED WINE AND
BLACK OLIVES

*A well-flavoured stew with red wine and olives, Boeuf à la Mode d'Arles* (berf ah lah mohd dahrl), *like all good stews,* *improves in flavour if it is prepared a day in advance and reheated before serving. Serve with plain boiled potatoes, followed by a crisp green salad.*

6 SERVINGS

7 oz. salt pork, cut into small dice
3 lb. good braising beef, cut into
  2-inch cubes
4 medium-sized onions, chopped
½ lb. streaky bacon, cut into small
  dice
1 teaspoon salt
½ teaspoon freshly ground black
  pepper
  bouquet garni, consisting of
  4 parsley sprigs, 1 thyme spray
  and 1 bay leaf tied together
2 tablespoons olive oil
1 tablespoon flour
1¼ pints [3 cups] red wine
1 lb. tomatoes or 14 oz. canned
  peeled tomatoes, drained
4 oz. black olives, stoned

Heat a large flameproof casserole and add the diced salt pork. With a metal spoon, turn the diced pork frequently so that the fat is released and the dice become brown. With a slotted spoon,

**Attractive and tasty, Boeuf à la Mode d'Arles is beef cooked in red wine with tomatoes and olives.**

remove the dice and place to one side on a plate.

Add the beef cubes, a few at a time, to the fat remaining in the casserole. Brown the pieces, stirring constantly. As the cubes brown, take them out of the pot with a slotted spoon and put them on a plate.

When all the meat has been browned and removed, add the onions, bacon, salt, pepper, bouquet garni, olive oil and the flour to the pot. Stir to mix the ingredients thoroughly.

Return the meat cubes to the pot. Pour in the red wine and stir to mix. Bring the liquid to the boil and cover the pot. Reduce the heat to low and simmer for 2 hours.

Remove the bouquet garni and discard it. Add the tomatoes and olives and simmer, uncovered, over low heat for 30 minutes.

Just before serving, if you like, add the salt pork dice.

201

## Boeuf à la Mode en Gelée
COLD BRAISED BEEF IN RED WINE IN ASPIC

*This cold braised beef in aspic is similar to Boeuf à la Mode. The method of preparation is the same, but when the meat and vegetables are cooked, they are not removed for serving, but are left to cool for 1 hour in the braising stock. The meat is then removed, the stock strained into a bowl, and the meat and vegetables are wrapped separately in aluminium foil. Then placed in the refrigerator for 1½ hours or until the stock is completely chilled.*

6 TO 8 SERVINGS

5 lb. braised beef with braising stock
10 fl. oz. to 1 pint [1¼ to 2½ cups] beef stock
½ oz. gelatine
2 egg whites
1 teaspoon lemon juice
½ teaspoon oregano
1 small bay leaf
½ teaspoon salt
½ teaspoon freshly ground black pepper

Low Cal

When the braising liquid is completely chilled and jellied, skim off any surface fat with a metal spoon. Spoon the jellied braising stock into a saucepan and slowly heat the jelly over moderate heat until it liquifies. Measure the liquid and add enough beef stock to make 2 pints [5 cups]. Return the liquid to the pan. Dissolve the gelatine in 4 tablespoons of the hot liquid and, when it is completely dissolved, add it to the rest of the liquid.

Beat the egg whites with a wire whisk until they are frothy. Stir the egg whites, lemon juice, oregano, bay leaf, salt and pepper into the stock and bring it to the boil over moderate heat. When the foam rises, remove the pan from the heat and set aside. Leave to cool for 5 minutes.

Line a fine strainer with a scalded muslin cloth, and place over a bowl. Pour the stock into the lined strainer and leave the liquid to drain through slowly. When all the liquid has drained through, discard the muslin cloth and set the bowl aside.

Cover the base of a large oval platter with a layer of the aspic stock and refrigerate for 30 minutes or until set. Thickly slice the cold beef. Place alternate layers of cold beef, carrots and onions on the aspic, ending with a layer of beef.

In a small saucepan, melt 16 fl. oz. [2 cups] of the aspic over low heat. As

---

*Cold braised beef and vegetables in aspic, Boeuf à la Mode en Gelée is an attractive summer buffet dish.*

soon as the aspic has dissolved, pour it into a bowl placed over crushed ice and stirring continuously until the mixture is syrupy and just on the point of setting.

Pour about ⅓ of the aspic over the layered meat and vegetables. Place in the refrigerator and chill for 10 minutes or until the aspic sets.

Heat, chill and spread the aspic twice more to make 3 coatings of aspic in all on the meat and vegetables.

Chill the dish in the refrigerator for 1 hour, or until the aspic coating is quite firm.

Pour the remaining jelly into a large shallow dish or tin and set it in the refrigerator until the jelly is thoroughly chilled and quite firm. Remove the pan from the refrigerator and chop the jelly into neat cubes. Decorate the platter with the chopped aspic.

## Boeuf Printanier
BEEF WITH VEGETABLES

*An elegant and substantial French pot roast, Boeuf Printanier (berf pran-tan-ee-yay) makes a perfect dinner party main dish. Serve it with mashed or boiled potatoes and a white Burgundy wine.*

6 SERVINGS

3 oz. [⅜ cup] butter
3 lb. top rump [bottom round] of
　beef in one piece
3 medium-sized onions, peeled and
　sliced
3 medium-sized carrots, scraped
　and cut into rounds
1 teaspoon dried thyme
2 bay leaves
1 teaspoon salt
½ teaspoon black pepper
1 bottle (26 fl. oz.) dry white wine
VEGETABLES
3 small lettuces, stripped of the
　outer leaves and halved
10 oz. streaky bacon, cut in small
　pieces
15 small white onions, peeled and
　left whole
8 medium-sized carrots, scraped
　and quartered
1 teaspoon dried thyme
1 bay leaf
8 fl. oz. [1 cup] chicken stock
½ teaspoon salt
¼ teaspoon black pepper

In a large saucepan, melt 6 tablespoons of butter over moderate heat. Add the beef and brown it, turning it to make sure that it cooks evenly on all sides.

Add the sliced onions, carrots, thyme, bay leaves, salt and pepper. Pour in the wine. Bring the cooking liquid to a boil. Lower the heat to very low and simmer the beef, covered, for 3 hours. Turn the beef at least once during the cooking period and baste it with the cooking liquid occasionally to keep it moist.

When the meat has cooked for 1½ hours, preheat the oven to warm 325°F (Gas Mark 3, 170°C).

Blanch the lettuces by plunging them into a large saucepan of boiling water and cooking over moderate heat for 5 minutes. Drain the lettuces. Using a sharp knife, cut out the lettuce cores and set the halves aside.

In a frying-pan over moderate heat brown the bacon pieces until they are cooked but not crisp. Add the onions, carrots, 1 teaspoon thyme and 1 bay leaf, stirring the mixture to mix it well.

Cook the vegetables and seasonings together for 5 minutes, stirring occasionally to prevent them from sticking to the bottom of the pan.

Using a slotted spoon, transfer the carrots and onions to a large, shallow, flameproof casserole. Spread the vegetables out in a layer on the bottom. Put the halved lettuces on top of the vegetable mixture. Pour in the chicken stock and add the salt and pepper.

Place the casserole over moderately high heat and bring the liquid to a boil. Cover the casserole and transfer it to the oven. Cook the vegetables for 1¼ hours.

Remove the meat and vegetables from the saucepan and place them on a heated serving dish with the vegetables surrounding the meat. Keep them warm.

Increase the heat under the pan to high and boil the cooking liquid very rapidly for 4 minutes, or until it reduces substantially. With a wooden spoon scrape in any brown bits that may have stuck to the bottom or sides of the pan. Pour the reduced cooking liquid over the meat in the serving dish.

When the lettuce mixture is cooked, use a pair of tongs to remove the lettuce halves. Place them on another serving dish. Drain the rest of the vegetables through a sieve, discarding the cooking liquid, and spoon them over the lettuces.

Serve immediately.

## Boeuf à la Russe

BEEF STUFFED CABBAGE ROLLS

*A tasty, inexpensive dinner dish, Boeuf à la Russe (berf ah lah roose) must be made with good quality beef. Serve it hot as a main dish or cold as a first course.*

4 SERVINGS

1 cabbage
1 lb. lean minced [ground] beef
2 tomatoes, blanched, peeled and
　finely chopped
2 tablespoons uncooked rice
　juice and grated rind of ½ lemon
½ teaspoon dried mixed herbs
½ teaspoon salt
½ teaspoon freshly-ground black
　pepper
5 tablespoons cooking oil
SAUCE
1 onion, finely chopped
1 garlic clove, crushed
¼ teaspoon dried basil
1 lb. tomatoes, blanched, peeled and
　chopped or 14 oz. canned Italian
　peeled tomatoes, drained and
　chopped
½ teaspoon salt
¼ teaspoon freshly-ground black
　pepper
1 teaspoon sugar

Trim the tough outer leaves from the cabbage. Place a large pan of water on high heat and, when it is boiling, put the cabbage in. Boil it for 4 minutes. Lift out the cabbage and drain it in a colander. When the cabbage is cool enough to handle, carefully detach the leaves and set them aside on a plate.

Put the minced beef in a medium-sized bowl with the tomatoes, rice, lemon juice and grated rind, the mixed herbs, salt and pepper. Mix well with your hands and shape into small sausages.

Wrap each meat sausage in a cabbage leaf. Make a neat parcel and tie with thread. Cover and set aside.

To make the sauce, heat 2 tablespoons of oil in a small saucepan over moderate heat. Put in the onion and fry gently until it is soft and turning brown. Add the crushed garlic and basil and cook for 1 minute. Put in the tomatoes, salt, pepper and sugar. Stir, cover, lower the heat and simmer for 35 to 40 minutes.

In a large, heavy pot, heat the remaining 3 tablespoons of oil over moderate heat. When the oil is hot, put in the cabbage rolls. When they are slightly brown, turn them over and brown them on the other side. Pour the tomato sauce over the cabbage rolls. Cover the pot, lower the heat and simmer for 1 hour.

Cut and remove the thread from the cabbage rolls. Put them in a warmed serving dish. Pour the sauce over them and serve immediately.

## Boeuf à la Vinaigrette

COLD BRISKET OF BEEF WITH OIL AND
VINEGAR DRESSING

*An unusual way to use leftovers, Boeuf à la Vinaigrette (berf ah lah vee-nay-gret) is an easy and appetizing cold luncheon or supper party dish. It can be served with a green or tomato salad.*

4 SERVINGS

3 tablespoons white wine vinegar
1 teaspoon French mustard
1 teaspoon salt
¼ teaspoon black pepper
8 tablespoons olive oil
1½ lb. cooked brisket of beef, thinly
　sliced
4 medium-sized potatoes, peeled,
　boiled, chilled and thinly sliced
1 medium-sized onion, finely
　chopped
4 tablespoons chopped fresh parsley

Combine the vinegar, mustard, salt and black pepper in a small bowl. Add the olive oil, a few drops at a time. Mix well and set aside.

Arrange the beef and potato slices alternately on a large, shallow serving dish. Sprinkle with the chopped onion and parsley.

Pour the dressing over the beef and potatoes, making sure that all the slices are well coated. Let the dish stand at room temperature for about 20 minutes before serving.

## Bogrács Gulyás
HUNGARIAN BEEF GOULASH

*A variation of the traditional Hungarian goulash, the sauce of Bogrács Gulyás (boh-grahch goo-yahsh) is flavoured with wine. This dish is best served with noodles.*

4 SERVINGS

2-2½ lb. chuck steak
4 tablespoons vegetable oil
3 large onions, chopped
1½ tablespoons paprika
1 tablespoon flour
2 tablespoons tomato purée
2 garlic cloves, crushed
16 fl. oz. [2 cups] red wine
   bouquet garni, consisting of 4
   parsley sprigs, 1´thyme spray and
   1 small bay leaf tied together
1 teaspoon salt
1 teaspoon black pepper
1 red pepper
½ teaspoon marjoram
3 large tomatoes
5 fl. oz. [⅝ cup] sour cream

Trim any excess fat from the meat and cut it into 1-inch cubes. Dry the cubes on kitchen paper towels.

Heat the oil in a large, flameproof casserole over moderate heat. Add the meat cubes, a few at a time, and brown them all over. With a slotted spoon, remove the meat cubes from the casserole when they are brown and set them aside.

When all the meat has been browned and removed from the casserole, lower the heat, add the onions to the casserole and fry for 5 minutes, stirring occasionally. Add the paprika to the pan and stir it in until the onions are well coated. Stir in the flour, and add the purée, garlic and wine. Continue stirring until the liquid comes to the boil.

Return the meat to the casserole with the bouquet garni, salt, pepper, and marjoram. Cover and simmer over low heat for 1½ hours, or until the meat is tender.

While the meat is cooking, cut the pepper into thin strips, removing the seeds and pith. Put the tomatoes in a bowl, cover with boiling water and leave to stand for 1 minute. Pour off the water,

*Easy-to-make Bogrács Gulyás is an interesting variation on the traditional Hungarian goulash.*

peel and chop the tomatoes coarsely.

When the meat is cooked, add the pepper and tomatoes to the casserole. Simmer for 5 minutes. Remove the bouquet garni and discard it.

Stir in the sour cream, cook for a further 5 minutes, and serve.

## Boil

Cooking a liquid at a temperature of 212°F (100°C) is called boiling, and liquid is said to be boiling when it is seething, rolling and bubbling.

In most recipes, the liquid is brought to boiling point (or the ingredients are put into boiling liquid), but the heat is then reduced and the cooking is carried out at a lower temperature. This is done because continued boiling may cause the ingredients to become tough, to shrink and to lose their flavour.

Sauces and gravies are often allowed to boil so that the quantity is reduced and the flavour more concentrated. Heavy puddings, such as suet pudding, and green and other vegetables are also boiled.

## Boiled Beef and Dumplings

*In England salt beef is traditionally used for Boiled Beef and Dumplings, a tasty and satisfying one-dish main course. Cook more meat than you need for a meal—cold salt beef is delicious with a salad or in a sandwich.*

8 TO 10 SERVINGS

5 lb. salt silverside or brisket of beef
8 black peppercorns
1 onion stuck with 2 cloves
  bouquet garni, consisting of 4 parsley sprigs, 1 thyme spray and 1 bay leaf tied together
12 small onions, peeled and left whole
12 small carrots, scraped and left whole
1 turnip, quartered
1 stalk celery, chopped
DUMPLINGS
7 oz. [1¾ cups] self-raising flour
1 oz. [½ cup] fresh breadcrumbs
½ teaspoon salt
3 oz. [⅜ cup] suet, shredded
7 tablespoons cold water

Put the beef in a large saucepan and cover it completely with cold water. Bring the water to the boil and immediately pour off the water to remove excess salt. Fill the pan with fresh water. Place the pan over moderate heat and bring the liquid to the boil. As the scum rises to the surface, skim it off with a metal spoon.

Add the peppercorns, onion and cloves and bouquet garni.

Half cover the pot, reduce the heat to low and simmer for 1½ hours.

Remove the pan from the heat. Remove and discard the onion and clove and bouquet garni. Add the prepared onions, carrots, turnip and celery. Return the pan to the heat and simmer for a further 45 minutes.

Meanwhile prepare the dumplings. Sift the flour and salt into a medium-sized bowl, add the breadcrumbs and suet and mix thoroughly. Stir in the water with a fork, if necessary adding more water in order to make a light dough. Divide the dough into 12 small pieces. Roll into balls about 1-inch in diameter.

Remove the pan from the heat. Take out the meat and vegetables and arrange them on a heated platter and keep hot. Return the stock to the heat, and turn the temperature up to high. When the liquid boils, add the dumplings. Boil them for 20 minutes.

Remove the cooked dumplings with a slotted spoon and arrange them in a circle around the cooked meat and vegetables. Serve immediately.

## Bok Choy

A variety of Chinese cabbage, Bok Choy is similar in appearance to celery, with smooth white stalks about 12 to 16 inches long and light green leaves. It has a subtle flavour and crisp texture. Sold in bunches or by weight, it is generally available in some Chinese provision stores. If you are unable to obtain Bok Choy, you may substitute celery or cabbage in Chinese recipes.

## Bollito Misto

ITALIAN BOILED BEEF, CHICKEN AND
SAUSAGE

*Bollito Misto (boh-LEE-toh MEES-toh) is a
famous Italian stew. The name means,
literally, "mixed boil" and the dish consists
of meat, poultry and vegetables boiled
together. The cooking stock makes an
excellent meaty soup. The stew is usually
served with a green sauce or tomato sauce
and is a filling family meal.*

8 TO 10 SERVINGS

1 veal knuckle
1 teaspoon salt
1 x 4 lb. chicken
1½ lb. topside [top round] beef
6 black peppercorns
2 bay leaves
1 teaspoon dried oregano
1 teaspoon dried basil
½ teaspoon dried thyme
2 leeks, washed and coarsely
 chopped
2 stalks celery, chopped
1 lb. carrots, scraped and sliced
12 small white onions, peeled and
 left whole
1 medium-sized white cabbage,
 quartered
2 lb. medium-sized potatoes,
 peeled and sliced
1 Italian boiling sausage

Place the veal knuckle in a large heavy
saucepan. Half fill the pan with water.
Add 1 teaspoon of salt. Bring the water
to the boil over moderate heat. Remove
any scum with a metal spoon and boil the
knuckle for 45 minutes.

Remove the pan from the heat, add the
whole chicken and the piece of beef.
Season with black peppercorns, bay
leaves, dried oregano, basil and thyme.

Remove the pan to a moderate heat,
and bring the stock to the boil. Cover the
pan, reduce the heat to low and simmer
for 1½ hours.

Return the pan to the heat, add the
leeks, carrots, celery, onions, cabbage,
potatoes and sausage. Top up the water
to almost cover the vegetables. Return to
the heat, stir with a wooden spoon and
continue to simmer, uncovered, for a
further hour or until the vegetables are
completely cooked and the meat is tender.

Remove the veal knuckle and discard.
Remove the meat, chicken and sausage
from the stock. Carve the meat into slices,
cut the chicken into serving pieces and
chop the sausage into bite-sized chunks.

Place on a heated platter and surround
with the vegetables. Moisten the meat and
vegetables with 5 tablespoons of the stock,
reserving the remaining stock for soup.

## Bolognese Sauce

ITALIAN MEAT AND VEGETABLE
PASTA SAUCE

*A tasty combination of minced meat and
vegetables, flavoured with white wine, this
famous Italian Bolognese (boh-loh-nays)
Sauce is served over pasta.*

4 SERVINGS

1 oz. [2 tablespoons] butter
1 tablespoon olive oil
4 oz. lean ham, finely chopped
1 medium-sized onion, finely
 chopped
1 carrot, scraped and finely chopped
1 celery stalk, finely chopped
½ lb. lean minced [ground] beef
¼ lb. chicken livers, finely chopped
14 oz. canned peeled Italian
 tomatoes, drained
2 tablespoons tomato purée
5 fl. oz. [⅝ cup] dry white wine
10 fl. oz. [1¼ cups] chicken stock
1 teaspoon dried basil
1 bay leaf
½ teaspoon salt
4 grindings black pepper

Heat the butter and oil in a medium-
sized saucepan over moderate heat. When
the butter foam subsides, add the ham,
onion, carrot and celery. Stirring occasionally, cook for 8 to 10 minutes, or
until the vegetables begin to brown.

Add the minced beef to the pan and,
stirring, cook for about 10 minutes, or
until the meat is well browned.

Continue stirring and add the chicken
livers, tomatoes, tomato purée, wine,
stock, basil, bay leaf, salt and pepper.
Reduce the heat to low, cover the pan and
simmer for 1 hour. Remove the bay leaf.

Pour the sauce over pasta and serve.

## Bombay Duck

Bombay Duck is the Western name, of
unknown origin, for a small, flat fish
found in the Arabian Sea and the Bay of
Bengal. In India, Bombay Duck is dried
and salted and served as an accompaniment to curries. It is exported throughout
the world.

## Bombe

A bombe is an ice-cream dessert which is
made by freezing ice-cream in a conical
mould. A bombe may be made with more
than one kind of ice, such as two flavours
of ice-cream, or a mixture of ice-cream
and sorbet. Alternatively, the mould
may be lined with ice-cream and the
centre filled with a mousse. Fruit or nuts
may also be added.

## Bombe Coppelia

COFFEE AND RUM ICE-CREAM
FILLED WITH PRALINE

*A rich and unusual dessert, Bombe Coppelia
is a mouth-watering combination of coffee
ice-cream and praline. To make this dessert
you will require either a large frozen food
compartment in your refrigerator or a home
freezer.*

10 TO 12 SERVINGS

3 pints coffee-flavoured ice-cream,
 slightly softened in the
 refrigerator
8 egg yolks
4 oz. [½ cup] sugar
3 tablespoons dark rum
1 tablespoon water
10 fl. oz. double [1¼ cups heavy]
 cream
PRALINE
1 tablespoon vegetable oil
3 oz. [⅜ cup] castor sugar
3 oz. [½ cup] blanched almonds

Prepare a chilled 3-pint bombe mould by
spooning a little of the ice-cream into the
base. Working quickly, so that the ice-
cream does not thaw too much, spoon
scoops of the ice-cream into the mould
and, with the back of a metal spoon, pat
the ice-cream firmly against the sides of
the mould. Press a chilled glass bowl,
1-inch smaller than the mould, inside the
mould so that the ice-cream forms a solid
wall between the bowl and the mould.
With a knife, cut out more slices of ice-
cream to fill up any gaps in the walls.

Place the mould, with the bowl in the
freezer, and chill for 1 hour or until the
ice-cream is completely firm. Chill the
remaining ice-cream in a separate bowl
for later use.

While the ice-cream is freezing, prepare
the praline filling. Using a pastry brush,
coat a baking sheet with the vegetable oil.

Stir the castor sugar in a small saucepan
over very low heat until the sugar dissolves. Add the almonds to the saucepan
and cook, turning the nuts constantly
with a metal spoon until they are browned.
Remove the pan from the heat. Pour the
praline mixture on to the greased baking
sheet. Leave the mixture to cool for about
10 minutes, or until it is firm.

Place the pieces of praline mixture
between greaseproof or waxed paper.
Pound them to a coarse powder with a
wooden mallet or a rolling pin.

Set the praline aside while you prepare

*A rich dessert, Bombe Coppelia is a
mouth-watering combination of coffee
ice-cream, rum and praline.*

the bombe mixture. In a large mixing bowl, beat the egg yolks with a wire whisk until they are pale yellow and form a ribbon trail on themselves when the whisk is lifted.

Place the sugar, rum and water in a large saucepan and cook over moderate heat, stirring continuously with a wooden spoon. When the sugar has dissolved, bring the liquid to the boil. As soon as the syrup reaches a temperature of 230°F on a sugar thermometer, or a few drops of the syrup spooned into cold water immediately form a soft ball, remove the pan from the heat.

Slowly pour the hot syrup into the egg yolks, beating continuously with a wooden spoon. Continue to beat the mixture as it cools. Beat in the praline.

Whip the cream with a wire whisk in a chilled bowl until it stands in peaks. Gently fold the cream into the praline mixture with a metal spoon. Continue folding until all the cream is blended.

Remove the ice-cream mould from the freezer and pour the praline mixture into the centre of the ice-cream shell. Return the mould to the freezer for 2-3 hours, or until the praline feels firm.

Remove the remaining ice-cream from the freezer, and allow to thaw for a few minutes, until it is soft enough to spread, but is not melting. With a rubber spatula, smooth the slices of ice-cream over the praline filling and ice-cream shell in the mould. Cover the mould with aluminium foil. Return the bombe to the freezer for 8 hours or overnight.

Chill a serving plate for 15 minutes.

When you are ready to serve the bombe, unmould it by dipping the mould in hot water for about 30 seconds. Place the chilled plate upside-down on top of the mould. Pressing the plate down firmly on to the mould, turn the mould and plate over quickly. The bombe should slip out smoothly. Serve at once.

## Bombe Framboises

MOULDED ICE CREAM WITH RASPBERRIES

*An old recipe, Bombe Framboises (Bom frahm-bwahs) is not a traditional bombe, but moulded macaroons and brandy flavoured cream served with a sauce made from puréed fruit. Bombe Framboises is impressive and easy to prepare. To make this dessert you require a large frozen food storage compartment in your refrigerator or a home freezer.*

10 TO 12 SERVINGS

½ lb. macaroons
10 fl. oz. double cream [1¼ cups heavy cream]

3 tablespoons brandy
2 tablespoons castor sugar
2 egg whites, stiffly beaten
1 lb. raspberries

With your fingertips, coarsely crumble the macaroons into a medium-sized mixing bowl.

In another bowl, whip the cream with a wire whisk until it stands in stiff peaks. With a metal spoon, fold the brandy and 1 tablespoon of castor sugar into the whipped cream. Fold in the stiffly beaten egg whites. Taste and add more sugar if necessary. Add the whipped cream to the pieces of macaroon and stir just enough to mix the ingredients.

Spoon the mixture into a chilled 3-pint mould. Cover the top of the mould with aluminium foil and place it in the freezer for at least 2 hours.

While the bombe is freezing, prepare the sauce. With a wooden spoon, press the fruit through a sieve into a small bowl. Sweeten the purée with 1 tablespoon of sugar. Taste and add more sugar if necessary. Chill in the refrigerator.

Remove the mould from the freezer and dip it in hot water. Place a chilled serving dish upside-down over the mould. Holding the dish and mould firmly together, turn them over and bang them sharply on the table. Pour the fruit sauce around the bombe. Serve at once.

## Bombe Marie-Claire

MOULDED VANILLA ICE-CREAM WITH APRICOT FILLING

*Bombe Marie-Claire is an elegant dessert. Although this recipe uses canned apricots, you may substitute strawberries or black-currants. Bombe Marie-Claire may be accompanied by sponge fingers. To make this dessert, you require either a large frozen food storage compartment in your refrigerator or a home freezer.*

10 TO 12 SERVINGS

3 pints vanilla ice-cream, slightly softened in the refrigerator
10 oz. canned, drained apricots
5 egg yolks
2½ oz. [5 tablespoons] sugar
4 fl. oz. [½ cup] Marsala
2 tablespoons lemon juice
8 fl. oz. double cream [1 cup heavy cream], chilled

Prepare a chilled 3-pint bombe mould by spooning a little of the ice-cream into the base. Working quickly, so that the ice-cream does not thaw too much, spoon scoops of the ice-cream into the mould and, with the back of a metal spoon, pat the ice-cream firmly against the sides of the mould. Press a chilled glass bowl, 1-inch smaller than the mould, inside the mould, so that the ice-cream forms a solid wall between the bowl and the mould. With a knife, cut out more slices of ice-cream to fill up any gaps in the walls.

Place the mould, with the bowl, in the freezer, and chill for 1 hour or until the ice-cream is completely firm. Chill the remaining ice-cream in a separate bowl for later use.

While the ice-cream is freezing, prepare the apricot filling. Purée the apricots in an electric blender or, with the back of a wooden spoon, rub the apricots through a sieve placed over a bowl. Set aside.

Place the chilled cream in a medium-sized mixing bowl, chilled, and beat with a fork or wire whisk until the cream is stiff and stands in peaks. Set aside.

Place a glass mixing bowl in a larger mixing bowl filled with hot water. Beat the egg yolks and sugar together with a wire whisk for 3 to 4 minutes, or until the yolks are pale yellow in colour and form a ribbon trail on themselves when the whisk is lifted. Still beating, add the Marsala and lemon juice.

Lift the bowl out of the water, beat in the apricot purée and fold in the whipped cream with a metal spoon. Place the mixture in the refrigerator for half an hour to chill.

Remove the bombe mould from the freezer. Lift out the glass bowl in the centre. If it sticks, pour a little hot water into the bowl and let it stand for 20 seconds. The bowl should now slide out easily.

Remove the chilled apricot mixture from the refrigerator and spoon it into the cavity in the centre of the bombe, filling it almost to the top. Place the mould in the freezer for 2 to 3 hours or until the apricot filling is quite firm. Then remove the mould and the remaining ice-cream from the freezer and place a lid of ice-cream slices on top of the apricot mixture. Smooth with a knife.

Cover the mould carefully with aluminium foil and freeze the bombe for 6 hours, or until it feels completely firm to the touch.

Fifteen minutes before serving, place a serving plate in the freezer to chill it thoroughly.

When you are ready to serve the bombe, unmould it by dipping the mould in hot water for about 30 seconds. Place the chilled plate upside-down on top of the mould. Pressing the plate down firmly on to the mould, turn the mould and plate over quickly. The bombe should slip out smoothly.

Serve at once.

## Bone-Marrow

Bone-marrow, the soft, fatty substance which is contained in long bones, commonly called marrow bones, has a variety of cooking uses.

Cut into fairly thick slices and poached in salt water, the marrow may be used to garnish steaks. Beef bone-marrow, diced, poached and drained, is also used in various brown sauces.

## Bonito

The bonito is a small species of tuna fish which may be up to 30 inches in length. Bonito is sold in cans and may be prepared in the same ways as tuna. Dried and flaked bonito is a popular ingredient in Japanese cooking.

## Bonne Femme, à la

A French culinary term, *à la bonne femme* (ah lah bohn fahm) is applied to soup, meat or fish which is cooked in a simple housewifely style and garnished with fresh vegetables.

## Bookmaker's Sandwich

*A mammoth sandwich of cold steak and mustard in a Vienna loaf, the Bookmaker's Sandwich is so called because the Irish would take it to race meetings for a good satisfying lunch. If you like, chopped pickles or chutney may also be used.*

4 SERVINGS

1 long, fresh, crusty Vienna loaf
4 to 6 oz. [½-¾ cup] butter
1½ lb. fillet steak, cut 1-inch thick
½ teaspoon salt
4 grindings black pepper
3 tablespoons prepared mustard or horseradish

Slice the loaf in half lengthways and butter it.

Preheat the grill [broiler] to high.

Grill the steaks for 2 to 3 minutes or more on each side, according to whether you like your steaks rare, medium or well-done.

Place the hot steaks on one-half of the loaf. Sprinkle the salt and pepper over the meat and spread it with the mustard. Put the top of the loaf on over the meat and press down.

Wrap the loaf in greaseproof paper or aluminium foil. When the meat is cold slice the sandwiched loaf into wedges and serve.

## Borage

A little herb with bright blue flowers, borage is native to the eastern Mediterranean and is grown elsewhere in the Northern hemisphere. Borage leaves, which have a distinct cucumber flavour, are used to flavour claret cups, fruit drinks and salads.

## Borani Esfanaj

SPINACH AND YOGURT SALAD

*In the Middle East, it is believed that eating yogurt ensures a long life, good looks and eternal youth. In this Iranian recipe, yogurt combines with spinach to make an unusual salad. Borani Esfanaj (BOH-rah-nee ESS-fah-nahj) may be served as an hors d'oeuvre or as an accompaniment to such meat dishes as Shish Kebab.*

4 SERVINGS

2 lb. fresh spinach
10 fl. oz. [1¼ cups] cold water
1 tablespoon lemon juice
1 shallot, finely chopped
½ teaspoon salt
½ teaspoon black pepper
10 fl. oz. [1¼ cups] plain yogurt
1 garlic clove, crushed
1 tablespoon finely chopped fresh mint

*Low Cal*

*Bookmaker's Sandwich is a mammoth sandwich of cold grilled steak, spread with mustard, in a Vienna loaf.*

Wash the spinach by plunging it alternately into two bowls of cold water, lifting it out with your hands from one bowl to the other, until no sediment remains at the bottom of either bowl. The water in the bowls should be changed between each rinsing. Drain the spinach well on kitchen paper towels. Strip the leaves from the stalks. Throw away the stalks and old leaves.

In a medium-sized saucepan, bring the water to the boil over high heat. Put the spinach leaves into the water. Bring the water to the boil again and cook for 10 minutes.

Remove the spinach from the pan, drain it in a sieve and squeeze it dry by pressing it down into the sieve with a metal spoon. When the spinach has cooled to room temperature, transfer it to a wooden board and chop it finely.

Place the spinach, lemon juice, shallot, salt and pepper in a large salad bowl. Toss the mixture with a spoon. Stir in the yogurt and garlic clove and mix all the ingredients well together.

Cover the bowl with a plate and refrigerate for 1-2 hours until the Borani is well chilled. Pile it in a chilled serving dish. Sprinkle the top with the chopped mint and serve.

## Bordeaux Wines

Bordeaux, on the southwest coast of France, is generally acknowledged to be the greatest wine-producing region of France and, thus, of the world. The history of wine-making in this region extends back over 2,000 years and the area was already famous for its wines during the days of Imperial Rome. The Senechaussée of Bordeaux (Gascony) belonged to the English crown from the twelfth to the fifteenth century. During this time English merchants developed a flourishing trade and firmly established the popularity of Bordeaux wines in England. The red wines of Bordeaux were then called claret (literally, 'light-coloured') by the Gascons, which soon became corrupted into the English word claret. Claret has now become a general descriptive term for red Bordeaux wines.

The soil of the region produces only the finest quality of grape, for it is composed of limestone, gravel and sand with a clay subsoil. Bordeaux is one of the areas covered by the appellation contrôlée laws enacted by the French government during the 1930's, which strictly maintain the standards of wine-making and labelling and even designate the wine districts, what type of grapes can be grown on them and how much wine can be produced per acre.

Bordeaux wines differ widely in character, with each district producing a readily identifiable and distinct type. They are, therefore, assessed and labelled according to the locality in which they are grown, and within each main area are many sub-districts. Individual vineyards are referred to as *châteaux*, after the country houses or storage buildings which most of them contain, and almost every bottle of Bordeaux wine carries its *château* name on its label. Those wines bottled at the vineyard—*mis en bouteille au château* or, literally, château-bottled—are the best of the Bordeaux wines.

Bordeaux is divided into five main wine-producing areas, three of which produce red wine (Médoc, St. Emilion and Pomerol), one which produces white wine (Sauternes) and one which produces both red and white wine (Graves).

The wines of the Médoc are probably the best-known of the Bordeaux reds, and 62 of the leading vineyards of this region were, in 1855, subjected to classification by a group of wine brokers in Bordeaux —rankings ranging from *premiers crus* (first growths) through *cinquièmes crus* (fifth growths). Despite some controversy, the rankings have generally stood the test of time and today there are still only four Médocs meriting the description *premiers crus* (Château Lafite, Château Latour, Château Margaux and Château Mouton-Rothschild). Wines which failed to make the list at all were given the general description of *crus bourgeois*, and these wines still form a major part of the claret trade. Twenty-two of the white wines of the Sauternes were also classified by the 1855 committee, one, the 'Queen of Sauternes', Château d'Yquem, being of such outstanding quality that a special category was created for it of

*grand premier cru*. Eleven Sauternes wines were classed as *premiers crus*.

The wines of St. Emilion and both the red and white wines of Graves were ranked in a similar way during the 1950's —Château Ausone and Château Cheval-Blanc being considered the best of the St. Emilions, Château Haut Brion leading the red Graves and Château Carbonnieux being considered the most distinguished white Graves. The wines of the Pomerol have not been officially classified, but Château Petrus and Château Certan are generally considered to be the leading wines of this area.

Clarets go well with roast chicken, turkey, veal, fillet of beef, ham, liver, lamb, pheasant and such soft, fermented cheeses as CAMEMBERT. Dry white Graves wine can be drunk with veal, poultry or ham dishes while medium sweet whites usually accompany dessèrt mousses, creams, soufflés and cakes. Those rich golden Sauternes should be served chilled at the end of, or after, the meal.

## Bordelaise, à la

A French culinary term, *à la bordelaise* (ah lah bord-layz) is used to describe dishes served with any of four garnishes. It is most commonly used for those dishes served with a bordelaise sauce, but it is also applied to those served with a mirepoix, or a garnish which features cèpes (flat mushrooms), or another composed of artichokes and potatoes.

## Bordelaise Sauce

SAUCE WITH RED WINE, SHALLOTS
AND BEEF MARROW

*A variation of the classic Marchand de Vins sauce, Bordelaise Sauce is served with grilled steak. It may be served in a sauce-boat or poured over the steaks on the serving dish.*

4 SERVINGS

2 oz. [¼ cup] butter
4 shallots, finely chopped
1 garlic clove, crushed
3 fl. oz. [⅜ cup] red wine
8 fl. oz. [1 cup] brown sauce
½ teaspoon thyme
1 small bay leaf
2 oz. beef marrow, sliced
juice of ½ lemon
½ teaspoon salt
4 grindings black pepper
1 teaspoon chopped parsley

In a medium-sized saucepan, melt 2 tablespoons of butter over moderate heat.

When the foam subsides, add the shallots and garlic and fry for 2 minutes, stirring constantly.

Add the wine to the pan and cook for 5 to 8 minutes, or until the liquid has reduced by half.

Add the brown sauce, thyme and bay leaf to the pan and simmer for 15 minutes.

While the sauce is simmering, place the slices of beef marrow in a small saucepan and barely cover them with water. Bring the water to the boil over moderate heat. Reduce the heat and simmer for 2 minutes. Remove the marrow from the pan with a slotted spoon and transfer it to the sauce.

Remove the pan with the sauce from the heat. Stir in the remaining butter. When the butter has melted, add the lemon juice, salt and pepper to the sauce.

Remove the bay leaf from the pan and discard it. Pour the sauce into a warmed sauce boat or over the steak in the serving dish. Finish with a sprinkle of parsley and serve at once.

## Bordure de Pommes de Terre

POTATO BORDER

*An attractive way to serve potatoes, Bordure d'Pomme de Terre (bohr-dure d'pohm d' tair) may be used to surround slices of cooked fish covered with Mornay Sauce, a selection of shellfish, meat hashes or vegetables cooked in butter.*

4 SERVINGS

1½ pints [3¾ cups] water
1¼ teaspoons salt
1 lb. potatoes, peeled and quartered
1½ oz. [3 tablespoons] butter
4 grindings black pepper
⅛ teaspoon grated nutmeg
2 egg yolks, lightly beaten
2 tablespoons grated Parmesan cheese

Bring the water to the boil in a medium-sized saucepan over moderate heat. Add 1 teaspoon of salt and the potatoes to the water. Boil the potatoes for 25 to 40 minutes, or until they are tender when pierced with a skewer. The time taken depends on the kind of potatoes you are using.

Remove the pan from the heat. Pour away the water and drain the potatoes well.

With a wooden spoon, rub the potatoes through a sieve set over the saucepan. Stir the puréed potatoes in the saucepan for 1 minute over low heat to dry them thoroughly. Add the butter, the remaining salt, the pepper and the nutmeg to the potatoes. Mix well with a wooden spoon.

When the butter has melted, remove the pan from the heat and mix in the beaten egg yolks. Set aside a little of the egg yolk for later use.

Put the potato mixture in a forcing bag and while the potatoes are still hot, pipe around the edge of a flameproof serving dish to make a border.

Brush the top of the potato border with the reserved beaten egg and sprinkle it with the grated Parmesan cheese. Brown the potato lightly in a hot oven or under the grill [broiler]. Fill the centre with cooked fish, meat or vegetable and serve immediately.

## Börek

A savoury-filled pastry, börek (bur-REK) is traditionally made in Turkey and in the Balkans.

## Borjúpörkölt

VEAL STEW WITH TOMATOES, PAPRIKA AND GREEN PEPPER

*A colourful, tasty stew from Hungary, Borjúpörkölt (BOHR-yoo-PUR-kutt) may be served for a family lunch or informal dinner party. It may be accompanied by boiled new potatoes, dumplings or noodles.*

6 SERVINGS

2 oz. [¼ cup] butter
1 tablespoon vegetable oil
2 large onions, finely chopped
2 garlic cloves, crushed
1½ tablespoons paprika
3 lb. shoulder of veal, cut into 1-inch cubes
2 teaspoons salt
1 teaspoon freshly ground black pepper
6 tomatoes, blanched, peeled, seeded and coarsely chopped
2 large green peppers, seeds and white pith removed and coarsely chopped

In a large, flameproof casserole, melt the butter and heat the oil over moderate heat. When the butter foam subsides, add the onions and garlic. Cook for 10 minutes, or until the onions are golden brown.

Remove the casserole from the heat and stir in the paprika. When the onions are well coated with paprika, add the veal, salt and pepper. Cover the casserole, reduce the heat to very low and simmer for 40 minutes.

Add the tomatoes and peppers to the casserole. Recover the casserole and simmer for 1 hour, stirring occasionally,

or until the meat is tender when pierced with the point of a knife.

Taste for seasoning and add more salt and pepper if necessary. Serve at once.

## Borscht

BEETROOT [BEET] SOUP

*This is a classic summer Borscht, a light clear soup that may be served hot or cold. It is traditionally served hot with boiled potatoes as well as with sour cream. This recipe can be varied by whisking two beaten eggs into the hot soup just before serving.*

6 SERVINGS

5 large, raw beetroots [beets], peeled and coarsely grated
3 pints [7½ cups] water
1 onion, chopped
3 fl. oz. [⅜ cup] tomato puree
1 tablespoon lemon juice
1 teaspoon salt
6 grindings black pepper
1 teaspoon sugar
6 fl. oz. [¾ cup] sour cream

Place the beets, water and onion in a large saucepan over high heat. Bring the liquid to the boil, cover the pan, reduce the heat to low and simmer for 45 minutes.

Add the tomato purée [paste], lemon juice, salt, pepper and sugar to the saucepan. Cover and cook the soup over moderately low heat for 45 minutes.

Remove the pan from the heat. Strain the soup through a sieve into a soup tureen. Discard the vegetables. Serve topped with spoonfuls of sour cream.

*A light, clear beetroot soup, Borscht may be served either hot or cold, with sour cream.*

## Borscht Ukrainian

UKRAINIAN BEETROOT SOUP

*A hearty soup full of meat and vegetables, Borscht Ukrainian is a meal in itself. Serve it with hot crusty bread.*

6 SERVINGS

1¾ pints [4⅜ cups] cold water
1 lb. stewing beef, cut into 1-inch cubes
1 marrow bone, cracked
8 oz. lean fresh pork, sliced
8 oz. boiled ham, diced
1 small bay leaf
5 peppercorns
1 garlic clove, crushed
3 medium-sized tomatoes, blanched and skinned
1 celery stalk, sliced
1 parsnip, peeled and chopped
5 medium-sized raw beetroots [beets]
1 small white cabbage, shredded
1 large onion, chopped
2 medium-sized potatoes, peeled and diced
1 teaspoon salt
1 tablespoon red wine vinegar
1 teaspoon sugar
4 oz. canned kidney beans, drained
2 tablespoons chopped parsley
5 fl. oz. [⅝ cup] sour cream

Bring the water to a boil in a large saucepan. Add the beef and the bone. Cover,

211

reduce the heat and simmer for 1 hour.

Add the fresh pork, the boiled ham, bay leaf, peppercorns, garlic, tomatoes, celery and parsnip to the pan. Cover and raise the heat. Bring the soup to the boil. Reduce the heat to low and simmer gently for 1½ hours.

While the soup is simmering, boil 4 of the beetroots [beets], unpeeled, in water, until they are tender when pierced with a knife. Drain the beetroots [beets] in a colander. When they are cool enough to handle, remove the skins and coarsely chop each beetroot [beet].

Peel the remaining raw beetroot [beet]. Grate it and mix it with 4 tablespoons of cold water. Set aside.

Remove the bone and meats from the pan. Discard the bone. Strain the soup through a sieve and discard the vegetables and flavourings. Return the meats and strained soup to the pan. Add the cooked beetroots [beets], cabbage, onion, potatoes, salt, vinegar and sugar. Simmer the soup, covered, over low heat for 45 minutes.

Add the beans to the pan and simmer, covered, for a further 10 minutes.

With a metal spoon, skim the fat off the surface of the soup. Add the grated raw beetroot [beet] to the soup. Return the soup to a boil. Taste the soup and add more salt and sugar if necessary. Pour the soup into a tureen, sprinkle with parsley and serve with the cream.

## Boston Baked Beans

*Flavoured with molasses and baked to a dark, rich brown, Boston Baked Beans are traditionally American. In colonial New England, this nourishing combination of beans, salt pork and molasses was often baked in the oven with the week's bread and then eaten with thick slices of the steaming hot, brown bread. Today, Boston Baked Beans are usually served with roast pork or ham.*

6 TO 8 SERVINGS

8 oz. fat salt pork
2 lb. dried haricot, pea or kidney beans, washed and drained
2 teaspoons salt
1 large onion
3 oz. [⅓ cup] brown sugar
6 tablespoons molasses or black treacle
3 teaspoons dry mustard
1 teaspoon black pepper

Put the salt pork in a large bowl. Add cold water to cover. Soak the salt pork for 3 hours and drain well.

Place the beans in a large saucepan

and add enough cold water to cover. Add 1 teaspoon of salt. Bring the water to the boil over high heat. Boil the beans for 2 minutes. Remove the pan from the heat and let the beans soak in the water for 1 hour.

Return the pan to the heat and bring the beans to the boil again. Reduce the heat to very low, partially cover the pan and slowly simmer the beans for 30 minutes. Drain the beans and discard the liquid.

Preheat the oven to very cool 250°F (Gas Mark ½, 130°C).

Place the whole onion in the bottom of a large flameproof casserole. Add a layer of the cooked, drained beans to the casserole.

Thickly slice the drained salt pork and cut each slice into small chunks. Arrange a layer of salt pork over the beans in the casserole. Add another layer of beans and finish with a layer of salt pork.

In a small bowl, with a wooden spoon mix together the brown sugar, molasses, or treacle, mustard, black pepper and the remaining 1 teaspoon of salt. Spoon the mixture over the beans and pork. Add enough boiling water to cover the beans.

Cover the casserole and place it in the oven. Bake for 5 hours, adding boiling water from time to time so that the beans are always just covered.

Remove the lid of the casserole and bake uncovered for 45 minutes. Serve straight from the casserole.

## Boston Brown Bread

*This is the authentic recipe for the unusual American steamed bread which was made in colonial New England. It is easy to prepare and, although it must steam for 3½ hours, it is well worth waiting for.*

2 LOAVES

2 teaspoons vegetable oil
18 fl. oz. [2¼ cups] commercial buttermilk
6 fl. oz. [¾ cup] molasses, or dark treacle
6 oz. [⅞ cup] seedless raisins
6 oz. [1¼ cups] cornmeal
6 oz. [1¼ cups] rye flour
6 oz. [1¼ cups] wholewheat flour
2 teaspoons baking powder
1 teaspoon salt

Using a pastry brush, lightly oil two 2-pint, round, plain moulds or pudding basins.

Pour the buttermilk, molasses, or dark treacle, and raisins into a medium-sized mixing bowl and beat together.

Put the cornmeal, rye flour, whole-

wheat flour, baking powder and salt into a large mixing bowl. Stir to mix. Pour in the buttermilk mixture and continue to stir until well mixed.

Divide the mixture between the two moulds or basins. Cover them very securely with greased aluminium foil, tied tightly with string under the lip of each basin.

Place a rack in the bottom of a large, deep saucepan which is wide enough to hold both the basins. Put the basins on the rack and pour in enough boiling water to come halfway up around the basins. Cover the saucepan and boil steadily, over moderate heat, for 3 to 3½ hours. Add more water when necessary to keep the water at the original level.

Preheat the oven to cool 300°F (Gas Mark 2, 150°C).

After taking the basins out of the saucepan, remove the foil covers and place the basins in the oven for about 15 minutes. This will remove any excess moisture from the bread.

Turn the bread out on to a rack. Serve hot or cold.

## Boti Kebabs

GRILLED LAMB ON SKEWERS

*Spicy lamb cubes marinated in a yogurt mixture, threaded on skewers and grilled, Boti Kebabs (BOH-tee k'bahb) are very easy to make. This adaptation of a popular Indian dish is usually eaten with chapatis, but it may also be served with rice as part of an Indian meal.*

4 SERVINGS

2 lb. boned leg of lamb, cut into 1-inch cubes
5 fl. oz. [⅝ cup] plain yogurt
1 tablespoon ground coriander
1 teaspoon ground turmeric
½ teaspoon chilli powder
1 teaspoon salt
2 garlic cloves, crushed
1-inch piece fresh ginger, grated or finely chopped
1 tablespoon chopped fresh coriander leaves
2 lemons, cut into wedges

Put the lamb cubes into a large mixing bowl.

Put the yogurt in a small mixing bowl and beat it well with a wooden spoon. Add the ground coriander, turmeric, chilli powder, salt, garlic and

---

*Beans cooked with salt pork and molasses, Boston Baked Beans is eaten with Boston Brown Bread.*

ginger and stir well to mix. Pour this mixture over the lamb cubes and mix well. Cover the bowl with aluminium foil and leave it in the refrigerator for at least 6 hours or overnight.

Preheat the grill [broiler] to high. Stir the meat mixture well with a wooden spoon. Thread 8 or 12 skewers, depending on the size of your skewers, with the meat cubes. Line your pan with aluminium foil to keep it clean. Grill [broil] the kebabs for 4 minutes on each side, 8 minutes in all.

Place the skewers on a serving dish, sprinkle the kebabs with the coriander leaves and garnish with lemon wedges. Serve immediately.

# Bottling

Bottling is a method of preserving fruit in sterilized and hermetically sealed jars. Properly prepared, the fruit will keep for a long time provided it is stored in a cool, dark place.

### BOTTLING VEGETABLES

It is generally considered unsafe to bottle vegetables in a water bath or in the oven, since the temperature reached is not high enough to kill the yeasts, moulds and bacteria. Vegetable bottling, therefore, must be done in a pressure cooker where a sufficiently high temperature can be reached. It is not, however, recommended that vegetables be bottled at home.

### BOTTLING FRUIT

There are two important precautions to take when bottling fruit. First, the fruit must be heated properly to destroy any yeasts, moulds or bacteria. Second, the bottles must be absolutely airtight.

### EQUIPMENT

There are three kinds of jars suitable for bottling—Kilner jars, snap-closed jars and jars with a Porosan metal cap. The jars should not be cracked or nicked at the edges and the covers must fit perfectly. The rubber rings should be exactly the right size and, to make sure that they are as elastic as they should be, they should be soaked in water for 10 minutes and then dipped in boiling water just before using.

A pair of tongs for lifting the jars, a long-handled wooden spoon and a bottle brush will also be needed.

Whatever vessel you use for sterilizing must be fitted with a rack or raised inner bottom to prevent the jars from coming into contact with the heated base of the pan, which will crack them.

Complete sterilizers with thermometers and raised inner bottoms can be bought, but a large pan or even a thick metal bucket will do.

### PREPARATION OF FRUIT

Wash and, if necessary, hull the fruit, discarding any which is bruised or over-ripe. Raspberries, blackberries and loganberries should first be soaked in a salt and water solution to draw out any maggots or grubs, and then carefully washed and drained in a colander. Peaches, plums, apricots and nectarines may be bottled whole or halved and stoned. Pears and apples may be halved or quartered and cored, or they can be bottled whole.

### SYRUPS

Fruit may be bottled in water or syrup. However, fruit bottled in syrup generally has a better flavour. The syrup may be thin, medium or thick, depending on the tartness of the fruit being used. For a thin syrup, use 4 ounces of sugar to 1 pint of water. For a medium syrup, use 8 ounces of sugar to 1 pint of water. For a thick syrup, the proportions are 1 pound of sugar to 1 pint of water. Average proportions are 8 ounces of sugar to 1 pint of water. This is suitable for all but very acid fruits, such as blackcurrants and damsons.

Tomatoes, unlike other fruits, are not bottled in syrup. Tomatoes may be bottled whole, peeled or unpeeled, peeled and pulped in their own juice or as a purée. If they are to be bottled whole, they should be covered in hot or cold brine. To make the brine, add 1 tablespoon of salt and $\frac{1}{2}$ tablespoon of sugar to 2 pints of water and bring to the boil.

### PACKING THE JARS

Wash the jars in hot, soapy water, rinse them in cold water, then drain them, leaving the insides wet. Fill the jars with the prepared fruit, packing it in carefully and tightly, using the handle of a wooden spoon if necessary. Leave $\frac{1}{2}$ inch between the top of the fruit and the cover.

### METHODS OF BOTTLING

There are six methods of bottling.

*1. Slow Heating in a Water Bath*
For this method you require a pan which is deep enough for the jars to be completely immersed in water and which has a rack or inner bottom. Wash the jars, drain them and then fill them with fruit. Pour in the cold syrup or water. Put on the rubber rings and lids tightly, then very slightly loosen the screw-bands or grips on the lids to allow for expansion.

Stand the sealed jars in the pan so that they do not touch each other or the sides of the pan. Completely cover the jars with cold water, cover the pan (if it does not have a lid, use a pastry board) and heat the water slowly. See the processing chart for times and temperatures.

Using the tongs, lift the jars out of the pan, one at a time, and stand them

*Carefully, but tightly, pack the fruit into the prepared jars.*

*Depending on the fruit used, top up the jars with syrup, water or brine.*

*After bottling, test the seals by lifting the jars by the lids.*

# Fruit processing chart

| | Preparation | Method 1 | | Method 2 | | Method 3 | Method 4 | | Method 5 | |
|---|---|---|---|---|---|---|---|---|---|---|
| | | Temp. °F. | *Time maintained min. | Temp. °F. | *Time maintained min. | Time maintained at 5 lb. pressure min. | Time 1-4 lb.* min. | 5-10 lb.* min. | Time 1-4 lb.* min. | 5-10 lb.* min. |
| **Apples** (in syrup) | Peel, core and slice. Keep under salted water (1 level tablespoon salt to 1 quart water). Drain and rinse before bottling. | 165 | 10 | 190 | 2 | 1 | Not recommended | | 30–40 | 45–60 |
| **Apples** (solid pack) | Prepare as above. Blanch in boiling water for 2 to 3 minutes or steam over boiling water until just tender. Pack warm. | 180 | 15 | 190 | 20 | 3–4 | Not recommended | | 50–60 | 65–80 |
| **Apricots** | Remove stalks. Pack whole or in halves. | 180 | 15 | 190 | 10 | 1 | Not recommended | | 40–50 | 55–70 |
| **Blackberries** | Remove stalks and leaves. | 165 | 10 | 190 | 2 | 1 | 45–55 | 60–75 | 30–40 | 45–60 |
| **Cherries** | Remove stalks. | 180 | 15 | 190 | 10 | 1 | 55–70 | 75–90 | 40–50 | 55–70 |
| **Cherry Plums** | Remove stalks. | 180 | 15 | 190 | 10 | 1 | 55–70 | 75–90 | 40–50 | 55–70 |
| **Currants** (Black, Red, White) | Remove stems and broken fruit. | 180 | 15 | 190 | 10 | 1 | 55–70 | 75–90 | 40–50 | 55–70 |
| **Damsons** | Remove stems. | 180 | 15 | 190 | 10 | 1 | 55–70 | 75–90 | 40–50 | 55–70 |
| **Gooseberries** (for pies) | Top and tail. If using syrup, nick the ends to prevent shrivelling. | 165 | 10 | 190 | 2 | 1 | 45–55 | 60–75 | 30–40 | 45–60 |
| (for dessert) | | 180 | 15 | 190 | 10 | 1 | 55–70 | 75–90 | 40–50 | 55–70 |
| **Greengages** | Remove stalks. This fruit is often cloudy when bottled. | 180 | 15 | 190 | 10 | 1 | Not recommended | | 40–50 | 55–70 |
| **Loganberries** | Remove stalks. This fruit attracts maggots so pick over carefully. | 165 | 10 | 190 | 2 | 1 | 45–55 | 60–75 | 30–40 | 45–60 |
| **Peaches** | Peel (see Tomatoes). Pack in halves or whole. | 180 | 15 | 190 | 20 | 3–4 | Not recommended | | 50–60 | 65–80 |
| **Pears** | Prepare as for apples in syrup. Pack and process as quickly as possible after preparing. Cooking pears should be stewed until tender. | 190 | 30 | 190 | 40 | 5 | Not recommended | | 60–70 | 75–90 |
| **Plums** | Remove stems. Fruit may rise. | 180 | 15 | 190 | 10 | 1 | 55–70 | 75–90 | 40–50 | 55–70 |
| **Plums** (halves) | Cut in half, remove stones, replace a few kernels if desired. | 180 | 15 | 190 | 20 | 3–4 | Not recommended | | 50–60 | 65–80 |
| **Raspberries** | See Loganberries. | 165 | 10 | 190 | 2 | 1 | 45–55 | 60–75 | 30–40 | 45–60 |
| **Rhubarb** (for pies) | Preserved when young so no need to peel. Wipe and cut stalks. | 165 | 10 | 190 | 2 | 1 | 45–55 | 60–75 | 30–40 | 45–60 |
| (for dessert) | | 180 | 15 | 190 | 10 | 1 | 55–70 | 75–90 | 40–50 | 55–70 |
| **Strawberries** | Remove hulls. This fruit loses colour and rises on bottling. It is better made into jam. | 165 | 10 | 190 | 2 | Not recommended | Not recommended | | 30–40 | 45–60 |
| **Tomatoes** (whole) | Remove calyx. Preserve with or without skins. The skins can easily be peeled off if the tomatoes are put into boiling water for 5 to 15 seconds and then dipped in cold water. | 190 | 30 | 190 | 40 | 5 | 80-100 | 105-125 | 60–70 | 75–90 |
| **Tomatoes** (solid pack) | Peel, cut in halves or quarters. Pack tightly in the jars, sprinkling salt on each layer—2 level teaspoons to every 2 pounds of tomatoes. A teaspoon of sugar added to each jar will improve the flavour. Press the tomatoes well down in the jars but do not add any liquid. | 190 | 40 | 190 | 50 | 15 | Not recommended | | 70–80 | 85-100 |

*Increase process time for large jars (Methods 1 and 2)

3 and 4 lb. size by   5 min. all packs except Tomatoes Solid Pack  10 min.

5 and 6 lb.  „   „   10 „   „   „   „   „   „   „   „   20 „

7 and 8 lb.  „   „   15 „   „   „   „   „   „   „   „   30 „

(Note: Method 6 is similar to Method 1.)

on a wooden table or board. Tighten the screw-band or grip on each jar as soon as it is lifted out of the water. Leave the jars to cool for 24 hours, then test the seal by unscrewing the screw-bands or removing the seal closures and lifting the bottles by their lids. If the lids come off the bottles, they must be sterilized again, or the fruit must be eaten within two or three days.

## 2. Quick Heating in a Water Bath

Follow the instructions given for Method 1, but use hot syrup or water (about 140°F) to fill the jars and warm water (about 100°F) in the bottling pan. Twenty-five to 30 minutes after the processing is begun, the water should reach simmering point (about 190°F). It should be kept simmering throughout the bottling process. Remove and finish the jars as directed in Method 1. Test the seal before storing.

## 3. Processing in a Pressure Cooker

For this method you will need a pressure cooker fitted with a gauge or weight for 5-pound pressure. The quantity of water will depend on the size of the pan. Put a rack or inner bottom in the pan and pour in the water. Add a little vinegar to prevent the pan from staining. Bring the water to the boil. Place the filled and sealed jars on the rack in the pan and put on the lid. Heat the pan and process the fruit for the length of time given in the processing chart. Remove the pan from the heat and allow it to cool for 10 minutes before removing the lid. Remove and finish the jars as described in Method 1. Test the seal before storing.

## 4. Slow Oven Method

With oven bottling it is more difficult to control the heating because the temperature in the oven varies from one part to another. Oven bottling is also less economical because only one batch of fruit can be processed at one time.

This method is suitable for gooseberries and dark-coloured fruit, but it is not recommended for such light-coloured fruits as apples, pears, peaches, light-coloured plums or solid pack tomatoes. The fruit will turn brown and the temperature is not high enough to penetrate the solid pack tomatoes.

Preheat the oven to very cool 250°F (Gas Mark $\frac{1}{2}$, 130°C). Fill the washed and drained jars with fruit, but do not pour over the syrup or water. Stand the jars on an asbestos mat, or on a baking sheet lined with newspaper, on a shelf in the middle of the oven. Process the fruit for the time given in the chart, remembering to vary the time according to the quantity of jars in the oven. Two 2-pound jars, for example, should be given the same time as four 1 pound jars.

Remove the jars from the oven, one at a time, and place on a heat proof surface. As each jar is removed from the oven, fill it to the brim with boiling syrup or water (or brine for tomatoes) and seal it. Remember to soak the rubber rings in boiling water just before sealing. Fill

and seal each jar before the next one is taken from the oven. Cool the jars for 24 hours. Test the seal before storing.

## 5. Moderate Oven Method

Any kind of fruit can be processed by this method, using whole fruit or solid pack. Preheat the oven to cool 300°F (Gas Mark 2, 150°C). Fill the washed and drained jars with fruit and pour over boiling syrup or water. Cover the jars with the lids, but do not put the screw-bands on. Stand the jars about 2 inches apart on a baking sheet lined with news-paper on a shelf in the middle of the oven. Process the fruit according to the times given in the chart. After processing, remove the jars from the oven and place them on a wooden board. Put on the screw-bands or grips. Cool for 24 hours, then test the seal before storing.

## 6. Pulping

This is a simple way of bottling stewed fruit, whether soft or hard, and it is an especially useful method for windfall apples or bruised plums, providing the bruised parts are removed first. Stew the fruit in a little water and add sugar if necessary. For tomatoes, you should add 2 teaspoons of sugar and 1 teaspoon of salt to bring out the flavour. When the fruit is completely soft and pulped, pour it into the hot jars and seal them. Slightly loosen the screw-bands or grips on the lids to allow for expansion.

Place the jars in a pan similar to that used for Method 1 and cover them with boiling water. Boil for 5 minutes, except tomatoes, which require 10 minutes' boiling. Remove and finish the jars as described in Method 1. Test the seal before storing.

### BOTTLING FAULTS AND CAUSES

Rising fruit may be caused by the fruit being packed too loosely in the jars, by over-heating during processing or by using too heavy a syrup. However, do not worry about the fruit rising—it will still keep well.

Mould may be caused by allowing too short a time and/or using too low a temperature for processing so that the fruit in the centre of the jar is not heated through, by putting too many jars in the oven at one time, by not completely covering the jars with water if using Methods 1 or 2, or by having a leak in the seal.

If there is only a small spot of mould, this may be removed and the rest of the fruit can be used. However, the flavour may not be very good.

Fermentation may be caused by any of the causes suggested for mould or by using over-ripe fruit. The seal of the jar will be broken if fermentation occurs.

There may be white sediment in the jar. Such sediment is usually due to the action of the fruit acid on hard water. If the fruit has fermented, however, the sediment may be due to yeast cells.

If a seal fails after only a short period, this is probably caused by allowing too

short a time for processing. It may also be due to a pin-hole in the rubber ring or a faulty cover. The fruit may be used for cooking.

If the fruit turns dark at the top of the jar, it may have been processed at too low a temperature or insufficient water was used in the deep pan in Methods 1 and 2.

## Botulinum

Botulinum are bacteria which live in the soil and which may grow in some improperly tinned foods. The foods in which the botulinum bacteria may be present are usually low-acid, such as meat and some vegetables. The bacteria may or may not give an indication of its presence. If the spores have been active, the food may be of a soft consistency and some gas may be present. The lids of the cans may bulge. The toxin that this bacteria produces, however, may be present without showing any evidence. Botulinum spores can remain resistant to temperatures as high as 212°F after several hours of processing and, consequently, can produce a deadly toxin in the tinned product. The toxin can cause the sometimes fatal disease botulism.

If the cans are slightly bulging, it is advisable not to open them. Either throw them away or, if they have been bought recently return them to the shop.

## Bouchées

Puff pastry patties, bouchées are filled with mixture of various meats. These tiny hors d'oeuvre get their name from the French word *bouchée* (boo-shay), which means 'mouthful'.

## Bouchées aux Fruits de Mer

PUFF PASTRY CASES FILLED WITH
MUSSELS AND PRAWNS

*Little puff pastry cases filled with mussels and prawns in cream sauce, Bouchées aux Fruits de Mer (boo-shay oh fwee d'mair) may be served as a first course for dinner or as a main dish at lunch.*

*Puff pastry is not difficult to make, but special care is needed when preparing it. Choose a time when you will not be interrupted for an hour or two. The best time would be early morning before the kitchen has become hot from cooking. Do not choose a warm day, as the dough will be sticky and difficult to roll.*

*The ingredients, the mixing bowl, the pastry board, rolling pin and your hands*

*Bouchées aux Fruits de Mer are flaky puff pastry cases filled with mussels and prawns or shrimps.*

*should all be cold. The butter should be cool and firm, but not completely hard. If the butter is too hard, place it between greaseproof or waxed paper and beat it 2 or 3 times with a rolling pin.*

*The method of rolling is important. Keep the pressure of the rolling pin even and roll away from yourself. Always roll in the same direction. Lift the rolling pin at the end of a stroke and begin again. Do not roll backwards. Avoid rolling so hard that the butter is pushed through the dough.*

*Do not turn the dough over; it should be rolled only on one side. If the fat breaks through the dough, dust it lightly with flour and place in the refrigerator for 15 minutes. Uncooked puff pastry will keep in the refrigerator for 24 to 48 hours if it is wrapped in greaseproof paper, so you can prepare it the day before you make the bouchées. The bouchée cases may also be baked a day or two before they are required if stored in an airtight tin.*

12 BOUCHEES

PUFF PASTRY CASES
8 oz. [2 cups] flour, cool
⅛ teaspoon salt
8 oz. [1 cup] butter, cool and firm
1 teaspoon lemon juice
5 fl. oz. [⅝ cup] water, ice cold
1 egg beaten with ½ teaspoon salt

FILLING
1 lb. mussels
5 fl. oz. [⅝ cup] white wine or water
1 tablespoon butter
1 small onion, finely chopped
2 oz. mushrooms, chopped
10 fl. oz. [1¼ cups] Béchamel sauce
6 oz. prawns or shrimps, shelled and chopped
5 fl. oz. double cream [⅝ cup heavy cream]
¼ teaspoon salt
4 grindings black pepper
1 tablespoon chopped parsley

Sift the flour and salt into a medium-sized bowl. Cut off about 1 tablespoon of butter. With your fingertips, rub it into the flour. Mix the lemon juice with the water. Make a well in the flour and pour in two-thirds of the liquid. Stir it with a table knife until a dough begins to form and add the rest of the liquid.

Lightly dust a marble slab, plastic work top or a board with flour. Put the dough on it and knead it with the heels of your hands for 2 minutes.

Roll the dough out to a square shape about ½-inch thick. Place the butter between two sheets of greaseproof paper and flatten it slightly with a rolling pin.

Place the butter in the centre of the dough. Fold the dough up over the butter to enclose it and make a parcel. Wrap the dough in waxed paper and put it in the refrigerator for 15 minutes.

Lightly flour your work surface. Remove the dough from the refrigerator, unwrap it and place it on the work surface with the join facing towards you.

With a strong firm pressure, roll the dough, just to the edge, about 4 times, to flatten it.

The dough should be a rectangular shape about ½-inch thick. Fold the dough as carefully as possible into 3, bringing the ends to the middle, like a parcel. With your fingertips, press the edges at both ends to seal it. Turn the dough around so that one edge faces you. Roll it out again and fold it in 3. Wrap it in waxed paper and refrigerate for 15 minutes. Repeat this process, giving 4 more 'turns' with a 15 minute rest in the refrigerator after each 2 turns. If the pastry looks streaky, give it an extra 'turn'.

To make the bouchées, on the lightly floured work top, roll out the pastry to a ½-inch thick square. With a pastry brush, evenly paint the pastry with the beaten egg-and-salt mixture. Cut out bouchée rounds with a 2½-inch round fluted cutter. Cut them as close to each other as possible so that no pastry is wasted.

Sprinkle cold water on a baking sheet to dampen it. Arrange the pastry rounds on it. With a 1½-inch round fluted or plain cutter make shallow cuts (not all the way through to the baking sheet) for the lid in the centre of each bouchée.

Place the baking sheet with the bouchées in the refrigerator to chill for 15 minutes.

Preheat the oven to hot 425°F (Gas Mark 7, 220°C).

Transfer the baking sheet to the top part of the oven and bake for 15 to 20 minutes, or until the bouchées are golden brown. Remove the baking sheet from the oven. Arrange the bouchées on a wire rack to cool. With the point of a small sharp knife, lift away the centre lid and, with a teaspoon, scoop out any soft centre.

To make the filling, scrub the mussels well under cold running water with a hard brush and tug out their beards. Discard any mussels which are not completely closed. Leave them to soak in a bowl of cold water for 1 hour, then drain and rinse them again.

Preheat the oven to hot 425°F (Gas Mark 7, 220°C).

Bring the wine or water to a boil in a medium-sized saucepan over moderate heat. Add the mussels to the boiling water, cover the pan and boil for 5 minutes or until the mussels have opened.

Lift them out with a slotted spoon. Scoop out the mussels from their shells. Set the mussels aside in a bowl and discard the shells.

Melt the butter in a small, heavy saucepan and add the chopped onion to it. Cook over low heat, stirring occasionally, for 10 minutes. Add the mushrooms and cook for a further 5 minutes. Remove the pan from the heat.

Put the béchamel sauce in a medium-sized saucepan and stir in the chopped onion and mushroom. Add the mussels and prawns and stir in the double cream. Add the salt and pepper. Taste the mixture and add more seasoning if necessary.

Place the bouchée cases back on the baking sheet and spoon the filling into them. Fill the cases almost to overflowing. Replace the bouchée lids, or sprinkle parsley over the tops. Place in the oven for 10 minutes or until the bouchées and filling are thoroughly heated.

## Bouchées au Jambon
PUFF PASTRY CASES FILLED WITH HAM

*This tasty ham and mushroom mixture makes another delicious filling for bouchées.*

12 BOUCHEES

12 baked bouchée cases

FILLING

2 tablespoons butter

4 oz. button mushrooms, wiped clean and sliced

8 oz. cooked ham, cut in one piece and diced

10 fl. oz. [1¼ cups] bechamel sauce

1 teaspoon prepared mustard

⅛ teaspoon salt

6 grindings black pepper

In a medium-sized saucepan melt the butter over low heat. Add the mushrooms to the pan and cook them for 3 to 4 minutes or until they are soft, shaking the pan occasionally so the mushrooms do not stick. Stir in the ham, béchamel sauce, mustard, salt and pepper.

Increase the heat to moderate and cook the mixture, stirring constantly, for 10 minutes or until it is hot.

With a teaspoon fill the hot bouchée cases with the mixture and serve at once.

## Bouchées Newburg
PUFF PASTRY CASES FILLED WITH LOBSTER

*This alternative filling for bouchées is based on a classic recipe. If you prefer, other shellfish may be used instead.*

12 BOUCHEES

12 baked bouchée cases

FILLING

1 tablespoon butter

1 small onion, finely chopped

12 oz. cooked lobster meat, cut in small pieces

2 tablespoons brandy

10 fl. oz. single cream [1¼ cups light cream]

3 egg yolks

¼ teaspoon salt

4 grindings black pepper

In a medium-sized frying-pan melt the butter over moderate heat. Add the onion to the pan and fry it for 6 to 8 minutes or until it is soft but not brown. Stir in the lobster meat and cook for 10 minutes or until the lobster is hot, stirring occasionally.

Pour in the brandy and with a match set it alight. Remove the pan from the heat and allow the flames to die out.

In a small bowl, beat the cream and egg yolks together with a fork. Pour the cream-and-egg yolk mixture over the lobster mixture in the pan. Stir in the salt and pepper.

Return the pan to low heat and cook and stir the mixture until it is thick.

Remove the pan from the heat. With a teaspoon fill the hot bouchée cases with the mixture and serve at once.

## Bouchées Parmentier au Fromage
POTATO CHEESE STICKS

*A French recipe, Bouchées Parmentier au Fromage (boo-shay pahr-mont-yay oh froh-mahj) are small mouthfuls of cheese and mashed potato. They are ideal to serve at a cocktail party. They will keep for about a week if they are wrapped in waxed paper and stored in an airtight tin.*

ABOUT 60 STICKS

2 large potatoes, washed, peeled and sliced

6 oz. [1½ cups] flour

4 oz. [½ cup] butter, softened

2 small eggs

6 oz. Emmenthal cheese, grated

¼ teaspoon white pepper

⅛ teaspoon grated nutmeg

¼ teaspoon caraway seeds

½ teaspoon salt

Preheat the oven to hot 425°F (Gas Mark 7, 220°C). Line two baking sheets with waxed paper or vegetable parchment.

In a medium-sized saucepan, cover the potatoes with water and bring to the boil over moderate heat. Continue boiling for 15 to 20 minutes, or until the potatoes are tender when pierced with a fork. Remove the pan from the heat, drain and return them to the empty saucepan.

Mash the potatoes well with a potato masher or fork. Beat in the flour. Add the butter, little by little. When all the butter has been absorbed, beat in the eggs, cheese, pepper, nutmeg, caraway seeds and salt. Taste and add more seasoning if necessary.

Using a forcing bag, fitted with a fluted pastry nozzle about $\frac{1}{4}$-inch in diameter, pipe the mixture into 2-inch lengths on to the baking sheets.

Place the baking sheets in the oven and bake for about 15 minutes, or until the sticks are lightly brown.

Remove the baking sheets from the oven and leave the sticks to cool for 5 minutes. Transfer the sticks, with a spatula, from the baking sheets to a wire rack. Cool to room temperature before serving.

## Bouillabaisse

FISH SOUP SERVED WITH PIECES OF FISH

*A filling fisherman's soup from the South of France, Bouillabaisse (bwee-yah-behz) makes a wonderful main dish for a lunch or dinner party. It is eaten in large soup plates and the pieces of fish and the soup are served separately. It is usually accompanied by a side dish of Rouille (ruee), a garlic, pimiento and chilli pepper sauce which enhances the flavour of the soup. Each guest spoons a little into his soup according to taste. Accompany this dish with hot crusty French bread and butter.*

*All the fish except the lobster can be cleaned, scaled and sliced well in advance and kept, covered, in the refrigerator. The court bouillon may also be made in advance and stored in a covered container in the refrigerator.*

6 TO 8 SERVINGS

FISH
2 lb. mussels
2 x 2 lb. lobsters (optional)
1 lb. each of 3 kinds of the following white fish, washed, cleaned, scaled and cut into 1-inch pieces: halibut, red snapper, bass, haddock, cod, sole or rockfish
2 lb. scallops, cut in halves

COURT BOUILLON
5 fl. oz. [$\frac{5}{8}$ cup] olive oil
2 large onions, thinly sliced
2 leeks, washed and thinly sliced
2 garlic cloves, crushed
8 tomatoes, blanched, peeled and coarsely chopped
2 pints [5 cups] water and 1 pint [$2\frac{1}{2}$ cups] white wine
1 lb. fish heads, bones and trimmings
1 teaspoon dried tarragon
2 tablespoons fresh lemon juice
2-inch strip lemon peel
1 teaspoon dried thyme
1 tablespoon chopped parsley
1 bay leaf
1$\frac{1}{4}$ teaspoons crushed saffron threads
$\frac{1}{2}$ teaspoon salt
8 grindings black pepper

ROUILLE
1 large green pepper, the white pith removed, seeded, and finely chopped
1 green chilli pepper, finely chopped
7 fl. oz. [$\frac{7}{8}$ cup] water
3 canned pimientos, drained and dried
3 garlic cloves, crushed
2 fl. oz. [$\frac{1}{4}$ cup] olive oil
1 to 2$\frac{1}{2}$ tablespoons dried breadcrumbs
$\frac{1}{4}$ teaspoon Tabasco sauce

CROUTES
14 slices French bread, 1-inch thick
2 teaspoons olive oil
1 large garlic clove, cut in half

To prepare the mussels for cooking they must be thoroughly scrubbed with a stiff brush. Discard any mussels which are not tightly shut or any mussels that seem too heavy, as they will be full of sand. With a small sharp knife, scrape off the tufts of hair, or beards which protrude from between the closed shell halves. Place the mussels in a basin of cold water for 2 hours so they disgorge their sand. Wash and drain them again before cooking.

To make the court bouillon, heat the oil in a large, heavy, flameproof casserole over moderate heat. Reduce the heat to low and add the onions and leeks. Cook them slowly for 5 minutes, or until they are tender, stirring occasionally. Stir in the garlic and chopped tomatoes. Raise the heat to moderate and cook for 5 minutes more. Add the water, the wine, the fish trimmings, herbs and seasonings to the saucepan and cook, uncovered, over low heat for 40 minutes.

While the court bouillon is cooking, make the Rouille. Put the green pepper and chilli pepper in a small saucepan. Add the water and simmer over low heat for 10 minutes until the peppers are tender. Drain them through a sieve and pat them dry with kitchen paper towels. Put the peppers, pimiento and garlic in a large mortar and mash them with a pestle to a smooth paste, or put the peppers, pimiento and garlic in a mixing bowl and mash with a wooden spoon. Gradually beat in the olive oil, a few drops at a time. When all the oil has been

beaten in, add enough breadcrumbs to make a sauce thick enough to hold its shape when a little is spooned on to a plate. Stir in the Tabasco. Taste and add salt and pepper if necessary.

Set the Rouille aside in a bowl.

Preheat the oven to warm 325°F (Gas Mark 3, 170°C).

To make the croûtes, place the slices of bread in one layer on a baking sheet and bake in the oven for 10 minutes. Then, with a pastry brush, lightly coat the slices with olive oil. Turn the slices over on to the side which was uppermost in the first baking and bake for another 10 minutes, or until the bread is dry and golden brown. Rub each slice of bread with the cut side of the garlic and set aside, covered with aluminium foil.

When the court bouillon is ready, strain it through a large, fine sieve into another large saucepan, pressing down with the back of a metal spoon to squeeze out the juices from the vegetables and fish trimmings. Discard the vegetables and trimmings. Cover the saucepan and place it to one side.

Now prepare the lobsters. Tie the claws together and wash each lobster. Lay it on its underbelly on a chopping board and, with a towel wrapped around one hand for protection, grasp the lobster firmly. With a large, heavy, sharp knife, cut through the lobster behind the head to sever the spinal cord. This kills the lobster. Slice the tail in half lengthways and then into 4 or 5 pieces crossways. (Do this by putting the knife in position and hitting the back of it sharply with a hammer.) Remove the lobster's intestinal tract. Cut off the claws and separate the joints from the claws. Crack the flat side of each claw. Remove the feelers and cut the body section in half lengthways. Remove and discard the gelatinous sac near the head, but scoop out and reserve the liver and coral.

Bring the court bouillon to a boil over moderately high heat. Add the lobster pieces and liver and coral to the bouillon. Boil briskly for 5 minutes. Add the white fish and cook for 5 minutes more. Add the mussels and scallops, cover the pan and boil for 5 minutes longer or until the mussels open and the fish is tender when pierced with a fork. Do not overcook the fish or it will not stay in firm pieces.

To serve, remove the fish carefully from the bouillon with a slotted spoon and transfer it to a warmed serving dish.

---

*A hearty Mediterranean fish soup, Bouillabaisse is traditionally served with hot, crusty French bread.*

Pour the soup into a large tureen. Add just enough of the soup to the Rouille to thin it. Pour the thinned Rouille into a sauce boat to be served separately.

At the table put 1 croûte in the middle of each individual soup bowl. Ladle the soup into each bowl and top with some pieces of fish. Serve very hot.

## Bouillabaisse de Cabillaud
COD SOUP

*Unlike most fish soups, which are made from a variety of fish, this Bouillabaisse de Cabillaud (bwee-yah-bahz d'cah-bee-yoh) is made only with cod. The fish and potatoes are served separately from the soup, so that the dish is almost a meal in itself.*

6 TO 8 SERVINGS

3 tablespoons olive oil
3 onions, chopped
3 garlic cloves, chopped
4 large tomatoes, blanched, peeled and chopped
4 pints [5 pints] water
½ teaspoon crushed saffron threads
bouquet garni, consisting of 4 parsley sprigs, 1 thyme spray, and 1 bay leaf tied together
1 teaspoon grated orange rind
½ teaspoon cayenne pepper
½ teaspoon black pepper
½ teaspoon salt
10 potatoes, peeled and sliced into ½-inch rounds
2 lb. cod fillets, cut into chunks

Heat the oil in a large saucepan over moderate heat. Add the onions and garlic and cook gently for 10 minutes, stirring frequently with a wooden spoon. Add the tomatoes, stir to mix and cook for another 2 minutes. Stir in the water, saffron, bouquet garni, orange rind, cayenne pepper, black pepper and salt. Reduce the heat to very low and simmer the soup for 20 minutes.

Drop the potato slices into the soup and cook for 10 minutes. Add the pieces of cod and cook, stirring occasionally, for another 15 minutes, or until the fish is cooked.

With a large slotted spoon, remove the fish and potatoes from the soup and place them on a heated dish. Pour the soup through a sieve into a large, heated tureen, pressing the vegetables and flavourings with the back of a wooden spoon to extract as much of their juices as possible. Discard the vegetables and flavourings.

Serve immediately.

*For clarified bouillon, bring the liquid to the boil, skimming off the scum with a slotted spoon.*

*Strain the bouillon through a wire sieve into a pan and discard the meat, bones and vegetables.*

*Whisk the egg whites and egg shells into the boiling bouillon. Be careful not to break the crust.*

*After the third boiling, allow the liquid to cool, then strain it slowly through a cloth into a bowl.*

## Bouillon

*Bouillon (bwee-yon) is a beef and veal bone stock which is enriched with the addition of meat. Like stock, bouillon is used as a base for sauces and gravies, as well as for consommé. You can serve the meat and vegetables separately as a main course, but if you do, the finished bouillon will not be strong enough for a consommé.*

ABOUT 5½ PINTS

1 veal bone
2 lb. rolled ribs of beef, with the bones
6 pints [15 cups] plus 6 fl. oz. [¾ cup] cold water
2 teaspoons salt
4 carrots, scraped and sliced into 2-inch pieces
1 turnip, peeled and quartered
3 leeks, washed and cut in halves
1 celery stalk, sliced into 2-inch pieces
1 parsnip, peeled and quartered
2 onions, each stuck with 1 clove
bouquet garni, consisting of 3 parsley sprigs, 1 thyme spray and 1 bay leaf tied together

*Low Cal*

Wash the bones and put them in a large stock pot or saucepan and pour over the 6 pints of water. Add the 2 teaspoons of salt.

Place the pot over low heat and bring the liquid slowly to the boil, allowing at least 30 minutes for the liquid to heat. As the liquid heats, scum will rise to the surface. With a slotted spoon, skim this scum off at regular intervals.

When the liquid reaches boiling point, add 2 fluid ounces [¼ cup] of water. Bring the liquid slowly to the boil again, skimming off the scum. When it boils add another 2 fluid ounces [¼ cup] of water. Repeat this process once more to clear the bouillon.

Add all the vegetables to the pot. Bring the liquid to the boil and skim off the scum. Put in the bouquet garni. Half cover the pan with the lid on a slant and reduce the heat to low. Simmer the bouillon for 3 hours.

Strain the bouillon through a fine wire sieve into a glass or enamel pan. Discard the meat, bones and vegetables.

Leave the bouillon to cool and then cover the jug or bowl. Do not break the layer of fat that forms on the surface of the bouillon until you are ready to use it.

If you want to serve the boiled beef and vegetables, use a slotted spoon to take them out of the pot after the bouillon has simmered for 1½ hours. Then continue simmering the bouillon with just the bones for 1½ hours longer.

## Bouillon, Clarified

*Clarified Bouillon (bwee-yon) is used for making clear consommés. It is a simple process, providing certain points are remembered. The bouillon should be cold and of a clear, brown colour. It is impossible to clarify a cloudy bouillon properly. An enamel or glass saucepan should be used rather than an aluminium pan, which tends to make the bouillon cloudy. The pan and whisk should be scalded before use. The egg whites should be beaten only to a froth, and when the white crust forms on top of the bouillon as a result of adding the egg whites, it should not be broken, since it acts as a filter when straining the bouillon.*

MAKES 1½ PINTS

1½ pints [3¾ cups] of cold bouillon
2 egg whites, lightly beaten
2 crushed
egg shells

*Low Cal*

Bring the bouillon to the boil in an enamel or glass saucepan over moderate heat. Add the beaten egg whites and the crushed egg shells to the bouillon and, with a wire whisk, whisk it vigorously. The whisking should be done in the reverse of the usual movement, or anti-clockwise. This will more thoroughly mix the egg whites into the bouillon.

As soon as the bouillon begins to boil again, stop whisking and allow it to rise to the top of the pan.

Remove the pan from the heat until the bouillon has settled.

Repeat the boiling process twice more. Be careful not to break the white crust which forms on the top.

After the third boiling, allow the liquid to stand for 5 minutes in the pan, then slowly strain it through a scalded, clean, flannel cloth into a jug or mixing bowl. Do not squeeze the cloth. This will make the bouillon cloudy. Again, do not break the egg white crust. If the bouillon is not absolutely clear, strain it again through the cloth and egg white crust.

## Boules de Neige au Chocolat

POACHED MERINGUES ON
CHOCOLATE CUSTARD

*A delectable dessert, Boules de Neige au Chocolat (bool d' nayj oh shoh-koh-lah)*

*Poached meringues in a rich chocolate custard, Boules de Neige au Chocolat is a delectable cold dessert.*

---

*are meringues which are poached in milk and then arranged on a rich chocolate custard. Serve in one large serving bowl or spooned into individual sundae glasses. This dessert may be accompanied by a bowl of whipped cream.*

6 SERVINGS

1 pint [2½ cups] milk
1 teaspoon vanilla essence
6 oz. [¾ cup] castor sugar
2 egg whites
CHOCOLATE CUSTARD
2 oz. [¼ cup] castor sugar
3 tablespoons cocoa
4 egg yolks

In a medium-sized saucepan, simmer the milk, vanilla essence and 2 ounces [¼ cup] of sugar over low heat, stirring occasionally until the sugar has dissolved.

In a medium-sized mixing bowl, beat the egg whites with a wire whisk until they form stiff peaks. Beat 2 teaspoons of the sugar into the egg whites for 1 minute. Then, using a metal spoon or spatula, carefully fold the remaining sugar into the meringue.

Using a large spoon, drop balls of meringue on to the simmering milk. Simmer for 4 to 5 minutes, stirring the milk once, or until the meringues are firm. Carefully remove the meringues from the milk and set them on kitchen paper towels. Reserve the milk.

To make the custard, mix the sugar, the cocoa and egg yolks in a medium-sized mixing bowl. Gradually stir in the sweetened hot milk reserved from poaching the meringues.

Place the bowl over a pan of barely simmering water and, stirring constantly with a wooden spoon, cook the custard until it is thick enough to coat the spoon in a thin film.

Remove the custard from the heat and leave it for a few minutes to cool. Pour the chocolate custard into a glass serving bowl or individual sundae glasses. Place the meringues on top. Chill in the refrigerator for at least 2 hours.

## Bouquet

The fragrance and aroma of wine is called its bouquet.

## Bouquet Garni

A bouquet garni (booh-kay gahr-nee) is the French culinary term for a bunch of herbs, usually including a bay leaf and sprigs of parsley and thyme, tied together (or often put in a piece of thin cloth) and cooked in stews, soups and sauces to give flavour. It is removed before the dish is served. A bouquet garni was known by the English as a faggot of herbs, a term which is rarely used today.

## Bourbon

The famous American whisky made from corn or maize, Bourbon was originally produced in Bourbon County, Kentucky, in the late eighteenth century. United States Federal law requires that all bourbon be made from a mash of at least 51 per cent corn. The best bourbon is 'straight', which means that it is the product of a single distillery during a given year and is not blended with other distillations. Straight bourbon labelled 'bottled in bond' is the best of all. Bourbon is an ingredient in Mint Juleps and Old-Fashioneds.

---

*A bouquet garni is a bunch of fresh or dried herbs, used to flavour stews, soups and sauces.*

## Bourbon-glazed Ham

*Baked ham coated with a bourbon, brown sugar and mustard glaze and garnished with orange segments is an American speciality, and it is a magnificent main dish for a dinner party. The ham may be served with a green vegetable and mashed potatoes. It is best to buy as large a ham as possible, since glazed ham is delicious both hot and cold. You should allow 20 to 30 minutes per pound for the boiling, but, if it is a small ham, allow a little longer.*

10 TO 12 SERVINGS

10 lb. smoked ham, well scrubbed
    bouquet garni, consisting of 4
    parsley sprigs, 1 thyme spray and
    1 bay leaf tied together
8 peppercorns
1 onion, quartered
1 carrot, scraped and quartered
1 celery stalk, quartered
12 oz. [1½ cups] dark brown sugar
2 teaspoons dry mustard
5 fl. oz. [⅝ cup] bourbon whisky
12 whole cloves
2 oranges, peeled and segmented

Put the ham in a large bowl and cover it with cold water. Leave the ham to soak overnight. Drain the ham.

Transfer the ham to a large pan and cover it with water. Add the bouquet garni, peppercorns, onion, carrot and celery. Place the pan over moderately high heat and bring the water to the boil. Reduce the heat to low and simmer the ham gently for 4½ hours.

Remove the pan from the heat and leave the ham to cool in the liquid.

Preheat the oven to moderate 350°F (Gas Mark 4, 180°C).

To prepare the glaze mixture, combine the sugar, mustard and 2 fluid ounces of the bourbon in a small mixing bowl. Set the bowl aside.

With a sharp knife, cut away the rind of the ham. Then, using the point of the knife, score the fat in a diamond pattern, making cuts through the fat to the meat.

Put the ham on a rack in a roasting tin. Using a pastry brush, coat the scored ham with the remaining 3 fluid ounces of bourbon. With a rubber spatula, spread the prepared glaze mixture over the ham. Push the cloves into the fat. Arrange the orange segments on the top of the ham, securing each segment with a wooden cocktail stick.

Put the ham in the oven and bake it for 45 minutes to 1 hour.

## Bourgeoise, à la

A French culinary term, *à la Bourgeoise* (ah lah boor-jwahz) refers to various dishes which are cooked in a modest home style. Most of these dishes consist of large pieces of braised meat and always include sliced young carrots, turnips, small onions and diced lean bacon.

## Bourgueil

A light red wine from the Touraine area on the Loire River in France, Bourgueil (*boor-goy*), which should be drunk young, has the distinct flavour of raspberry.

## Bourguignonne, à la

*À la Bourguignonne* (ah lah boor-gheen-yon) is a French culinary term which refers to dishes in which red wine, usually a Burgundy, is used. Mushrooms, onions, and rolls of grilled [broiled] bacon are often included too.

# Bourride

PROVENÇAL FISH SOUP WITH GARLIC
MAYONNAISE

*An unusual fish soup, delicately flavoured
with herbs and wine and enriched with a
pungent garlic mayonnaise, Bourride (boo-
reed) is frequently served as a main course
in Provence with only fresh fruit and
cheese to follow.*

6 SERVINGS

2 tablespoons olive oil
1 medium-sized onion, thinly sliced
2 leeks, white part only, thinly
   sliced
2 large tomatoes, blanched, peeled
   and quartered
1 carrot, scraped and sliced
2 or 3 cod or haddock heads
2 tablespoons white wine vinegar
1 bay leaf
$\frac{1}{2}$ teaspoon dried thyme
$\frac{1}{2}$ teaspoon dried fennel
2 teaspoons salt
$\frac{1}{2}$ teaspoon dried tarragon
2 tablespoons lemon juice
3 pints [$7\frac{1}{2}$ cups] water
10 fl. oz. [$1\frac{1}{4}$ cups] white wine
4 egg yolks
2 lb. haddock or cod fillets, cut into
   1-inch pieces
4 tablespoons aioli

Heat the oil in a large, flameproof casserole, or soup pot, over moderate heat.
Add the onion, leeks, tomatoes and carrot.
Cover the casserole and reduce the heat to
moderately low. Cook the vegetables
for 20 to 25 minutes, or until they have
softened.

Add the fish heads, wine vinegar,
bay leaf, thyme, fennel, salt, tarragon,
1 tablespoon of lemon juice, the water
and the wine. Raise the heat and bring
the liquid slowly to the boil. Reduce the
heat to low again and gently simmer the
broth for 30 to 40 minutes or until it has
reduced slightly.

Strain the broth into a measuring jug.
Discard the fish heads, vegetables and
flavourings. Measure 3 pints [$7\frac{1}{2}$ cups] of
the broth (this is ample for 6 people) and
return it to the casserole.

In a medium-sized mixing bowl, using
a fork or a wire whisk, beat the egg yolks
together with the remaining 1 tablespoon
of lemon juice and 5 fluid ounces [$\frac{5}{8}$ cup]
of the hot, strained broth.

Stir the egg yolk mixture into the
broth and return the casserole to moderate heat. Add the pieces of fish and stir
the soup gently. Cook the soup for 6 to
8 minutes, or until the fish is still firm
but cooked and the soup is quite hot and
has thickened slightly. Do not let the
soup boil.

Remove the casserole from the heat.
Stir in the aioli. Serve the soup at once.
If you like, serve a sauceboat of aioli
separately.

# Boursin

Boursin (boor-san) is a French triple-
cream cheese.

# Boxty

IRISH POTATO PANCAKES

*'Boxty on the griddle, Boxty in the pan,
If you don't eat Boxty, you'll never get a
man.' Boxty are traditional Irish potato
pancakes which are served on the eve of
All Saints' Day. The pancakes may be
served alone or accompanied by a thick apple
sauce and slices of crisp bacon.*

TWELVE 3-INCH PANCAKES

$\frac{1}{2}$ lb. potatoes
$\frac{1}{2}$ lb. potatoes, boiled and mashed
2 eggs
2 tablespoons flour
1 teaspoon salt
$\frac{1}{2}$ teaspoon freshly ground black
   pepper
1 small onion, finely grated
2 fl. oz. [$\frac{1}{4}$ cup] milk
2 oz. [$\frac{1}{4}$ cup] butter

Peel the raw potatoes and coarsely grate
them on to a clean cloth. Wring the
cloth to extract as much moisture from
the potatoes as possible. Put the grated
potato in a large mixing bowl. Add the
mashed potatoes and beat in the eggs
with a wooden spoon.

Add the flour, salt, pepper, grated
onion and milk to the egg-and-potato
mixture. Stir with the wooden spoon
until all the ingredients are combined.

Melt the butter in a large frying-pan
over moderate heat. When the foam subsides, drop 2 or 3 large spoonfuls of the
mixture into the pan and cook for 3 to
4 minutes on each side, or until the pancakes are golden and crisp round the
edges.

Remove the pancakes from the frying-
pan, transfer them to a heated plate and
cover with aluminium foil to keep them
warm. Cook the remaining pancakes,
adding more butter to the pan if needed.
If necessary, the pancakes may be kept
warm in a very low oven. Serve the pancakes as soon as they are all cooked.

*Crisp potato pancakes, Boxty may be
served alone or with thick apple
sauce and fried bacon.*

## Brabançonne, à la

The French culinary term *à la Braban-conne* (ah lah BRAH-bun-SON) refers to meat dishes which are served with a garnish of endive and potato croquettes, to which hop shoots, cooked in butter or cream, are often added.

## Braciuolia di Manzo

GRILLED [BROILED] BEEF ROLLS

*An Italian recipe, Braciuolia di Manzo (brah-chyoh-lah dee MAHN-zoh) are grilled [broiled] beef rolls. This unusual lunch or supper dish may be served with creamed spinach, French fried potatoes and a tomato and onion salad.*

4 SERVINGS

- 2 lb. rump or sirloin steak, sliced about ¼-inch thick
- 1 large onion, finely chopped
- 2 garlic cloves, crushed
- 1 teaspoon dried basil
- ½ teaspoon salt
- ½ teaspoon freshly ground black pepper
- 6 bacon slices, cut in half lengthways

Preheat the grill [broiler] to moderate.

Place the slices of steak on a board and cut them into 2-inch squares. In a small bowl, mix together the onion, garlic, basil, salt and pepper. Put a small amount of this mixture in the centre of each square of meat. Roll the steak carefully around the mixture.

Wrap a piece of bacon around each steak roll and fasten with a wooden cocktail stick.

Place the rolls on the grill rack [broiler pan]. Grill [broil] the rolls for 5 minutes on each side, or until they are brown and tender.

Place the rolls on a warmed serving dish, sprinkle with salt and pepper and serve immediately.

## Braciuolia Ripiene

STUFFED VEAL ROLLS

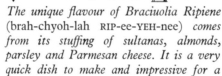

*The unique flavour of Braciuolia Ripiene (brah-chyoh-lah RIP-ee-YEH-nee) comes from its stuffing of sultanas, almonds, parsley and Parmesan cheese. It is a very quick dish to make and impressive for a dinner party.*

4 SERVINGS

- 8 escalopes of veal, pounded thin
- 8 slices of prosciutto
- 4 tablespoons chopped fresh parsley
- 2 tablespoons slivered almonds
- 2 tablespoons sultanas or raisins
- 3 tablespoons grated Parmesan cheese
- ½ teaspoon salt
- ¼ teaspoon freshly ground black pepper
- 2 oz. [¼ cup] butter
- 6 fl. oz. [¾ cup] Marsala

Put the escalopes of veal on a board. Place one slice of ham on each of the escalopes.

Combine the parsley, almonds, sultanas, cheese, salt and the pepper in a small mixing bowl. Place a spoonful of the mixture in the middle of each ham slice. Roll the meat and the filling in swiss [jelly] roll style. Tie the rolls with thread.

*Veal escalopes stuffed with prosciutto, almonds, sultanas and Parmesan cheese, Braciuolia Ripiene is a superb dinner party dish.*

In a large, heavy frying-pan, heat the butter over moderate heat until it is hot. Put the veal rolls in the pan and brown them on all sides. Add the Marsala, cover and simmer gently for 20 minutes. With a slotted spoon, take the rolls out of the pan. Remove the thread from the meat. Serve, with the wine sauce, on a bed of rice.

## Brains

*The brains of calf, sheep or pig are considered a culinary delicacy. Calves' brains are the most popular.*

*To prepare brains, soak them in cold water for at least 4 hours, changing the water frequently. Remove and discard the loose skin. Rinse the brains in tepid water to remove any clots of blood. The brains should then be gently poached in the following bouillon:*

2 pints [5 cups] water
1 teaspoon salt
1 onion, stuck with 2 cloves
2 tablespoons vinegar
    bouquet garni, consisting of 4
    parsley sprigs, 1 thyme spray
    and 1 bay leaf tied together
6 peppercorns

Sheep's brains should be simmered in the bouillon, over low heat, for 15 minutes. Calf's and pig's brains should be simmered for 20 to 25 minutes.

Once poached and drained, the brains are ready to be prepared in a variety of ways. One pound of brains will serve 4 people.

## Brains Baked with Eggs

*A quick and easy dish to prepare, Brains Baked with Eggs is ideal for a family lunch or supper. If you prefer, this dish may be made in one medium-sized casserole, rather than in individual cocotte dishes. Serve with sautéed potatoes and French beans.*

6 SERVINGS

3 oz. [⅜ cup] butter
3 sets of brains, soaked and poached
1 lb. tomatoes, blanched, peeled, seeded and coarsely chopped
2 tablespoons olive oil, heated
1 small onion, finely chopped
½ teaspoon dried basil
½ teaspoon salt
⅛ teaspoon cayenne pepper
¼ teaspoon black pepper
1 tablespoon chopped parsley
6 eggs
1 tablespoon lemon juice

Preheat the oven to moderate 350°F (Gas Mark 4, 180°C). Grease 6 cocotte dishes with one-third of the butter.

With a small, sharp knife, cut the brains into 1-inch cubes. Divide the brains equally among the cocotte dishes.

In a small mixing bowl combine the tomatoes, olive oil, onion, basil, salt, cayenne, black pepper and half the chopped parsley. Spoon the mixture over the brains in the cocotte dishes. Break 1 egg into each dish.

Place the dishes on a baking sheet in the oven and bake for 5 minutes, or until the eggs are firm.

While the brains are baking, melt the remaining butter in a small saucepan over moderate heat. Stir in the lemon juice.

Remove the brains from the oven. Pour the hot butter-and-lemon sauce over them. Sprinkle each dish with the remaining parsley. Serve at once.

## Brains in Butter

*An unusual light main dish for lunch or supper, Brains in Butter are very easy to prepare. Serve with cauliflower sautéed in butter, boiled new potatoes, and a light white wine.*

---

**Quick and easy to prepare, Brains in Butter flavoured with capers is an unusual and tasty light supper dish.**

6 SERVINGS

3 sets of calves' brains
2 pints [5 cups] cold water with
    3 teaspoons salt added
8 fl. oz. [1 cup] beef stock
2 celery stalks, sliced
1 onion, cut in half
1 bay leaf
¼ teaspoon dried sage
10 peppercorns
4 oz. [½ cup] butter
2 teaspoons white wine vinegar
1 tablespoon capers

Place the brains in a bowl and cover them with the salted water. Soak for 20 minutes.

Drain off the water and remove the membrane and veins from the brains.

Put the beef stock in a large saucepan and bring to a boil over high heat. Put the brains into the boiling stock and add the celery, onion, bay leaf, sage and peppercorns.

Reduce the heat, cover the pan and simmer for 25 minutes.

While the brains are cooking, put the butter in a small saucepan and melt it over moderate heat. Cook until it is nut brown, but do not let it burn. With a wooden spoon, stir in the vinegar and capers.

Remove the cooked brains carefully from the liquid with a slotted spoon. Discard the liquid. Place the brains on a warmed serving dish. Cover them with the browned butter mixture. Serve immediately.

## Brains, Breaded

*Brains rolled in breadcrumbs, cheese and parsley and quickly fried until the outsides are appetizingly crisp, this tasty Italian dish should be served very hot with a green salad.*

4 SERVINGS

2 sets of brains, soaked and poached
2 oz. [1 cup] fresh, white breadcrumbs
1 tablespoon chopped parsley
1 tablespoon grated Parmesan cheese
½ teaspoon salt
¼ teaspoon black pepper
4 tablespoons olive oil

Cut the brains into small pieces with a small, sharp knife.

In a small mixing bowl, combine the breadcrumbs, parsley, cheese, salt and pepper. Roll the brains in the mixture.

In a medium-sized frying-pan heat the oil over moderate heat. Fry the brains for about 5 minutes, or until they are brown. Lift the brains out of the pan with a slotted spoon, transfer them to a warmed serving dish and serve at once.

## Braise

A combination of steaming and baking which requires heat to be applied from above and below, braising is a method of cooking meat, fish, game, poultry and some vegetables. In France, in earlier times, braising was done in a special pan, called a *braisière*, which had a concave lid for holding hot charcoal. Later, the charcoal was replaced by boiling water and today, although braising pans are available and are used in professional kitchens, they no longer have concave lids. For domestic use a heavy saucepan or flameproof casserole may be used for braising.

Braising is done in part on top of the stove and then, for the greater part of the cooking time, in the oven. When a large piece of meat is braised it is first browned and then placed on a bed of vegetables, bacon and herbs. This bed of vegetables is used for flavouring and is discarded before the meat is served. A little liquid is added and after a preliminary simmer on top of the stove for up to an hour, the meat is cooked in the oven for 2 to 3 hours.

*A subtle blend of flavours, Braised Bass is a simple, interesting dish. If bass is not available, halibut or haddock may be used instead.*

## Braised Bass

*A simple yet interesting way to serve bass, this dish may be served with mashed or croquette potatoes.*

4 SERVINGS

6 oz. [¾ cup] butter
1 lb. carrots, scraped and finely chopped
2 medium-sized onions, chopped
1½ teaspoons salt
2 teaspoons finely chopped parsley
½ teaspoon dried tarragon
¼ teaspoon black pepper
1 bass, about 3 lb., cleaned and gutted
10 fl. oz. [1¼ cups] dry white wine
1 tablespoon melted butter
3 lemons, cut into slices

Preheat the oven to fairly hot 375°F (Gas Mark 5, 190°C).

Melt one-third of the butter in a medium-sized saucepan. When the foam subsides, add the carrots and onions.

Season with ½ teaspoon of salt. Cover the saucepan and cook the vegetables for 15 minutes over low heat.

In a small bowl, beat together another third of the butter, the parsley, tarragon, the remaining 1 teaspoon of salt and the pepper until the mixture is smooth and creamy. Spread the insides of the fish with the butter mixture.

Remove the vegetables from the saucepan and spread them over the bottom of a roasting tin or flameproof casserole. Place the fish on top of the vegetables. Pour the wine over them and sprinkle the top of the fish with the melted butter.

Put the tin or pot in the oven. Bake for 30 minutes, or until the fish is cooked and flakes easily. Remove the roasting tin from the oven. Transfer the fish to a warmed serving dish. Strain the vegetables and liquid into a small saucepan. Arrange the vegetables around the fish. Cover and keep the fish and vegetables hot while you make the sauce.

Place the saucepan over high heat and

bring the braising liquid to the boil. If the sauce is thin, boil it briskly to reduce it. Remove the pan from the heat and whisk in the remaining butter, a little at a time. When all the butter has been absorbed, pour the sauce over the fish. Garnish with the lemon slices and serve immediately.

## Braised Beef

*A hearty main dish to serve for a dinner party, this beef braised in red wine may be accompanied by steamed rice and broccoli.*

10 SERVINGS

5 lb. piece of beef for braising, topside or silverside [top round or brisket]
2 tablespoons flour
2 oz. [¼ cup] butter
1 medium-sized onion, chopped
1 large carrot, scraped and diced, plus 4 carrots, scraped and quartered

1 small turnip, peeled and diced, plus 2 small turnips, peeled and quartered
2 celery stalks, diced
1 garlic clove, crushed
8 fl. oz. [1 cup] dry red wine
8 fl. oz. [1 cup] beef stock
1 teaspoon salt
¾ teaspoon black pepper
1 bay leaf
¼ teaspoon dried marjoram
½ teaspoon dried thyme

Preheat the oven to warm 325°F (Gas Mark 3, 170°C). Dry the beef well with kitchen paper towels. Coat it with the flour.

Melt the butter in a large, flameproof casserole over moderate heat. When the foam subsides, add the beef to the casserole and brown it on all sides. Remove the beef from the casserole and place it to one side.

Add the chopped onion, diced carrot, diced turnip, celery and crushed garlic to the casserole. Add a little more butter

if necessary. Cover the casserole and cook the vegetables for 15 minutes over moderate heat, stirring occasionally.

Place the browned meat on top of the vegetables in the casserole. Add the wine, stock, salt, pepper, bay leaf, marjoram and thyme. Cover the casserole and bake in the oven for 3½ hours, or until the meat is almost tender when pierced with a fork. If necessary, add more stock or wine to the casserole while it is cooking.

Remove the beef from the casserole. Pour the gravy through a strainer placed over a large bowl. Discard the vegetables in the strainer. Return the beef and strained gravy to the casserole. Taste and add more salt and pepper if necessary.

Add the quartered carrots and turnips. Cover the casserole and return it to the oven. Cook for a further 30 minutes, or until the meat and vegetables are tender.

Place the meat on a warmed serving platter and surround it with the carrots and turnips. Pour a little gravy over the meat and the remainder into a warmed sauceboat.

## Braised Oxtail

*An inexpensive meat dish, Braised Oxtail may be served with mashed potatoes and green vegetables. Ask your butcher to cut the oxtail into pieces.*

6 SERVINGS

4 lb. oxtail, cut into 2-inch lengths
1½ teaspoons salt
½ teaspoon black pepper
4 oz. [1 cup] flour
1 tablespoon vegetable fat
2 carrots, scraped and coarsely chopped
2 turnips, peeled and chopped
2 celery stalks, coarsely chopped
2 onions, coarsely chopped
1½ pints [3¾ cups] beef stock
1 bay leaf
½ teaspoon dried thyme
4 parsley sprigs

Preheat the oven to warm 325°F (Gas Mark 3, 170°C).

Trim the pieces of oxtail and discard any excess fat. Sprinkle them with the salt and black pepper. Coat the oxtail pieces with the flour and shake off all the excess.

In a large, heavy frying-pan, melt the vegetable fat over high heat. When it is hot, lower the heat to moderate and add the oxtail pieces a few at a time. Cook them, turning frequently, until they are brown. Transfer the meat to a large flameproof casserole.

Add the carrots, turnips, celery and onions to the fat in the frying-pan, adding more fat if necessary. Cook them over moderate heat, stirring frequently, for about 15 minutes, or until the vegetables are lightly browned.

Put the vegetables on top of the oxtail pieces in the casserole. Add the stock, bay leaf, thyme and parsley. Place the casserole over high heat and bring the liquid to the boil.

Cover the casserole and place it in the centre of the oven. Bake for about 4 hours, or until the meat comes away easily from the bone.

Using a large spoon, skim off the surface fat. Taste and add more salt and pepper if necessary. Serve immediately.

## Braised Ribs of Beef

*A filling dish for a winter dinner, Braised Ribs of Beef can be served with mashed potatoes and spinach or Brussels sprouts. A glass of ice-cold lager would go very well with the ribs, but if you would prefer a wine, try a Spanish burgundy.*

4 SERVINGS

3 lb. lean ribs of beef, cut into 3-inch pieces
2 tablespoons seasoned flour, made from 2 tablespoons flour,
1 teaspoon salt and ½ teaspoon black pepper
1 oz. [2 tablespoons] butter
2 medium-sized onions, coarsely chopped
3 medium-sized carrots, scraped and coarsely chopped
1 large garlic clove, crushed
½ teaspoon dried marjoram
4 fl. oz. [½ cup] beef stock
1 bay leaf

Preheat the oven to very hot 475°F (Gas Mark 9, 240°C).

Dip the beef pieces into the seasoned flour, shaking off any excess. Arrange them on a rack in a shallow roasting pan. Brown the beef pieces in the oven for 20 minutes, watching carefully to make sure they do not burn. The meat should be a deep brown colour by the end of the cooking period.

While the meat is cooking, melt the butter in a large flameproof casserole over moderate heat. When the foam subsides, add the onions, carrots, garlic and marjoram and cook for 10 minutes, stirring from time to time.

Take the meat out of the oven and lower the oven temperature to warm 325°F (Gas Mark 3, 170°C).

Place the meat on top of the vegetables, Pour the beef stock into the roasting pan and swirl it around. Pour it over the meat-and-vegetable mixture. Add the bay leaf. Bring to a boil over high heat on the top of the stove.

Cover the casserole and transfer it to the middle of the oven. Cook for 1 hour.

Remove the meat from the casserole and set aside on a heated serving dish.

Strain the vegetables and cooking liquid into a medium-sized saucepan, pressing hard with the back of a wooden spoon to extract all the juices. Skim the fat from the surface of the sauce, taste it and add more salt and pepper if necessary. Put the saucepan over high heat and bring the sauce to the boil.

Pour the sauce over the meat and serve immediately.

## Braised Round of Beef

*A sumptuous dish, ideal for Sunday dinner, Braised Round of Beef can be served with parsley potatoes and, perhaps, a green salad. A hearty red wine would be best with this dish.*

6 SERVINGS

3 lb. lean beef (topside or silverside), prepared for roasting
2 oz. [½ cup] plus 1 tablespoon flour
2 oz. [¼ cup] butter
3 medium-sized onions, finely sliced
2 garlic cloves, crushed
5 medium-sized carrots, scraped and quartered
1 small turnip, peeled and diced
1 small head of fennel, sliced
3 slices streaky bacon
8 fl. oz. [1 cup] dry red wine
8 fl. oz. [1 cup] beef stock
1 teaspoon salt
½ teaspoon black pepper
1 bay leaf
1 teaspoon dried thyme
2 large potatoes, peeled and cut into squares

Preheat the oven to warm 325°F (Gas Mark 3, 170°C).

Coat the beef well with the 2 ounces [½ cup] of flour. In a large flameproof casserole melt the butter over moderate heat. Put the meat in the pan and, using tongs or two large spoons, turn and brown the meat well on all sides. Set the meat aside on a heated platter when it is completely browned.

Add two of the sliced onions, garlic cloves, half the carrots, turnip and fennel to the pan and cook them, uncovered, over moderate heat for about 5 to 6 minutes, stirring occasionally to prevent the vegetables from sticking to the bottom of the pan. Pour the vegetables and cooking juices out of the casserole into a small bowl and reserve them.

Place the bacon slices in the bottom of the casserole. Arrange the cooked vegetables and their cooking juices on top. Put the piece of meat on top of the vegetables. Pour the wine and beef stock into the casserole. Add the salt, pepper, bay leaf and thyme to the mixture. Bring to the boil over moderate heat.

Cover the casserole and place it in the centre of the oven. Cook for 2¾ hours, or until the meat is almost tender. Add more beef stock, or wine, if necessary during the cooking period.

Remove the meat from the pan and set it aside. Pour the pan juices and vegetables through a strainer, pressing down hard on the vegetables with the back of a wooden spoon to extract all the juices. Discard the vegetables and return the strained liquid to the casserole. Replace the meat and add the remaining carrot quarters, sliced onion and potatoes. Cover the casserole and return it to the

*A substantial dish for a winter dinner, Braised Oxtail is cooked in rich beef stock with onions, carrots, turnips and celery.*

oven. Braise for a further 45 minutes, or until both the vegetables and the meat are very tender when pierced with the point of a sharp knife.

Transfer the meat to a warmed serving dish and arrange the vegetables around it.

Thicken the braising liquid in the casserole by adding the remaining 1 tablespoon flour and mixing well over moderate heat on top of the stove. Cook for 1 minute or until the sauce is smooth and thick.

Pour some of the sauce over the meat and serve the rest separately, as gravy, in a sauce boat.

## Braised Steak

*This is a tempting and easy-to-prepare main dish. Serve it with buttered noodles, and sautéed courgettes [zucchini] or peas. If you prefer, you may cook this dish in a casserole in the oven preheated to warm 325°F (Gas Mark 3, 170°C) instead of in a frying-pan. The meat will require the same cooking time.*

4 TO 6 SERVINGS

4 tablespoons flour
1 teaspoon salt
½ teaspoon black pepper
2 lb. braising steak, 1-inch thick
2 oz. [¼ cup] butter
1 onion, thinly sliced
2 carrots, scraped and sliced
1 green pepper, white pith removed, seeded and diced
14 oz. canned tomatoes, undrained
1 bay leaf

*(Low Cal)*

Mix the flour, salt and pepper in a bowl. Coat the steak with the mixture.

Heat the butter in a large, heavy frying-pan over moderate heat. When the foam has subsided, put the meat in the pan and brown it for 5 minutes on all sides.

Add the remaining ingredients to the pan and stir well. Cover the frying-pan and simmer gently for 2 to 2½ hours, or until the meat is tender when pierced with a fork. Remove the bay leaf and serve immediately.

## Bramble

Bramble is another name for BLACKBERRY.

## Bramble Jelly

*A light, clear jelly made from fresh blackberries, Bramble Jelly is delicious spread on hot buttered toast or scones. In making a successful Bramble Jelly, the fruit should not be over-ripe. To strain the fruit pulp, you will need a jelly bag or a large square of cheesecloth. Since the straining takes a long time, you should plan to do it overnight, but do not leave the juice for more than 24 hours before making the jelly. First scald the bag or cloth by pouring boiling water through it. Hang the bag on a frame or tie the ends to the legs of an up-turned chair or stool and place a large bowl underneath. Do not squeeze the bag to hurry the process as this might make the jelly cloudy. Measure the juice after straining. You will require one pound [2 cups] of granulated or preserving sugar for every pint [2½ cups] of the strained blackberry juice.*

ABOUT 2½ POUNDS

4 lb. fresh blackberries, hulled and washed
10 fl. oz. [1¼ cups] water
2 tablespoons lemon juice
granulated or preserving sugar

Place the blackberries in a preserving pan or large saucepan with the water and lemon juice. Bring the water to the boil over high heat. Reduce the heat to low. Simmer the fruit, uncovered, for 1 hour, or until it is quite tender, occasionally mashing the fruit against the sides of the pan with a wooden spoon.

Hang the scalded jelly bag or piece of cheesecloth over a large bowl. Pour the blackberries into the cloth. Allow the juice to drain through the cheesecloth for at least 12 hours. When the juice has completely drained through the cheesecloth, discard the blackberry pulp.

Measure the juice before returning it to the rinsed preserving pan. Add 1 pound of sugar to every pint [2½ cups] of

*Light and clear, Bramble Jelly is made from ripe blackberries.*

liquid. Stir to dissolve the sugar, over low heat. When the sugar is completely dissolved, raise the heat to high and bring the mixture to the boil. Boil briskly, without stirring, for about 10 minutes, or until the jelly has reached setting point. Remove the pan from the heat. Test it by spooning a little of the jelly on to a cold saucer. Cool it quickly. If the surface is set and crinkles when pushed with your finger, it is ready. Skim the foam off the surface of the jelly with a metal spoon.

Ladle the jelly into hot, clean, dry jam jars, leaving half an inch at the top of each jar. Press a circle of waxed paper on to the surface of the jam in each jar. Wipe the jars with a damp cloth. Cover them with jam covers and secure with rubber bands. Label the jars and store them in a cool, dark, dry place.

## Bramborová Polevka
POTATO SOUP

*A satisfying and easy-to-prepare soup from Czechoslovakia, Bramborová Polevka (bram-bore-oh-vah po-LEHV-ka) is ideal to serve as a first course for winter lunches or dinners.*

4 SERVINGS

2 lb. potatoes
3 oz. [⅜ cup] butter
4 celery stalks, chopped
1 small turnip, diced
1 medium-sized onion, finely chopped
4 carrots, scraped and diced
2½ tablespoons flour
2 pints [5 cups] chicken stock
¼ teaspoon dried oregano
1 tablespoon chopped parsley
1 teaspoon salt
1 teaspoon black pepper
1 green pepper, white pith removed, seeded and chopped

Place the potatoes in a large saucepan and cover them with water. Bring the water to a boil over high heat and boil for 8 minutes. Drain the potatoes. Peel and cut them into cubes.

Melt the butter in a large, heavy saucepan or flameproof casserole over moderate heat. Add the potatoes, celery, turnip, onion and carrots to the pan. Fry the vegetables, stirring occasionally, for 8 minutes, or until they are brown.

Stir the flour into the vegetables and mix well. Cook for 1 minute. Add the stock, oregano, parsley, salt, pepper and the green pepper. Stirring continuously, bring the soup to a boil over high heat. Cover the pan, reduce the heat to low and simmer gently for 40 minutes, or until the potatoes and vegetables are tender.

If the soup is too thin, cook uncovered until the liquid is reduced. Taste and add more salt and pepper if necessary. Pour the soup into a warmed soup tureen and serve immediately.

## Bramborové Knedliky
POTATO DUMPLINGS

*In Czechoslovakia, dumplings of all shapes and sizes are part of most main meals. One of the tastiest and easiest to make of Czechoslovakian dumplings are Bramborové Knedliky (bram-bore-oh-vey k'ned-lee-kee). They go well with roast chicken or pork or boiled beef. They may also be cooked in a chicken soup and, if you prefer, may be served in the soup.*

ABOUT 12 DUMPLINGS

5 pints [3 quarts] water
2 lb. potatoes, boiled and mashed
2 oz. [½ cup] flour
2 oz. [½ cup] semolina
½ teaspoon salt
1 egg, lightly beaten
1 tablespoon milk
1 tablespoon chopped parsley

In a large saucepan, bring the water to a boil over moderate heat.

In a large mixing bowl, mix the mashed potatoes, flour, semolina, salt, egg and milk together with a wooden spoon and beat until the mixture is completely smooth.

With floured hands, form the mixture into balls about the size of large walnuts. Put the dumplings into the boiling water. When the water returns to the boil, reduce the heat and simmer the dumplings for 10 minutes, or until they rise to the surface of the water. With a slotted spoon transfer the dumplings to a serving dish. Sprinkle the dumplings with parsley and serve.

## Bran
The brown outer layer of a cereal, such as wheat, bran is obtained in the flour-making process. It is mainly used to feed livestock, but it is also prepared for human consumption, principally as a breakfast cereal.

## Bran Nut Muffins

*Bran Nut Muffins have a coarse, nutty texture and are quick and easy to make.*

12 MUFFINS

2 oz. [¼ cup] butter, melted and cooled, plus ½ tablespoon butter
4 oz. [1 cup] flour
4 oz. [¾ cup] bran
2 oz. [¼ cup] sugar
½ teaspoon salt
2 teaspoons baking powder
2 oz. [⅓ cup] chopped nuts
1 egg, beaten
8 fl. oz. [1 cup] milk

Preheat the oven to fairly hot 400°F (Gas Mark 6, 200°C). Lightly grease two muffin tins with ½ tablespoon butter. Sift the flour, bran, sugar, salt and baking powder into a large mixing bowl. Add the chopped nuts.

In a medium-sized mixing bowl, combine the beaten egg with the milk.

Make a well in the centre of the dry ingredients and pour the egg and milk mixture into it. With a wooden spoon, stir the mixture until all the ingredients are well blended but not smooth. For perfect muffins the batter should be slightly lumpy. Overbeating will produce unsatisfactory results.

Fold the melted butter into the batter. Turn the mixture into the greased muffin tins. Bake for 25 minutes. Remove the muffins from the tins and serve.

## Brandade de Morue
A famous French dish traditionally served for lunch on Friday, *Brandade de Morue* (BRAHN-dad d'moh-roo) consists of salt cod, soaked and poached and then pounded together with milk and oil until the mixture becomes a smooth, thick cream. Pepper, freshly grated nutmeg, lemon juice and crushed garlic are added to taste.

Originally brandade was made at home, but as it is a difficult and time-consuming dish to prepare, most French housewives now buy it ready-made.

Brandade may be served either hot or cold. It is served hot in a vol-au-vent case. Cold, it is served surrounded by triangles of fried bread or pastry.

## Brander
Brander is a Scottish name for a gridiron or grill [broiler].

## Brandied Cherries

*This is a quick and easy way to conserve cherries in brandy. Other fruits, such as peaches, greengages, plums or apricots, may also be used. The stones may be removed, but if they are the fruit may lose its shape. Brandied Cherries, which should be aged for four to six months, may be served as a dessert since they have a rich, thick juice, or as a garnish. Use, if possible, wide-necked bottling jars or Kilner jars as these have rubber seals and clip covers which make sealing easy.*

2 POUNDS

2 lb. cherries
3 lb. sugar
2 pints [5 cups] water
brandy

Remove the stalks from the cherries and wash in cold water. In a large saucepan dissolve 1 pound of sugar in the water over moderate heat. Bring the syrup to the boil, skimming off any froth which may rise to the surface.

When the syrup is clear, add the cherries, a few at a time, and boil for 1 minute. Remove the cherries from the pan with a slotted spoon and set them aside on a plate to cool.

Measure 1 pint [2½ cups] of the syrup and put it in a pan with the remaining sugar.

Place the pan over low heat and allow the sugar to dissolve slowly. When the sugar is completely dissolved raise the heat and boil rapidly, removing any scum with a metal spoon.

Continue boiling until the syrup is clear or reaches 213°F (100°C) on a sugar thermometer.

Remove the pan from the heat and leave to cool slightly. Then strain the syrup through a clean cloth into a jug.

Measure the strained syrup, add an equal quantity of brandy and stir well.

Pack the cherries into the jars and pour the syrup over them, ensuring that the cherries are covered.

Seal the jars and leave them in a cool, dry place for at least 4 to 6 months.

## Brandy

Brandy, an English corruption of the Dutch *brandewijn*, which literally means burned wine, is a spirit distilled from the fermented juice of fruits, especially grapes. Brandy is made wherever wine is produced and, like wine, varies greatly in appearance, from almost colourless to deep glowing amber, in alcohol by volume, in quality, from the smooth mellowness of *grande champagne* Cognac to the rough fierceness of local *grappa*, and, naturally, in price, which depends on national or even regional origins. Its alcohol (strength), however, remains constant. The world's largest producers of brandy are France and the United States. Spain, Portugal, South Africa, Greece and Italy also produce large amounts of brandy.

France is generally considered to produce the finest quality brandy in the world and in France, as in other brandy-producing countries, the industry is rigidly controlled by law. Brandy produced in the Charente, for example, is exactly identified by specific geographic area, is required to be distilled twice in copper-pot stills and is then aged for several years in special oak casks before it is blended, bottled and sold as Cognac. In the United States the government is even more closely involved and the origin, proof and substances added during distillation are federally regulated.

Of the other brandies, Armagnac, from the Gers area of Gascony, is considered to be of especially fine quality. Some of the brandies produced from fruit other than grapes are also excellent and are, by law, always clearly identified with the fruit of origin, such as apricot brandy, plum brandy and cherry brandy. CAL-VADOS, an apple brandy from Normandy, is the best known of the fruit brandies and is, when well aged, a superior liqueur.

Most European and American vintners also produce a spirit from the pomate or pulp that remains after juice has been extracted from the fruit. Colourless, odourless and fiery to taste, it is drunk in large quantities by those who distill it and is called *marc* (pronounced mahr) in France and *grappa* in both Italy and the United States.

Brandy is usually drunk as an after-dinner liqueur and a ritual has grown up around its consumption. Large balloon-shaped goblets are said to improve the bouquet, as is the practice of slightly heating the glass before the liqueur is drunk. In most countries the human hand was used for this function but special allowances were made for the British indoor winter and so the brandy-warmer or flame was born!

Brandy can be added to coffee, or served as an accompaniment to coffee. It is also a popular ingredient in many desserts. It can be warmed slightly over a chafing dish or similar gentle heat and either set alight and poured over the fruit to be flambéed or—the safer method, perhaps—poured over the fruit and then set alight.

## Brandy Alexander Pie

*This brandy-flavoured cream pie is an attractive and delicious dessert. It may be made a day in advance and left in the refrigerator to chill.*

ONE 9-INCH PIE

7 oz. [¾ cup] finley crushed digestive
  biscuit [graham cracker]
  crumbs
2 oz. castor sugar [¼ cup
  superfine]
3 oz. [6 tablespoons] butter or
  margarine, melted
FILLING
3½ fl. oz. [7 tablespoons] cold water
  4 teaspoons gelatine
3 oz. castor [⅜ cup superfine]
  sugar
½ teaspoon salt
3 eggs, separated
2 fl. oz. [¼ cup] brandy
2 fl. oz. [¼ cup] creme de cacao or
  other coffee-flavoured liqueur
12 fl. oz. [1½ cups] thick [heavy]
  cream
2 oz. [2 squares] piece of plain
  chocolate, at room temperature

Mix all the biscuit crust ingredients well together. Cover the bottom and sides of a round 9-inch pie dish or tin with the mixture, pressing it down firmly. Chill for 30 minutes in the refrigerator until the mixture is firm.

Meanwhile, make the filling. Pour the water into a small mixing bowl and sprinkle in the gelatine. Stand the bowl in hot water to dissolve the gelatine. Add half the sugar, plus the salt and egg yolks. Mix well.

Cook the mixture over low heat, stirring constantly, until the mixture thickens. Do not allow it to boil.

Remove the mixture from the heat and mix in the brandy and crème de cacao. Pour the mixture into a bowl and leave to cool, then chill in the refrigerator until it begins to set.

Whisk the egg whites until soft peaks form. Add the remaining sugar, a little at a time, and continue whisking until the whites are stiff. Carefully fold the whites into the thickened egg yolk mixture with a large metal spoon or spatula.

Whisk 8 fl. oz. [1 cup] cream in a chilled bowl until thick, then gently fold into the egg mixture.

Pour the filling into the chilled piecrust and smooth the top with the back of a spoon. Cover with foil and chill for several hours or overnight in the refrigerator.

Just before you are ready to serve the pie, stiffly whip the remaining cream and pipe in a decorative pattern around the edge of the pie.

Make chocolate curls by shaving the chocolate block with a potato peeler and decorate the pie centre. Handle the chocolate as little as possible. Draw the peeler along the wide surface of the chocolate for large curls and along the narrow side of the block for small, slim curls.

A spring-clip or loose-bottomed tin makes serving easier and improves the presentation.

## Brandy Blazer

*A warming after-dinner drink for cold nights, Brandy Blazer is ignited in the glass and served flaming.*

1 SERVING

1 sugar lump
1 strip lemon rind
1 strip orange rind
4 fl. oz. [½ cup] warmed brandy

Warm a thick glass and into it put the sugar, lemon rind, orange rind and brandy. Stir the ingredients with a long-handled spoon to dissolve the sugar. With a match, ignite the brandy and serve.

## Brandy Butter

*Also known as hard sauce, Brandy Butter is traditionally served with Christmas puddings, plum puddings and mince pies. It may be stored in the refrigerator for 2 weeks in a screw-topped jar.*

ABOUT 6 SERVINGS

4 oz. [½ cup] unsalted butter
4 oz. [½ cup] castor sugar
4 tablespoons brandy

Put the butter in a medium-sized mixing bowl. Cream it with a wooden spoon until it is quite soft. Beat in the sugar a little

*Rich, brandy-flavoured cream in a crumb crust, Brandy Alexander Pie is a mouth-watering dessert.*

*For brandy snaps, beat the flour, ginger and lemon juice into the melted butter, sugar and golden [corn] syrup.*

*Drop teaspoonfuls of the mixture on to a buttered baking sheet, leaving about 4 inches between each teaspoonful.*

at a time. When all the sugar has been incorporated, add the brandy a teaspoon at a time and beat well.

Add as much brandy as will give the butter a good flavour, but be careful not to add too much, as the butter will curdle.

Pile the brandy butter in a serving bowl and chill in the refrigerator.

## Brandy Cocktail

*A classic Brandy Cocktail this is usually served before dinner, or sometimes after a formal lunch.*

1 COCKTAIL

½ teaspoon castor sugar
2 drops Angostura bitters
3 fl. oz. [⅜ cup] brandy
2 ice cubes
3 strips orange rind

Place the sugar, bitters and the brandy in a cocktail shaker, or covered container, and stir with a spoon to dissolve the sugar. Add the ice cubes. Twist the strips of orange rind and drop them into the shaker. Cover the shaker and shake vigorously. Pour into a chilled glass.

## Brandy Punch

*Brandy punch makes a delightful apéritif with the addition of just a little soda water. For a long cool drink add more ice cubes and soda water.*

1 SERVING

1¼ teaspoons castor sugar
4 fl. oz. [½ cup] brandy
3 ice cubes
1 teaspoon lemon juice
  soda water
1 slice of lemon
1 mint sprig

Mix the sugar and brandy in a tall glass and stir with a spoon to dissolve the sugar. Add the ice and lemon juice. Add enough soda water to fill the glass. Garnish the punch with the lemon slice and mint sprig.

## Brandy Snaps

*These attractive, crisp biscuits [cookies] may take a bit of time and trouble to prepare, but they are well worth the effort. Filled with brandy-flavoured cream, they may be served as a special dessert.*

15-20 BISCUITS

3 oz. [⅜ cup] plus 1 tablespoon
  butter
2 oz. [¼ cup] sugar
3 fl. oz. golden syrup [⅜ cup light
  corn syrup]
2 oz. [½ cup] flour
1 teaspoon ground ginger
  juice of ½ lemon
6 fl. oz. double cream [¾ cup heavy
  cream]
2 tablespoons brandy

Preheat the oven to moderate 350°F (Gas Mark 4, 180°C). Grease a large baking sheet with half the tablespoon of butter. Coat the handle of a long wooden spoon with the rest of the tablespoon of butter.

In a medium-sized saucepan melt the remaining butter, the sugar and golden syrup over moderate heat. Remove the pan from the heat and beat in the flour, ginger and lemon juice. Continue beating until the mixture is smooth.

Drop teaspoonfuls of the mixture on to the buttered baking sheet, leaving about 4 inches between each teaspoonful.

Place the baking sheet in the oven

and bake for 8 to 10 minutes, or until the biscuits are golden brown.

Turn off the heat and open the oven door, but leave the biscuits in the oven to keep them warm. If they are allowed to cool they will harden and break.

With a palette knife, remove one brandy snap at a time from the baking sheet and curl it around the butter-covered spoon handle. Slide the brandy snap off the handle and on to a wire cake rack. Repeat the process with the other brandy snaps, using additional butter to coat the handle each time.

Just before serving beat the cream with a wire whisk or rotary beater until it is very thick. Add the brandy and continue beating the cream until it is stiff. Fill a forcing bag with the brandied cream and pipe it into both ends of the brandy snaps. Serve at once.

## Brazilian Macaroons

*Crunchy little coconut macaroons from Brazil these are especially good served with an ice-cream or fruit dessert.*

40 BISCUITS

1 teaspoon butter
7 oz. [⅞ cup] sugar
6 tablespoons water
4 egg yolks, lightly beaten
4 tablespoons flour, sifted
9 oz. desiccated coconut [2¼ cups
  shredded coconut] or 16 oz. [3⅜
  cups] grated fresh coconut
½ teaspoon vanilla essence

Preheat the oven to fairly hot 375°F (Gas Mark 5, 190°C). Grease a baking sheet with the butter.

Put the sugar and water into a medium-

*Remove one brandy snap at a time from the baking sheet and curl it round a butter-coated wooden spoon handle.*

*Pipe the stiffly beaten cream, flavoured with brandy, into both ends of the brandy snaps.*

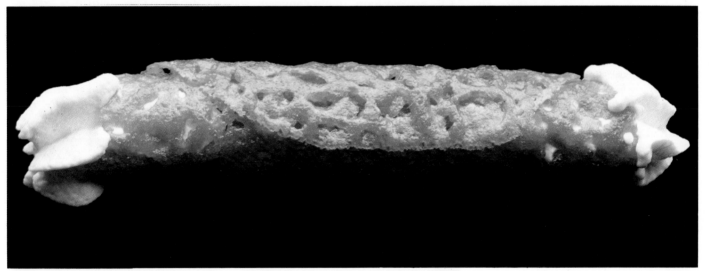

sized, heavy saucepan and cook over moderate heat, stirring with a metal spoon, just until the sugar dissolves. When the sugar has dissolved, raise the heat and boil the syrup until it reaches a temperature of 230°F on a sugar thermometer, or when a small amount dropped into iced water forms a thread and immediately hardens. Remove the saucepan from the heat.

In a medium-sized bowl, beat the egg yolks and flour together with a wooden spoon until they are well blended. Stirring the egg yolk-and-flour mixture continuously, add 1½ tablespoons of the hot syrup to it. Slowly pour the egg yolk-and-syrup mixture back into the pan of syrup, stirring continuously. Gradually add the coconut.

Replace the saucepan on very low heat and, stirring continuously, simmer the mixture gently until it becomes very thick and stiff. Do not allow it to come to the boil.

Remove the saucepan from the heat. Stir in the vanilla essence and leave the

mixture to cool to room temperature. Place the pan in the refrigerator and chill the macaroon mixture for 30 minutes or until it is completely cold.

Remove the saucepan from the refrigerator. Shape the mixture into small balls by rolling it between your hands.

Arrange the balls on the baking sheet. Place it in the oven. Bake for 15 minutes, or until the macaroons are light brown. Remove from the oven and transfer the macaroons to a wire rack to cool.

## Bratwurst

A sausage of German origin, Bratwurst (BRAHT-voorst) is made of lean pork and heavily seasoned with herbs and spices.

## Bratwurst Sausages in Sour Cream Sauce

*A German sausage dish which is easy to prepare, Bratwurst Sausages in Sour*

*Cream Sauce makes an unusual main dish for a family lunch or supper, accompanied by boiled new potatoes or dumplings. Bratwurst sausages are available in most delicatessen shops.*

4 SERVINGS
8 bratwurst sausages, separated
1 oz. [2 tablespoons] butter
8 fl. oz. [1 cup] sour cream
1 tablespoon flour
½ teaspoon salt
¼ teaspoon white pepper
1 tablespoon chopped parsley

Half fill a large saucepan with water and bring it to the boil over high heat. Put the bratwurst into the boiling water and cook them for 15 minutes. With a slotted spoon, remove the bratwurst from the pan. Allow them to drain on kitchen paper towels and then slice them into ½-inch pieces.

In a large frying-pan, melt the butter over moderate heat. When the foam subsides add the bratwurst slices to the pan and brown them well on all sides for

237

about 10 to 15 minutes.

In a medium-sized mixing bowl beat the sour cream, flour, salt and pepper together with a wire whisk until they are well blended.

Pour the sour cream mixture into the frying-pan. Reduce the heat to low and, stirring constantly, heat the sour cream sauce thoroughly without letting it come to the boil. If the sauce is too thick, add 1 to 2 spoonfuls of boiling water.

Turn the bratwurst and sour cream sauce into a warmed serving dish and sprinkle with parsley.

Serve immediately.

## Brawn

*Brawn is often made from pig's head, but calf's or sheep's head may be used instead. Most butchers, with a few day's notice, will supply the head already salted, but if you cannot obtain a salted head, the head should be soaked in brine for one day. Brawn is traditionally served on a bed of fresh parsley with mustard sauce.*

6 SERVINGS

1 salted pig's head
10 peppercorns
2 teaspoons salt
2 bay leaves
2 teaspoons marjoram
1 carrot, scraped and chopped
1 small turnip, peeled and diced
1 large onion, sliced
1 hard-boiled egg, sliced

Wash the head thoroughly in cold water. Cut off the ears and cook them in boiling water for 1 minute, then scrape them free of hair.

Place the ears in a large pan with the head, peppercorns, salt, bay leaves, marjoram, carrot, turnip and onion. Add enough cold water to cover. Bring the water to the boil over high heat. Remove any scum which rises to the surface with a slotted spoon.

Reduce the heat to low, cover the pan and simmer for 2½ to 3 hours, or until the meat is tender.

Strain and reserve the liquid. Discard the vegetables and flavourings. Remove the meat from the head and cut it into small pieces, removing any fat or gristle. Cut the ears into strips.

Arrange the slices of egg in the bottom of a large mould. Press the meat in tightly on top of the egg.

Return the liquid to the saucepan with the head bones and bring to the boil over high heat. Skim off any fat that rises to the surface. Lower the heat to mod-

erate and continue boiling until the liquid is reduced by half.

Pour enough of the liquid over the meat in the mould to come just level with the top of the meat. Place a weighted plate on the mould and leave until the next day, when the brawn will be set.

To turn the brawn out, dip the mould into hot water and turn it upside-down on to a serving plate.

## Brazilian Aubergines

*A wonderful supper or lunch dish, Brazilian Aubergines is easy to make, looks attractive and tastes delicious. It need be accompanied by only a tossed salad.*

4 SERVINGS

4 small aubergines [eggplant]
1 lb. cooked ham, finely chopped
3 hard-boiled eggs, chopped
8 oz. tomato puree [paste]
4 fl. oz. [½ cup] water
½ teaspoon dried marjoram
½ teaspoon dried basil
½ teaspoon salt
½ teaspoon white pepper
1 oz. [¼ cup] cheese, grated

Preheat the oven to fairly hot 400°F (Gas Mark 6, 200°C).

Fill a deep roasting tin one-third full of boiling water. Arrange the aubergines in the tin and put them in the oven to bake for 25 minutes.

Remove the aubergines from the oven and set them aside to cool slightly. Reduce the oven temperature to moderate 350°F (Gas Mark 4, 180°C).

Slice the aubergines in half. Using a large spoon, remove the flesh leaving only a ½-inch thick shell. Set the shells aside in a shallow ovenproof casserole and transfer the pulp to a large mixing bowl. Add the cooked ham and the eggs to the aubergine pulp and blend well.

Pile the mixture into the aubergine shells.

In a small saucepan, heat the tomato purée with the water over moderate heat, stirring constantly, until it is very hot. Stir in the marjoram, basil, salt and pepper. Remove the pan from the heat and spoon the sauce over the stuffed

*Succulent cold pork set in its own jelly, Brawn is traditionally made from salted pig's head.*

aubergines. Sprinkle the tops of the stuffing with the grated cheese.

Place the casserole in the oven and bake the stuffed aubergines for 20 minutes. Remove from the oven and serve immediately.

## Brazilian Rice

*This is a tasty and simple Brazilian way of cooking rice. It may be served instead of plain boiled rice with chicken or meat.*

4 SERVINGS

4 tablespoons olive oil
1 large onion, thinly sliced
12 oz. [2 cups] long-grain rice, washed, soaked in water for 30 minutes and drained
2 tomatoes, blanched, peeled and chopped
1 teaspoon salt
1¼ pints [3 cups] boiling water

Heat the oil in a large saucepan over moderate heat. Add the onion and fry, stirring constantly, for 8 minutes or until the onion is soft but not brown. Add the rice and fry for 5 minutes, stirring continuously.

Add the tomatoes and salt. Cook for 2 minutes and then pour in the boiling water.

Reduce the heat to low, cover the pan and simmer for 15 to 20 minutes, or until the rice is cooked and all the liquid has been absorbed.

Turn the rice into a warmed serving dish and serve immediately.

## Brazilian Swiss Roll

*A more sophisticated version of the English Swiss [jelly] roll, this Brazilian Swiss Roll is a popular South American cake with a rich rum-cream filling.*

6 SERVINGS

2 tablespoons butter, softened
6 tablespoons flour
4 egg whites
4 egg yolks
2 oz. [¼ cup] castor sugar
⅛ teaspoon salt
3 tablespoons icing [confectioners'] sugar
FILLING
15 fl. oz. [1⅞ cups] milk
2 egg yolks
2 oz. [¼ cup] castor sugar
4 tablespoons flour
½ teaspoon ground cinnamon
½ teaspoon vanilla essence
1 tablespoon rum

Preheat the oven the fairly hot 400°F (Gas Mark 6, 200°C). Grease the inside of a 10½ x 15½-inch Swiss [jelly] roll tin with half the butter. Line the tin with greaseproof or waxed paper, leaving a 2-inch extension of the paper at each end of the tin. With a pastry brush, grease the paper with the remaining butter and dust with half the flour. Tip and rotate the tin to distribute the flour evenly, then turn the tin over and knock it on the bottom to shake out the excess flour.

Put the egg whites in a medium-sized bowl and beat them with a wire whisk, or rotary beater, until they form stiff peaks.

Put the egg yolks, sugar and salt into another medium-sized bowl and beat them until the mixture is pale yellow and will make a ribbon trail on itself when the whisk is lifted.

Sprinkle the remaining flour over the beaten egg whites. Pour the egg yolks over the top of the flour and, with a metal spoon, gently fold together until the batter is well blended.

Pour the batter into the prepared tin and bake in the centre of the oven for 8 minutes or until a knife plunged into the centre of the cake comes out clean and dry.

Take the cake out of the oven and gently turn it out of the tin on to another large piece of greaseproof or waxed paper lightly sprinkled with castor sugar. Carefully peel off the layer of paper which is now on top.

Beginning at the long end of the cake, roll the cake into a cylinder with the paper inside, taking care not to break it. Place the rolled cake to one side and leave it to cool.

To make the filling, put the milk in a medium-sized, heavy saucepan. Bring the milk to the boil over moderate heat. Remove the pan from the heat, cover and set it aside to allow the milk to cool to lukewarm.

In a large mixing bowl beat the egg yolks and sugar with a wire whisk, or rotary beater, until the mixture is a light yellow colour and falls from the whisk in a smooth ribbon.

Beat in the flour 1 tablespoon at a time. When all the flour has been mixed into the egg mixture, gradually beat in the milk, pouring it in a thin stream through a strainer. Add the cinnamon and vanilla essence.

Pour the mixture back into the saucepan and cook it over very low heat, stirring constantly, until the mixture thickens and comes to the boil. Stir in the rum, remove the pan from the heat and set it aside to cool. Stir occasionally to prevent a skin forming on the surface.

When the cream has cooled to room

temperature and the cake is quite cool, unroll the cake, peel off the paper and spread the filling evenly over it. Carefully roll up the filled cake and sprinkle the icing [confectioners'] sugar over the top and sides. It is now ready to serve.

## Brazil Nut

Also known as the Para or cream nut and, in Brazil, as the *castanha*, the Brazil nut, with its tough, angular shell, is the edible seed of one of the largest trees of the Amazon forest.

The nuts are contained in a spherical, thick, hard, woody fruit which is up to six inches in diameter, and weighs three or four pounds. The nuts, about 12 to 24 of them, are developed in the fruit like the segments of an orange. The nuts have to be cracked to obtain the white-fleshed kernel, which is the part eaten.

Brazil nuts can easily be ground, sliced or chopped. They can be eaten plain or used in cooking and baking. Like other nuts, they contain fat and protein.

## Brazil Nut Banana Cake

*A tempting combination of bananas, Brazil nuts and whipped cream, this cake is an ideal dinner party dessert.*

ONE 8-INCH CAKE

4 oz. [½ cup] plus 1 tablespoon vegetable fat
9 oz. [2¼ cups] flour
6 oz. [¾ cup] sugar
2 teaspoons baking powder
½ teaspoon bicarbonate of soda [baking soda]
¼ teaspoon salt
2 eggs, lightly beaten
4 large bananas, mashed
4 oz. [½ cup] Brazil nuts, toasted and ground
10 fl. oz. double cream [1¼ cups heavy cream], stiffly whipped
2 oz. [½ cup] Brazil nuts, toasted and slivered

Preheat the oven to fairly hot 375°F (Gas Mark 5, 190°C). Grease two 8-inch cake tins with 1 tablespoon of the fat.

Sift the flour, sugar, baking powder, soda and salt into a large mixing bowl. With a wooden spoon, cream the remaining fat into the flour mixture. Beat in the eggs, bananas and ground Brazil nuts.

Turn the mixture into the greased cake tins. Bake for 25 minutes. Leave the cakes to cool for 5 minutes, then transfer them from the tins to a wire cake rack.

When the cakes are completely cool

spread half the whipped cream on top of one cake and place the other cake on top of it. Spread the remaining cream on top of the cake and decorate it with the Brazil nut slivers.

## Brazil Nut Cake

*A rich, nutty cake, this American recipe utilizes a small quantity of leftover plain or chocolate cake crumbs. The cake crumbs must not be stale or the cake will be dry.*

ONE 12-INCH CAKE

8 oz. [1 cup] plus ½ tablespoon butter
2 tablespoons plain [all-purpose] flour
10 oz. [1¼ cups] sugar
1 teaspoon salt
2 tablespoons clear honey
8 eggs
4 oz. [1½ cups] crumbs from leftover white or chocolate cake
8 oz. [2 cups] self-raising flour
8 oz. [1 cup] Brazil nuts, toasted and ground

Preheat the oven to warm 325°F (Gas Mark 3, 170°C). Grease a 12-inch cake tin with ½ tablespoon of butter and lightly flour it with the 2 tablespoons of plain [all-purpose] flour, knocking out any excess flour. Set the tin aside.

In a large mixing bowl cream the remaining butter and the sugar together with a wooden spoon until the mixture is light and fluffy. Stir the salt and honey into the mixture. Beat in the eggs, one at a time. Fold in the crumbs and the self-raising flour. When the mixture is well blended quickly stir in the nuts.

Pour the batter into the prepared cake tin and place it in the oven. Bake for 1¼ hours, or until a skewer inserted into the centre of the cake comes out clean.

Remove the cake from the oven and leave it to cool for 5 minutes before turning it out on to a wire cake rack.

## Brazil Nut and Chive Spread

*This unusual spread of chives, cream cheese and Brazil nuts may be served on small circles of toast as a cocktail savoury or as an elegant snack.*

5 OUNCES

3 oz. cream cheese
⅛ teaspoon cayenne pepper
1 tablespoon finely chopped chives
2 oz. [⅓ cup] Brazil nuts, finely chopped

In a medium-sized mixing bowl, using a wooden spoon blend the cream cheese thoroughly with the cayenne.

Mix in the chives and then stir in the Brazil nuts. Turn the spread into a serving dish and keep it, covered with plastic wrap, in the refrigerator until you are ready to serve it.

## Brazil Nut Piecrust

*A lovely change from the usual pie pastry, this Brazil Nut Piecrust may be used with a variety of sweet fillings, such as chocolate, butterscotch or fruit mousse.*

ONE 9-INCH PIECRUST

5 oz. [⅝ cup] Brazil nuts, ground
2 tablespoons sugar

Preheat the oven to fairly hot 400°F (Gas Mark 6, 200°C).

Put the ground Brazil nuts and the sugar into a small mixing bowl. With a wooden spoon mix the nuts and sugar together well.

Spoon the mixture into a 9-inch pie dish and, with your fingers, press the mixture evenly against the sides and bottom of the dish.

Bake the crust in the oven for 8 minutes, or until it is lightly browned. Cool before adding the filling.

## Brazil Nut Stuffing

*Unusual and tasty, this Brazil Nut Stuffing is excellent for chicken or turkey. The stuffing may be prepared a day in advance and kept covered in the refrigerator.*

STUFFING FOR ONE 6-POUND FOWL

4 oz. [½ cup] butter
6 oz. mushrooms, finely chopped
4 celery stalks, finely chopped
4 oz. [⅔ cup] Brazil nuts, chopped
2 medium-sized onions, chopped
½ teaspoon salt
½ teaspoon black pepper
½ teaspoon dried thyme
6 oz. [3 cups] fresh breadcrumbs
1 egg, lightly beaten
juice of ½ lemon

In a medium-sized saucepan melt the butter over moderate heat. When the butter foam subsides, add the mushrooms, celery, Brazil nuts, onions, salt, pepper and thyme. Cook for 10 minutes, stirring frequently.

Turn the mixture into a medium-sized mixing bowl and add the breadcrumbs, beaten egg and lemon juice. Stir the mixture with a fork until all the ingredients are well combined.

## Bread

The history of bread is concurrent with that of civilization. The remains of coarse-grained Stone Age bread have been discovered. Some early breads were made from crushed acorns and beechnuts. Unleavened bread, in the form of flat cakes, was included in the diets of the early Egyptian, Hebrew and Chinese civilizations. The Egyptians were the first to discover, no doubt by accident, fermented or leavened bread. The Romans developed public bakeries. Large-scale commercial production of bread became possible towards the end of the nineteenth century by the development of special strains of yeasts.

Bread is one of the cheapest sources of food energy since it contains proteins, iron, calcium and B vitamins. Despite controversy, there is no significant difference between commercial brown and white bread. Although white flour has less calcium, iron and B vitamins, these nutrients are added to white bread to enrich it.

Raised bread is overwhelmingly preferred in Europe and in the United States. Unleavened or flat bread is still widely eaten throughout Asia and Africa, in addition to raised bread.

# Bread-Making

It is easy to buy a commercially made loaf of bread or even freshly baked bread from a bakery, but neither of these will give you the sense of satisfaction you will have when your family and friends tuck into a loaf of bread you have made yourself.

Making bread is an art, but, contrary to some opinion, it can be easily mastered. Bread recipes vary considerably and the general guidelines set out here will not fit all of them exactly, but if you understand what each ingredient is meant to do and what the techniques are, you will be on your way to successful bread-making.

INGREDIENTS
*Flour*
The type, or types, of flour you use for your bread is really a matter of personal taste, but the best flours for both bread and yeast doughs are milled from hard wheat. These flours have a high gluten content which produces a more elastic springy dough, while soft-wheat flours make a rather sticky dough.

Almost all the white flour sold commercially is soft household flour. Health food stores, however, usually stock wholewheat flour, stone-ground flour, 100 percent wholemeal flour (the whole grain of the wheat with nothing removed and nothing added) and 85 percent or 90 percent wholemeal flour (the husk and the bran removed). And some stores and supermarkets sell strong plain [all-purpose] or baker's white flour which is particularly good for bread-making.

You can mix several different kinds of flour together. For example, you can make a good loaf of pale brown bread if you use a mixture of 4 ounces [1 cup] of 100 percent wholemeal flour and 12 ounces [3 cups] of ordinary soft household flour. Even better bread is produced if you use 85 percent or 90 percent wholemeal flour with strong plain or baker's white flour in the same proportions.

When making bread, it is best if the temperature of the flour is the same as that of the room and of the liquid used in the recipe. If the flour is too cold, you can warm it in the oven.

*Yeast*
The most important thing to remember about yeast is that it is a living cell which must be provided with a 'friendly' environment if it is to do its job properly.

Yeast is a very tiny fungus which grows by sending off buds to form new plants, and by forming spores which may also become new plants. As yeast grows it gives off carbon dioxide gas. This gas, when the yeast is mixed into the dough, causes the elastic cell walls of the gluten in the flour to expand—the phenomenon of the dough rising.

The yeast also gives off alcohol which, if growth is allowed to continue too long, develops into acetic acid and causes the dough to become sour. The heat of baking, however, drives off the alcohol.

Controversy still rages over fresh yeast versus dried yeast. Fresh bakers' yeast or compressed yeast (*not* brewers' yeast) is sold by health food shops and by some bakers and supermarkets. Because the plants in fresh yeast are active and alive it is highly perishable and can be kept only for four to five days in an airtight container in the refrigerator. Fresh yeast should feel cool and like putty to touch. It should be grey in colour and practically odourless. When you use it, it should break with a clean edge and crumble easily. Do not use yeast that is

*1 In a large warmed bowl, make a well in the flour, salt and sugar. Pour in the liquid ingredients.*

*2 Using your hands, or a spatula, mix the ingredients together until all the flour is incorporated.*

*3 On a floured surface, knead the dough for about 10 minutes, or until it feels smooth and elastic.*

dry or sour-smelling or has dark streaks.

Dried yeast in granule form (activated dried yeast) will keep for 6 months in a cool place because the plants are inert and will not become active until they are mixed with a warm liquid.

The quantity of yeast given in all our bread recipes is for fresh yeast. If you prefer to use dried yeast, the conversion is quite simple—half the quantity. In other words, use 1 ounce of fresh yeast or ½ ounce of dried yeast. As a guide, use ½ ounce of fresh yeast for 1 to 1½ pounds of flour and 1 ounce of fresh yeast for 3 pounds of flour.

Yeast is destroyed by extreme heat—over 110°F. If you add hot water to yeast, or try to speed up the rising process by leaving the dough in a very hot place, the yeast will be killed. You can use cold water to dissolve the yeast and leave the dough to rise in the refrigerator overnight (this prolongs the rising process), but the yeast will develop most satisfactorily if the room temperature, the temperature of the flour and the temperature of the liquid are all between 75°F and 85°F.

*Sugar*

Sugar provides food for the yeast which helps it to grow and also adds flavour to the bread. Sugar also plays a part in browning the crust. If there is not very much sugar in the dough, the yeast will use it all in making carbon dioxide and alcohol, and the baked bread will not be golden brown.

Too much sugar, however, retards the yeast's activity and the dough will take longer to rise.

*Liquid*

The moisture in the dough is supplied by water or milk or a mixture of the two, and may be cold when it is added. The ideal temperature, however, is lukewarm (80°F to 85°F). Test the milk on the inside of your wrist.

Milk should be scalded (brought to just under the boiling point) and then cooled to lukewarm before it is added to the flour. This scalding destroys certain bacteria in the milk which could cause the dough to sour. It also makes the dough easier to handle.

*Salt*

Salt should never be mixed directly with the yeast because it slows down the fermentation process. But a sufficient amount of salt must be added to the dough or the bread will have a very uninteresting flavour.

*Eggs and butter or oil*

Eggs and butter or oil are variables. When eggs are added to the dough, as in sweet breads or French brioches, the finished bread is richer and more yellow. Butter or oil increase the volume of the baked bread because the gluten network of the dough is lubricated so that it expands more smoothly and easily. Butter or oil also improve the flavour and keeping qualities of the bread.

TECHNIQUES

*Dissolving the Yeast*

Crumble the yeast into a small bowl. Using a fork cream a small amount of sugar with the yeast and add a little lukewarm water. Mix to a paste and set aside in a warm, draught-free place to ferment. At the end of 15 to 20 minutes the yeast will be puffed up and frothy.

An alternative method is to add the yeast paste to a quarter of the specified amount of flour and mix it to a soft dough. Cut a cross in the top of this yeast ball with a knife and set it aside in a warm, draught-free place for 20 to 30 minutes to ferment. At the end of this time the yeast ball will be doubled in size.

If you are using dried yeast, dissolve a small quantity of sugar in lukewarm water in a small bowl or teacup and sprinkle on the yeast. Leave it for 10

minutes to allow the yeast cells to separate, swell and become active.

The yeast is now ready to begin its work as soon as it is added to the dough.

*Mixing the Dough*

Put the dry ingredients, the flour, salt and sugar, in a large warmed bowl. Make a well in the centre and into this pour the liquid ingredients, the dissolved yeast, milk and/or water, butter melted in the milk, or oil. Then, using your fingers or a spatula, gradually draw the dry ingredients into the liquids and continue mixing until all the flour is incorporated and the dough comes away from the sides of the bowl. If the dough is too soft and wet, more flour may be worked in.

*Kneading*

Turn the dough out of the bowl on to a floured board or marble slab to knead. This will thoroughly mix the flour with the liquid. The kneaded dough will hold in the gas bubbles manufactured by the yeast.

Fold the dough over on to itself towards you and then press it down away from yourself with the heels of your hands. Turn the dough slightly and fold and press it again. Continue kneading for about 10 minutes until the dough feels smooth and elastic. Dough made with hard-wheat flours requires a little more kneading than dough made with soft flour.

If the dough feels sticky while you are kneading, you may work in a little more flour, but be careful not to add too much or the dough will become stiff.

*Rising*

Shape the kneaded dough into a ball and place it in a lightly greased bowl. Sprinkle the surface of the dough with a little flour and cover the bowl with a damp cloth. The flour will prevent the dough from sticking to the cloth as it rises and

*4 Leave it in a warm place for 1 to 1½ hours, or until the dough has almost doubled in bulk. Remove the cover.*

*5 When the dough has risen, punch it to break up the air pockets, and fold the edges to the centre.*

*6 Shape the dough into pieces and press them into greased loaf tins. Leave the dough to rise again.*

the cloth is dampened to increase the humidity. Do not cover the bowl tightly because to grow the yeast needs air as well as moisture, warmth and food. Place the bowl in a warm, draught-free place until the dough has almost doubled in bulk.

If your kitchen is cold you may want to place the bowl on top of the stove with the oven on at cool 300°F (Gas Mark 2, 150°C).

Rising times vary greatly depending on temperature, the amount of yeast in the dough and the kind of flour used, but, generally speaking, 1 to 1½ hours is adequate. The longer the fermentation, the better-flavoured and better-textured the bread will be. However, the dough should not be left to rise in a warm place for too long or it will become tough. You can tell if this is happening because a crust will form on the top of the dough.

If you want to speed up the rising process, place the covered bowl on an oven rack over a pan of boiling water. But be sure that the bottom of the bowl is not too close to the water or the heat will kill the yeast.

To test if the dough has risen sufficiently, press two fingers deep into the dough and withdraw them quickly. If the indentation remains the dough has risen enough.

If you are preparing the dough the day before the bread is to be baked, you can prolong the rising process by putting the covered bowl in a cool place or in the refrigerator for 8 to 10 hours or overnight. When the dough is fully risen it will be lighter and more spongy than dough which has risen in a warm place. It will require more kneading the second time as well as a longer proving. This slow rising method will, however, produce an excellent bread which will keep well.

*Second Kneading*
Push your fist into the centre of the dough and fold the edges to the centre. This punching down breaks up the large gas pockets and makes available a new supply of oxygen for the yeast plants.

Turn the dough out of the bowl on to the floured work surface. Knead it thoroughly and vigorously for 2 to 3 minutes (a larger batch of dough requires a longer kneading). This second kneading is more important than the first because it temporarily checks the action of the yeast.

Use a sharp knife to cut the dough into the number of loaves you are baking. With your hands, shape these pieces into balls.

*Proving*
What you are proving is that the yeast is still active. To do this the balls of dough are put into the greased tins and pushed out slightly so that they are roughly the shape of the tins. The tins should be only about half full. Sprinkle the surfaces of the loaves with a little flour. Cover the tins with a damp cloth and return them to a warm place for 45 to 60 minutes. During this time the dough will rise to the tops of the tins.

The proving may be done on an oven rack over a pan of boiling water, but be careful not to place the bottoms of the tins too close to the hot water.

If you want your bread to have a shiny crust, instead of sprinkling the dough with flour, just before baking brush the tops of the loaves with a mixture of beaten egg and milk.

A country-style finish can be produced by making a criss-cross gash in the top of the dough with a heated, sharp knife or kitchen scissors.

*Baking*
The bread must always be started in a hot oven so the oven should be preheated to the correct temperature before the dough is put in to bake. Baking stops the fermentation of the yeast and evaporates the alcohol.

Place the tins in the centre of the oven and bake for 15 minutes. In this initial stage the loaf rises dramatically. This is caused by the leavening gas expanding rapidly and the gluten cells stretching to accommodate it.

Transfer the tins to a lower shelf and reduce the oven heat. The gluten cells will gradually be set by the heat, and after 25 to 30 minutes the bread should be done, having shrunk slightly in the tins.

To increase the crustiness of the loaves, brush the tops of the loaves with lightly beaten egg white or cold water 10 minutes before the end of the baking time. For a soft crust, brush the tops with melted butter 10 minutes before the baking time is completed.

Remove the tins from the oven and turn the bread out, upside-down, on to a wire rack. Rap the bottoms of the loaves with your knuckles. If they sound hollow, like a drum, the bread is cooked. If they feel soft, return them, upside-down, to the oven with the heat reduced and bake for a further 10 to 15 minutes.

A shiny, glazed crust, characteristic of French and Vienna bread or rolls, can be obtained by placing a flat pan of boiling water in the bottom of the oven just before the bread is put in and leaving the tin in the oven throughout the baking. The steam from the water forms a coating of moisture on the surface of the dough which gives it time to expand and develop a crust.

*Cooling*
Bread should be cooled on a wire rack so that the air can circulate around it and prevent moisture from spoiling the crispness of the crust.

243

## American White Bread

*This is a smooth-textured, pleasant-tasting milk bread. It has a shiny, golden brown crust and is excellent for sandwiches. This dough recipe can also be used successfully for fruit or nut loaves. For a fruit loaf, during the second kneading add either 5 ounces [1 cup] of raisins or dates, for a nut loaf, 5 ounces [1 cup] of chopped walnuts, hazelnuts or almonds. For a fruit and nut loaf, add 5 ounces [1 cup] of dried fruit and 3 ounces [¾ cup] of chopped walnuts, hazelnuts or almonds.*

ONE 1-POUND LOAF

2 oz. [¼ cup] plus ½ teaspoon butter
½ oz. yeast
1 tablespoon plus 1 teaspoon sugar
3 teaspoons lukewarm water
10 fl. oz. [1¼ cups] milk
1 lb. [4 cups] flour
1 teaspoon salt
GLAZE
1 egg lightly beaten with 1
   tablespoon milk

Grease the loaf tin with the ½ teaspoon of butter and set aside.

Crumble the yeast into a small bowl and mash in the 1 teaspoon of sugar with a kitchen fork. Add the water and cream the water and yeast together to form a smooth paste. Set the bowl aside in a

*A smooth milk bread with a golden brown crust, American White Bread is perfect for sandwiches.*

warm, draught-free place for 15 to 20 minutes, or until the yeast has risen and is puffed up and frothy.

Pour the milk into a small saucepan, place it over moderately high heat and bring it to just below the boiling point. Then reduce the heat to low and add the remaining butter. When the butter has melted, remove the pan from the heat and allow the milk-and-butter mixture to cool to lukewarm.

Sift the flour, the remaining sugar and the salt into a large, warmed mixing bowl. Make a well in the centre of the flour mixture and pour in the yeast and the milk-and-butter mixture. Using your fingers or a spatula gradually draw the flour into the liquid. Continue mixing until all the flour is incorporated and the dough comes away from the sides of the bowl.

Turn the dough out on to a floured board or marble slab and knead for about 10 minutes, reflouring the surface if the dough becomes sticky. The dough should then be elastic and smooth.

Rinse, thoroughly dry and lightly grease the large mixing bowl. Shape the dough into a ball and return it to the

bowl. Dust the top of the dough with a little flour and cover the bowl with a clean, damp cloth. Set the bowl in a warm, draught-free place and leave it for 1 to 1½ hours, or until the dough has risen and has almost doubled in bulk.

Turn the risen dough out of the bowl on to a floured surface and knead for about 4 minutes. Roll and shape the dough into a loaf. Place the dough in the tin, cover with a damp cloth and return to a warm place for about 30 to 45 minutes, or until the dough has risen to the top of the tin.

Preheat the oven to very hot 475°F (Gas Mark 9, 240°C).

Using a pastry brush, paint the top of the loaf with the glaze. Place the tin in the centre of the oven and bake for 15 minutes. Then lower the temperature to hot 425°F (Gas Mark 7, 220°C), put the tin on a lower shelf in the oven and bake for another 25 to 30 minutes.

After removing the bread from the oven, tip the loaf out and rap the underside with your knuckles. If the bread sounds hollow, like a drum, it is cooked. If the bread does not sound hollow, lower the oven temperature to fairly hot 375°F (Gas Mark 5, 190°C), return the loaf, upside-down, to the oven and bake for a further 10 minutes.

Cool the loaf on a wire rack.

*Simple and inexpensive to make, white Household Bread is the ideal loaf for beginner bread-makers.*

## Household Bread

*Simple and economical to make, Household Bread is ordinary white bread, the type most often seen in shops. But like anything home-made, it certainly looks and tastes better. This recipe makes enough dough to fill four 1 pound loaf tins, but it is more interesting to bake the bread in different containers, or shape the dough into individual braids, rolls, long French-style loaves or round Italian-style loaves.*

FOUR 1-POUND LOAVES

2 teaspoons butter
1 oz. yeast
1 tablespoon plus 1 teaspoon sugar
1½ pints [3¾ cups] plus 4 teaspoons lukewarm water
3 lb. [12 cups] flour
1 tablespoon salt

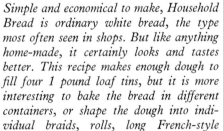

Grease the 4 tins with the butter.

Crumble the yeast into a small bowl and mash in 1 teaspoon of sugar with a kitchen fork. Add 4 teaspoons of water and cream the water and yeast together to form a smooth paste. Set the bowl aside in a warm, draught-free place for 15 to 20 minutes, or until the yeast has risen and is puffed up and frothy.

Put the flour, the remaining sugar and the salt into a warmed, large mixing bowl. Make a well in the centre of the flour mixture and pour in the yeast and the remaining lukewarm water. Using your hands or a spatula gradually draw the flour into the liquid. Continue mixing until all the flour is incorporated and the dough comes away from the sides of the bowl.

Turn the dough out on to a floured board or marble slab and knead for about 10 minutes, reflouring the surface if the dough becomes sticky. The dough should then be elastic and smooth.

Rinse, thoroughly dry and lightly grease the large mixing bowl. Shape the dough into a ball and return it to the bowl. Dust the top of the dough with a little flour and cover the bowl with a clean, damp cloth. Set the bowl in a warm, draught-free place and leave it for 1 to 1½ hours, or until the dough has risen and has almost doubled in bulk.

Turn the risen dough out of the bowl on to a floured surface and knead for about 8 to 10 minutes. Using a sharp knife, cut the dough into four pieces and roll and shape each piece into a loaf. Place the loaves in the tins, cover with a damp cloth and return to a warm place for about 30 to 45 minutes, or until the dough has risen to the top of the tins.

Preheat the oven to very hot 475°F (Gas Mark 9, 240°C).

Place the tins in the centre of the oven and bake for 15 minutes. Then lower the temperature to hot 425°F (Gas Mark 7, 220°C), put the bread on a lower shelf in the oven and bake for another 25 to 30 minutes.

After removing the bread from the oven, tip the loaves out of the tins and rap the undersides with your knuckles. If the bread sounds hollow, like a drum, it is cooked. If it does not sound hollow, lower the oven temperature to fairly hot 375°F (Gas Mark 5, 190°C), return the loaves, upside-down, to the oven and bake for a further 5 to 10 minutes.

Cool the loaves on a wire rack.

*This Quick Bread can be made when you're short of time since it requires only one rising and little kneading.*

## Quick Bread

*This bread differs from other breads in that it requires only one rising and very little kneading. It has a slightly rough texture and does not keep as well as breads prepared in the usual way.*

## Swedish Rye Bread

*The nutritious combination of rye and wholewheat flours makes light-textured, attractive brown bread. As with other wholewheat breads, Swedish Rye, wrapped in a clean dry cloth and stored in an airtight container, keeps extremely well.*

ONE 1-POUND LOAF

½ teaspoon butter
½ oz. yeast
1 teaspoon sugar
10 fl. oz. [1¼ cups] plus 3 teaspoons
   lukewarm water
12 oz. [3 cups] flour
4 oz. wholemeal flour [1 cup
   wholewheat flour]
1 teaspoon salt
1 tablespoon cracked wheat

*Low Cal*

Grease a loaf tin with the butter and set aside.

Crumble the yeast into a small bowl and mash in the sugar with a kitchen fork. Add 3 teaspoons of water and cream the water and yeast together to form a smooth paste. Set the bowl aside in a warm, draught-free place for 15 to 20 minutes, or until the yeast has risen and is puffed up and frothy.

Put the flour, the wholemeal [wholewheat] flour and the salt into a warmed, large mixing bowl. Make a well in the centre of the flour mixture and pour in the yeast and the remaining water. Using your fingers or a spatula gradually draw the flour into the liquid. Continue mixing until all the flour is incorporated and the dough comes away from the sides of the bowl.

Turn the dough out on to a floured board or marble slab and knead it for

*Made from rye and wholewheat flours, Swedish Rye Bread is flavourful and light-textured.*

about 3 minutes.

Roll and shape the dough into a loaf and place it in the tin. Cover the tin with a clean damp cloth and set it aside in a warm draught-free place for 1 to 1½ hours or until the dough has risen to the top of the tin.

While the dough is rising, preheat the oven to very hot 475°F (Gas Mark 9, 240°C).

Uncover the tin and sprinkle the top of the dough with the tablespoon of cracked wheat.

Place the tin in the centre of the oven and bake for 15 minutes. Then lower the temperature to hot 425°F (Gas Mark 7, 220°C), put the tin on a lower shelf in the oven and bake for another 25 to 30 minutes.

After removing the bread from the oven, tip the loaf out and rap the underside with your knuckles. If the bread sounds hollow, like a drum, it is cooked. If it does not sound hollow, lower the oven temperature to fairly hot 375°F (Gas Mark 5, 190°C), return the loaf, upside-down, to the oven and bake for a further 5 to 10 minutes.

Cool the loaf on a wire rack.

TWO 1-POUND LOAVES

1 teaspoon butter
¾ oz. yeast
1½ tablespoons plus 1 teaspoon
   brown sugar
3 teaspoons lukewarm water
1 pint [2½ cups] milk
1 lb. [4 cups] stone-ground rye flour
1 lb. [4 cups] stone-ground
   wholewheat flour
1½ teaspoons salt
2 teaspoons caraway seeds
   (optional)

Grease two loaf tins with the butter and set aside.

Crumble the yeast into a small bowl and mash in 1 teaspoon of sugar with a kitchen fork. Add 3 teaspoons of water and cream the water and yeast together to form a smooth paste. Set the bowl aside in a warm draught-free place for 15 to 20 minutes, or until the yeast has risen and is puffed up and frothy.

Pour the milk into a small saucepan,

*Sweet Bread dough may be made into buns and sprinkled with nuts to be served for breakfast or with coffee.*

place it over moderately high heat' and bring it to just below boiling point. Remove the pan from the heat and allow the milk to cool to lukewarm.

Put the rye flour, the wholewheat flour and the salt into a warmed, large mixing bowl. Add the remaining sugar and mix the ingredients together well.

Make a well in the centre of the flour mixture and pour in the yeast and all the milk. Using your fingers or a spatula, gradually draw the flour into the liquid. Continue mixing until all the flour is incorporated and the dough comes away from the sides of the bowl.

Turn the dough out on to a floured board or marble slab and knead for about 10 minutes, reflouring the surface if the dough becomes sticky. The dough should then be elastic and smooth.

Rinse, thoroughly dry and lightly grease the large mixing bowl, shape the dough into a ball and return it to the bowl. Dust the top of the dough with a little flour and cover the bowl with a clean, damp cloth. Put the bowl in a warm, draught-free place for 1 to 1½ hours, or until the dough has risen and has almost doubled in bulk.

Turn the risen dough out of the bowl on to a floured surface and knead vigorously for about 4 minutes. Knead in the caraway seeds, if you are using them. Using a sharp knife, cut the dough into two pieces. Roll and shape each piece into a loaf. Place the loaves in the tins, cover with a damp cloth and return to a warm place for about 30 to 45 minutes, or until the dough has risen to the top of the tins.

Preheat the oven to very hot 475°F (Gas Mark 9, 240°C).

Place the tins in the centre of the oven and bake for 15 minutes. Then lower the temperature to hot 425°F (Gas Mark 7, 220°C). Put the bread on a lower shelf in the oven and bake for another 25 to 30 minutes.

After removing the bread from the oven, tip the loaves out and rap the undersides with your knuckles. If the bread sounds hollow, like a drum, it is cooked. If the bread does not sound hollow, lower the oven temperature to fairly hot 375°F (Gas Mark 5, 190°C), return the loaves, upside-down, to the oven, and bake for a further 10 minutes.

Cool the loaves on a wire rack.

## Sweet Bread

*This basic Sweet Bread recipe can be used successfully in many ways. The dough baked in loaf tins can be served as a plain sweet bread spread with butter or jam. Baked in a ring mould filled with fruit and nuts or iced and sprinkled with chopped nuts it makes an attractive coffee cake. Alternatively, it may be shaped into buns, baked on a baking sheet, and served as sweet rolls for breakfast or with tea. If you are making a sweet fruit loaf or buns, add approximately 5 ounces [1 cup] of mixed fruit and candied peel for each 1 pound of flour.*

TWO 1-POUND LOAVES

4 oz. [½ cup] plus 1 teaspoon butter
½ oz. yeast
4 oz. [½ cup] plus ½ teaspoon sugar
3 teaspoons lukewarm water
8 fl. oz. [1 cup] milk
1½ lb. [6 cups] flour
1 teaspoon salt
2 eggs, lightly beaten
GLAZE
1 egg lightly beaten with
1 tablespoon milk

Grease the loaf tins with 1 teaspoon of butter.

Crumble the yeast into a small bowl and mash in ½ teaspoon of sugar with a kitchen fork. Add 3 teaspoons of water and cream the water and yeast together to form a smooth paste. Set the bowl aside in a warm, draught-free place for about 15 to 20 minutes, or until the yeast mixture has risen and is puffed up and frothy.

Pour the milk into a small saucepan. Place it over moderately high heat and bring it to just below the boiling point. Reduce the heat to low and add the remaining butter. When the butter has melted, remove the pan from the heat and allow the milk-and-butter mixture to cool to lukewarm.

Sift the flour, remaining sugar and salt into a warmed, large mixing bowl. Make a well in the centre of the flour mixture and pour in the yeast, milk-and-butter mixture and the 2 eggs. Using your fingers, or a spatula, gradually draw the flour into the liquid. Continue mixing until all the flour is incorporated and the dough comes away from the sides of the bowl.

Turn the dough out on to a floured board or marble slab and knead for about 10 minutes, reflouring the surface if the dough becomes sticky. The dough should then be elastic and smooth.

Rinse, thoroughly dry and lightly grease the large mixing bowl. Shape the dough into a ball and return it to the bowl. Dust the top of the dough with a little flour and cover the bowl with a clean, damp cloth. Set the bowl in a warm, draught-free place and leave it for 1 to 1½ hours, or until the dough has risen and has almost doubled in bulk.

Turn the risen dough out of the bowl on to a floured surface and knead it for about 4 minutes. Using a sharp knife cut the dough into 2 pieces. Roll and shape each piece into a loaf. Place the dough in the tins, cover with a damp cloth and return to a warm place for about 30 to 45 minutes, or until the dough has risen to the top of the tins.

Preheat the oven to very hot 475°F (Gas Mark 9, 240°C).

Using a pastry brush, paint the tops of the loaves with the glaze. Place the tins in the centre of the oven and bake for 15 minutes. Then lower the temperature to hot 425°F (Gas Mark 7, 220°C), put the tins on a lower shelf in the oven and bake for another 25 to 30 minutes.

After removing the bread from the oven, tip the loaves out and rap the undersides with your knuckles. If the bread sounds hollow, like a drum, it is cooked. If it does not sound hollow, lower the oven temperature to fairly hot 375°F (Gas Mark 5, 190°C), return the loaves, upside-down, to the oven and bake for a further 5 to 10 minutes.

Cool the loaves on a wire rack.

on to a floured surface and knead vigorously for about 10 minutes. Using a sharp knife, cut the dough into four pieces. Roll and shape each piece into a loaf. Place the loaves in the tins. If you prefer a country-style loaf, use a heated, sharp knife or kitchen scissors to make a deep gash on the top of each loaf and then dust them with a little wholewheat flour. Cover the tins with a damp cloth and return to a warm place for 30 to 45 minutes, or until the dough has risen to the top of the tins.

Preheat the oven to very hot 475°F (Gas Mark 9, 240°C).

Place the tins in the centre of the oven and bake for 15 minutes. Then lower the oven temperature to hot 425°F (Gas Mark 7, 220°C), put the bread on a lower shelf in the oven and bake for another 25 to 30 minutes.

After removing the bread from the oven, tip the loaves out of the tins and rap the undersides with your knuckles. If the bread sounds hollow, like a drum, it is cooked. If the bread does not sound hollow, lower the oven temperature to fairly hot 375°F (Gas Mark 5, 190°C), return the loaves, upside-down, to the oven and bake for a further 10 minutes.

Cool the loaves on a wire rack.

## Wholewheat Bread

*Home-made wholewheat bread is far superior to any commercial brown bread. Although it is most delicious when freshly baked and spread with butter, honey or cheese, stored correctly the bread keeps extremely well and can be served up to a week after baking. For variation the loaves may be baked in well-greased flower pots, or shaped into cottage loaves on a baking sheet.*

*To make cheese bread, add 12 ounces of finely grated Cheddar or any hard cheese to the flour with the yeast mixture.*

FOUR 1-POUND LOAVES

1½ teaspoons butter
1 oz. yeast
1 teaspoon brown sugar
1½ pints [3¾ cups] plus 4 teaspoons lukewarm water
3 lb. [12 cups] stone-ground wholewheat flour
1¼ tablespoon rock salt or 1 tablespoon table salt
2 tablespoons honey
1 tablespoon vegetable oil

*(Low Cal)*

Grease the 4 loaf tins with the butter.

Crumble the yeast into a small bowl and mash in the brown sugar with a kitchen fork. Add 4 teaspoons of water and cream the water, sugar and yeast together to form a smooth paste. Set

*For an attractive, unusual-shaped loaf, Wholewheat Bread can be baked in well-greased flower pots.*

the bowl aside in a warm, draught-free place for 15 to 20 minutes, or until the yeast has risen and is puffed up and frothy.

Put the flour and salt into a warmed, large mixing bowl. Make a well in the centre of the flour mixture and pour in the yeast mixture, the honey, the remaining lukewarm water and the oil. Using your fingers, or a spatula, gradually draw the flour into the liquid. Continue mixing until all the flour is incorporated and the dough comes away from the sides of the bowl.

Turn the dough out on to a floured board or marble slab and knead for about 10 minutes, reflouring the surface if the dough becomes sticky. The dough should then be elastic and smooth.

Rinse, thoroughly dry and lightly grease the large mixing bowl. Shape the dough into a ball and return it to the bowl. Dust the top of the dough with a little flour and cover the bowl with a clean, damp cloth. Set the bowl in a warm, draught-free place and leave it for 1 to 1½ hours, or until the dough has risen and has almost doubled in bulk.

Turn the risen dough out of the bowl

## Bread and Butter Pudding

*A perennial British favourite, Bread and Butter Pudding is easy and economical to make and delicious to eat. Its custard-like consistency is attractive to children.*

3 TO 4 SERVINGS

1 teaspoon butter, softened
6 thin slices of white bread, crusts removed and liberally buttered
3 oz. [¾ cup] seedless raisins
½ teaspoon grated nutmeg
2 tablespoons sugar
CUSTARD
2 eggs
15 fl. oz. [1⅞ cups] milk
1 tablespoon sugar
½ teaspoon vanilla essence

Grease the bottom and sides of a medium-sized, shallow baking dish with the butter.

Cut the slices of bread into quarters. Place a layer of bread (buttered side up) on the bottom of the dish and sprinkle with half the raisins, nutmeg and 1 tablespoon sugar.

Add a second layer of bread and sprinkle on the rest of the raisins, nutmeg and sugar. Top with a final layer of bread, buttered side up.

To make the custard, beat the eggs in a large mixing bowl with a wire whisk.

Heat the milk, sugar and vanilla essence. Add the heated milk mixture to the eggs, beating continuously to combine the ingredients well. Strain the mixture over the bread and let stand for at least 30 minutes, or until the bread has absorbed most of the liquid.

Preheat the oven to fairly hot 375°F (Gas Mark 5, 190°C).

Place the pudding in the centre of the oven and bake for 35 to 45 minutes, or until the top is crisp and golden.

## Breadcrumbs

There are three types of breadcrumbs used in cooking: fresh white bread-crumbs, dried white breadcrumbs and browned breadcrumbs.

Fresh white breadcrumbs are prepared from bread which is at least one day old. The crusts are removed and discarded and the remainder is either blended in a blender, grated with a hand grater or rubbed through a wire strainer with the palm of the hand. Fresh white bread-crumbs are used for panades, for stuffings and bread sauce and for some desserts and cakes. They will not keep long be-cause they soon become mouldy, but they will be all right for a day or two if they are stored in a screw-top jar. Put into polythene bags and frozen they will keep for several months.

Dried white breadcrumbs are prepared by drying fresh white breadcrumbs on a baking sheet in a very slow oven, so that the breadcrumbs do not brown. Dried white breadcrumbs are used for coating foods for frying. The fish or meat to be fried should be dipped in beaten egg and then coated with the crumbs before being fried in hot fat. This will give a firm, crusty surface. Dried white bread-crumbs will keep for several weeks in a screw-top jar.

Browned breadcrumbs are prepared by browning breadcrusts in a very slow oven and then crushing them finely with a pestle in a mortar, with a rolling pin or in a blender. They can be used for coating for frying, but they are more often used for covering the surface of ham before baking or for gratinés. They are also served hot, on their own, with game. Browned breadcrumbs will keep indefi-nitely in a screw-top jar provided they are stored in a cool, dry place.

## Breadcrumb Dumplings

*Quick and easy to make, these Breadcrumb Dumplings are light and puffy. They may be served with any meat stew or thick soup.*

4 TO 6 SERVINGS

3 oz. [1½ cups] fresh white breadcrumbs
3 oz. [¾ cup] self-raising flour
3 oz. [⅜ cup] shredded suet
1 tablespoon finely minced onion
1 egg
½ teaspoon salt
¼ teaspoon black pepper
1 tablespoon chopped fresh parsley
½ teaspoon dried mace

In a large mixing bowl, combine the breadcrumbs, flour, suet and minced onion, stirring until the ingredients are well blended together.

In a small bowl, beat the egg with a fork until it is frothy. Mix in the salt, pepper, parsley and mace.

Add the egg mixture to the breadcrumb mixture and beat well.

With your hands, gently form the mix-ture into small balls. Using a table-spoon, carefully drop the dumplings, one at a time, into the simmering stew or soup. Cover the pan and steam the dumplings for about 35 minutes or until they are light and puffy.

Serve immediately.

## Breadcrumb Stuffing

*This basic dry poultry stuffing is suitable for one large chicken or one small turkey. It is exceptionally easy to make and may be prepared a day or two in advance, if you keep it, covered, in the refrigerator until you are ready to use it.*

STUFFING FOR ONE 5-POUND FOWL

3 oz. [⅜ cup] butter
1 small onion, finely chopped
1 celery stalk, with leaves, finely chopped
2 teaspoons dried sage
½ teaspoon salt
¼ teaspoon black pepper
2 tablespoons chopped parsley
1 lb. white breadcrumbs, made from 3 days' old bread
2 to 3 tablespoons milk or water (optional)

In a medium-sized frying-pan, melt the butter over moderate heat. When the foam subsides, add the onion and the celery and fry them for 10 minutes, or until they are soft but not brown.

Remove the pan from the heat and transfer the onion and celery to a medium-sized mixing bowl. Add the sage, salt, pepper, parsley and breadcrumbs. With a fork blend the mixture thoroughly. If you prefer a moist stuffing, add 2 to 3 tablespoons of milk or water.

BREAD FRUIT.

## Breadfruit

The fruit of a tall tree of the mulberry family, breadfruit is a staple food in the South Pacific and is cultivated elsewhere in tropical areas. Breadfruit is large, greenish and spherical, with a rough surface and a white pulp. It differs from other fruits in that its main nutritional constituent is starch and it is gathered and cooked before it is ripe.

## Bread Sauce

*Traditionally served with roast turkey, chicken or pheasant, Bread Sauce should be neither too thin nor too thick, but the consistency is determined by individual taste. Coarse, crisply fried crumbs may be sprinkled on top of the sauce.*

4 SERVINGS

1 medium-sized onion, studded with 2 cloves
1 bay leaf
10 fl. oz. [1¼ cups] milk
2 oz. [1 cup] fresh white breadcrumbs
½ teaspoon salt
¼ teaspoon black pepper
1 tablespoon butter
1 tablespoon single [light] cream

Place the onion, bay leaf and milk in a medium-sized saucepan. Cover the pan and cook for 10 to 15 minutes over very low heat. In this time the milk will be-come infused with the flavour of the onion, cloves and bay leaf.

Remove the onion and bay leaf. Bring the milk to the boil and add the bread-crumbs. Reduce the heat to low and simmer for 3 to 4 minutes, or until the sauce is thick and creamy.

Remove the pan from the heat. Stir in the salt, pepper, butter and cream with a wooden spoon. Gently reheat the sauce over very low heat. Do not allow it to boil. Serve at once.

## Bread Sticks

*Bread sticks are nice to serve with soups or salads. They may be made with left-over ordinary bread dough, but the recipe given here, which is slightly richer than bread dough, will result in crunchier sticks. They will keep well if stored in an airtight tin. For an interesting variation, add $\frac{1}{4}$ teaspoon grated nutmeg, 1 teaspoon dried sage and 1 tablespoon caraway seeds to the dough before it is left to rise.*

32 STICKS

8 fl. oz. [1 cup] milk
$\frac{1}{2}$ oz. yeast
1 teaspoon sugar
1 lb. [4 cups] flour
1 teaspoon salt
1 oz. [2 tablespoons] butter
  milk or water (optional)
  crushed rock salt (optional)

Place the milk in a small saucepan and bring to just below the boiling point over moderately high heat. Remove the pan from the heat and allow the milk to cool to lukewarm.

Crumble the yeast into a small bowl. Add the sugar and cream it with the yeast. Stir in a little of the warmed milk to dissolve the yeast. Set the bowl in a warm place for 20 minutes. At the end of this time the yeast mixture will be frothy and almost doubled in bulk.

Sift the flour and salt into a warmed, medium-sized mixing bowl. Make a well in the centre of the flour and into this put the dissolved yeast.

Melt the butter in the warm milk and pour this into the well in the flour. Mix together the yeast mixture and the milk, and gradually draw in the flour. Continue mixing until a smooth dough is formed.

Cover the bowl with a clean cloth and leave the dough in a warm place to rise for 45 minutes.

When the rising is completed, turn the dough out on to a floured board or marble slab and knead it for 3 minutes until it is smooth.

Form the dough into a roll and cut it into 32 small pieces with a knife. Roll the pieces into sticks as thick as your little finger and 6 to 8 inches long. Place the sticks on a baking sheet and prove for 20 minutes.

Preheat the oven to fairly hot 400°F (Gas Mark 6, 200°C).

Bake the bread sticks in the oven for 10 minutes. Then lower the oven heat to moderate 350°F (Gas Mark 4, 180°C) and continue baking for a further 20 minutes. Remove the sheet from the oven and transfer the sticks to a wire

*An unusual change from rolls, these crunchy Bread Sticks go well with soups or salads.*

rack to cool.

To make salted bread sticks, before they are completely cool, brush the sticks with a little milk or water and then sprinkle them with crushed rock salt.

## Breakfast

"The moral and physical welfare of mankind depends largely upon its breakfast" —the words of Mrs. Beeton spoken almost a century ago still ring true today. Nutritional research has shown how important it is to eat a substantial breakfast. It has been proved that people are more alert and efficient after a well-balanced meal at the beginning of the day.

## Breakfast Buns

*These hot Breakfast Buns sprinkled with sugar and cinnamon are very simple to make. They can be prepared before you start to cook the rest of the breakfast.*

12 BUNS

2 oz. [¼ cup] butter
2 tablespoons vegetable fat
8 oz. [1 cup] sugar
1 egg
8 oz. [2 cups] flour
1½ teaspoons baking powder
½ teaspoon salt
¼ teaspoon ground nutmeg
4 fl. oz. [½ cup] milk
3 oz. [⅜ cup] melted butter
1 teaspoon powdered cinnamon

Preheat the oven to moderate 350°F (Gas Mark 4, 180°C).

Grease 12 cake patty tins with 1 tablespoon of butter. Set the greased tins aside.

In a medium-sized mixing bowl, beat together the remaining butter, the vegetable fat, half of the sugar and the egg with a wooden spoon or rotary beater until the mixture is smooth and creamy.

Sift together the flour, baking powder, salt and nutmeg into another bowl. Beat the flour mixture and the milk into the egg-and-fat mixture.

Spoon the mixture into the greased patty tins, filling them two-thirds full. Place the tins in the oven and bake for 25 minutes, or until the buns are a light brown.

Remove the tins from the oven and, with a palette knife, ease the buns out of the tins on to a wire rack. Brush the buns with the melted butter and sprinkle them with the remaining sugar and cinnamon.

Serve hot.

## Bream

A fish found in most European waters, the bream is a species of carp. The sea bream has a better flavour than the freshwater bream. All recipes for carp can be used for bream.

## Brèdes

A French colonial dish, *Brèdes* are made from the leaves of different vegetables, such as cabbage, spinach, lettuce and watercress.

*Sprinkled with sugar and cinnamon, these hot Breakfast Buns are very popular in the United States.*

## Brèdes de Chou
CABBAGE BREDES

*Cabbage steamed with bacon, tomatoes and ginger, Brèdes de Chou (bred d'shoo) is an interesting vegetable dish to accompany grilled [broiled] or roast meats, or it makes a light luncheon on its own.*

4 SERVINGS

1 medium-sized white cabbage
1 tablespoon butter
6 streaky bacon slices, rind removed and cut into 1-inch strips
½ teaspoon ground ginger
2 tomatoes, blanched, peeled, seeded and chopped
2 tablespoons water
1 teaspoon salt

Remove the leaves from the cabbage with a small, sharp knife. Cut out the centre vein from each leaf. Gather the leaves into small bundles and cut into thin strips. Set aside.

Melt the butter in a medium-sized saucepan over moderate heat. Add the bacon strips and fry for 5 minutes. Add the ginger, tomatoes, water and salt, cover the pan and simmer for 20 minutes.

Add the shredded cabbage to the sauce, recover the pan and cook over moderately low heat for 1½ hours.

Remove the pan from the heat, turn the cabbage into a vegetable dish and serve at once.

## Brèdes de Cresson
WATERCRESS BREDES

*An unusual way to serve watercress, Brèdes de Cresson (bred d'kreh-sawn) may be served as an accompaniment to almost any chicken or fish dish.*

4 SERVINGS

2 oz. [4 tablespoons] butter
5 oz. thickly sliced, lean bacon, rind removed and diced
1 small onion, coarsely chopped
2 garlic cloves, crushed
¼ teaspoon ground ginger
½ teaspoon salt
1 tomato, blanched, peeled, seeded and sliced
8 fl. oz. [1 cup] chicken stock
2 bunches watercress, washed and drained

Melt the butter in a medium-sized saucepan over moderate heat. Add the bacon and onion and fry them for 10 minutes, stirring frequently. Add the garlic, ginger, salt and tomato and cook for 2 minutes. Pour in the chicken stock and increase the heat to moderately high. Bring the sauce to a boil and simmer it, stirring occasionally, for 10 minutes.

Reduce the heat to low and add the watercress to the pan. Cook gently for 8 to 10 minutes.

Remove the pan from the heat and turn the brèdes into a warmed serving dish.

## Bremer Kuchen
BREMEN SWEET BREAD

*Bremer Kuchen* (bray-mer KOO-khen) *is a delicious yeast bread with fruit and nuts. It is traditionally made during the Christmas season in Bremen, West Germany, and is served with coffee in all the* konditoreien, *coffee houses, there.*

2 LOAVES

22 fl. oz. [2¾ cups] milk
3½ fl. oz. [7 tablespoons] water
4 oz. [½ cup] butter
3 lb. [12 cups] strong white flour
1 teaspoon salt
4 oz. [½ cup] sugar
½ teaspoon ground cardamom
   grated rind of 3 lemons
2 sachets easy-blend dried yeast
   oil, for geasing
5 oz. [⅔ cup] seedless raisins
2 oz. [⅓ cup] currants
2 oz. sultanas [⅓ cup golden raisins]
4 oz. [⅔ cup] slivered almonds
1 egg, beaten
   melted butter or sifted icing
   [confectioner's] sugar for
   decoration

Warm the milk with the water and the butter in a heavy-based saucepan over a low heat, stirring until the butter has melted.

Put the flour into a large, warmed mixing bowl with the salt, sugar, cardamom and lemon rind. Stir in the yeast. Make a well and pour in the milk mixture a little at a time. Using your fingers, gradually draw the flour into the liquid. Continue mixing with your fingers until all the flour is incorporated and the dough comes away from the sides of the mixing bowl.

Turn the dough out on to a floured surface and knead for about 10 minutes, or until smooth and elastic, reflouring the surface if the dough remains sticky, using 1 teaspoon of flour at a time.

Shape into a ball and place in a greased bowl. Cover with greased polythene and leave to rise in a warm place for 1-1½ hours, or until the dough has almost doubled in bulk.

Lightly grease 2 baking [cookie] sheets.

Turn the dough out on to a floured surface and knead for 2 minutes. Sprinkle the raisins, currants, sultanas [golden raisins] and half of the almonds over the dough, a handful at a time, and knead until all these ingredients are evenly incorporated.

Divide the dough into 2 pieces and shape each into a long loaf. Place on the prepared baking sheets and cover with greased polythene. Leave in a warm,

draught-free place for 30-45 minutes, or until each of the loaves have almost doubled in size.

Preheat the oven to fairly hot 375°F (Gas Mark 5, 190°C) and position the shelves just above and below the centre of the oven.

Uncover the loaves and brush with egg, then press the remaining almonds over the tops.

Bake for 1 hour or until the tops are crusty and golden.

Check that the loaves are cooked by tapping the undersides with your knuckles: they should sound hollow. If not, lower the oven temperature to cool 300°F (Gas Mark 2, 150°C) and return the loaves to the oven for another 5-10 minutes.

Place the loaves on a wire rack and brush the tops with melted butter or dust with icing [confectioners'] sugar, then set aside and leave to cool before serving.

If you want to freeze one of the loaves, place it in a rigid container, seal and label. It can be stored frozen for 3 months. Defrost in the wrappings at room temperature for 3-4 hours. Unwrap and refresh for 15-20 minutes.

## Bresse Bleu

A region in central eastern France, Bresse is best known for its blue cheese, *Bleu de Bresse,* as well as for its fine guinea fowl and other poultry. The yellow, maize-fed chicken, *poularde de Bresse,* are so highly regarded by gourmets around the world that they have their own appelation controlée.

## Bretonne, à la

This French term means literally 'Breton-style'. One of the best known of the Breton dishes is lamb with haricot beans. Fish or poultry from the region are usually served in a white wine sauce and artichokes are simmered in oil, butter, onions and cider.

## Brewer's Yeast

Brewer's yeast is a semi-liquid yeast which is used in the preparation of wines and beers. It can be obtained from some brewers and used for baking bread and rolls, but it is preferable to use fresh compressed or active dried yeast for baking because brewer's yeast has a bitter taste.

Two tablespoons of brewer's yeast are equivalent to 1 ounce of fresh compressed yeast, and 5 fluid ounces of a strong brewer's yeast or 7½ fluid ounces of a weaker type will raise a dough made from 7 pounds of flour.

Brewer's yeast can be strengthened by adding sugar, and the bitter taste may be removed by soaking the yeast in cold water for 1 day.

## Brick Cheese

An American original, brick cheese was created in Wisconsin in the 1870s. It is pale, supple-textured, mild in flavour, yet rather pungent smelling, and has numerous irregular holes throughout. The rind is naturally red, but is often removed before the cheese is sold. Whole cheeses weigh about 5½ lb. The name of the cheese may be derived from the shape of the whole cheese, or from the early custom of pressing it between bricks. The cheese is made from cows' milk with rennet.

## Bridge Rolls

*Bridge Rolls are quite easy to make and they may be split and filled with a variety of fillings. For this reason they are particularly suitable for an informal party. If you do not require such a large quantity of rolls, the ingredients can be halved.*

ABOUT 2 DOZEN ROLLS

7 fl. oz. [⅞ cup] milk
2 oz. [¼ cup] butter
1 lb. [4 cups] strong white flour
1 teaspoon salt
2 teaspoons easy-blend dried yeast
2 tablespoons sugar
4 eggs, lightly beaten
1 egg, lightly beaten with
   1 teaspoon salt, to glaze

Heat the milk until nearly boiling, add the butter and simmer gently until the butter has melted. Remove from the heat and cool to lukewarm.

Sift the flour and salt into a large bowl, then stir in the yeast and sugar. Make a well in the centre.

Mix the eggs with the lukewarm milk and pour the mixture into the well. Incorporate it into the flour to form a smooth dough.

Turn the dough on to a floured surface and knead for 5-10 minutes, until smooth and elastic. Put into a greased mixing bowl, cover with greased cling film and leave to rise in a warm, draught-free place for 2 hours.

Punch the dough down with your fist and knead again for 2-3 minutes. Turn it

*A German yeast bread rich with fruit and nuts, Bremer Kuchen is delicious served with morning coffee.*

out on to a floured surface and form it into a roll. Cut the roll into 24 pieces and form them into 24 individual finger-shaped rolls.

Grease a baking tray and arrange the rolls on it, fairly close together. Brush them with beaten egg. Put the tray in a warm place and leave for 30 minutes or until the rolls have risen and expanded. (Reserve the remaining egg.)

Preheat the oven to very hot 450°F (Gas Mark 8, 230°C), with the shelf above centre. Brush the rolls with beaten egg again and bake for 20 minutes or until golden brown. Transfer to a wire rack and leave until cold.

If the rolls brown too quickly reduce the oven temperature to fairly hot 375°F (Gas Mark 5, 190°C) for the last 10 minutes of the cooking time.

The dough can be frozen for up to 3 weeks after first rising. Defrost overnight in the refrigerator or for 6 hours at room temperature; punch down and knead. Baked rolls can be frozen for up to 4 months; refresh in a hot oven 425°F (Gas Mark 7, 220°C) for 5-10 minutes.

## Brie Cheese

Named after La Brie, the province in Northern France where it was first made, Brie Cheese is a round, soft, farm cheese. The best Brie is made in the autumn.

## Brie Cheese Croquettes

*Small balls of Brie cheese, coated with egg and breadcrumbs and served piping hot, these Brie Cheese Croquettes may be served with drinks.*

25 CROQUETTES

10 oz. Brie cheese
1½ oz. [3 tablespoons] butter
6 tablespoons flour
10 fl. oz. [1¼ cups] milk
¼ teaspoon white pepper
¼ teaspoon cayenne
1 egg yolk
1 egg, lightly beaten
2 oz. [⅔ cup] dry breadcrumbs
oil for deep-frying
½ teaspoon salt

Cut away and discard the rind from the Brie cheese. With a wooden spoon, press the cheese through a strainer.

Melt the butter in a medium-sized saucepan over moderate heat. Add the flour and, stirring, cook the mixture for 2 minutes. Remove the pan from the heat, and, stirring constantly, add the milk to the flour-and-butter mixture. When all the milk has been added and the mixture is smooth, return the pan to the heat. Bring the sauce to the boil, stirring continuously. Remove the pan from the heat. Stir in the pepper and cayenne. Allow the mixture to cool.

When the mixture is lukewarm, stir in the egg yolk and sieved cheese. Turn the mixture on to a plate and chill it in the refrigerator.

Dip your hands into flour and shape the mixture into walnut-sized balls on a floured board. Dip the balls in the beaten egg and then roll them in the breadcrumbs.

Heat the oil in a large, deep pan over high heat. When the oil is hot, place the cheese balls in a deep-frying basket and plunge them into the hot oil. Cook the balls for 1 minute, or until they are crisp and golden.

*Piping hot balls of Brie cheese, coated with egg and breadcrumbs - these croquettes go well with drinks.*

Remove the croquettes from the basket and drain them on kitchen paper towels. Sprinkle them with salt. Serve at once.

## Brill

A flat, oval-shaped, smooth-scaled European salt-water fish, similar to the turbot, brill is prized for its delicate and light flesh. Although brill is in season throughout the year, it is at its best from April to August.

## Brill with Aubergine
[Eggplant]

*Aubergine is a vegetable that goes well with fish and here it combines with brill to make a dish as pleasing to the eye as to the palate. This delicately flavoured fish dish may be served with boiled new potatoes and courgettes [zucchinis].*

4 SERVINGS

2 lb. brill fillets
1½ teaspoons salt
4 grindings black pepper
4 oz. mushrooms, sliced
5 fl. oz. [⅝ cup] white wine
2 aubergines [eggplant]
2 tablespoons flour
2 oz. [¼ cup] butter
6 tomatoes, cut in half
1 tablespoon chopped parsley
SAUCE
2 tablespoons butter
1 shallot, very finely chopped
3 tablespoons flour
10 fl. oz. [1¼ cups] milk
½ teaspoon salt
¼ teaspoon white pepper
2 tablespoons single [light] cream

Lay the fillets in a long flameproof dish. Sprinkle them with ½ teaspoon salt and the pepper and place the mushrooms on top. Pour over the wine. Put the dish over moderately low heat and poach the fish for 15 minutes.

While the fish is poaching, slice the aubergine [eggplant] and sprinkle the slices with 1 teaspoon salt. Leave for 15 minutes. Rinse the slices with cold, running water and pat dry with kitchen paper towels. Sprinkle them with the flour.

Melt 2 tablespoons of the butter in a medium-sized frying-pan. Fry the aubergine slices for 5 to 6 minutes on each side over moderate heat.

Remove the aubergine [eggplant] slices from the pan and place them in another flameproof dish.

Add the remaining butter to the frying-pan. When it is foaming, place the tomatoes in the pan, skin side down. Fry for 3 to 4 minutes over moderate heat.

Remove the fish fillets from their poaching liquid and place them on the aubergines in the dish. Arrange the tomatoes round the edge. Sprinkle the parsley over the tomatoes. Cover the dish with aluminium foil and keep hot while preparing the sauce. Remove the mushrooms from the poaching liquid and keep them warm. Reserve the liquid.

In a small saucepan, melt the butter over moderate heat. Add the shallot and fry it for 5 minutes, or until it is soft but not coloured. Stir in the flour with a wooden spoon and gradually add the milk, stirring constantly. Boil the sauce for 2 to 3 minutes, or until it has reduced a little. Add the liquid in which the fish was poached and blend thoroughly. Stir in the salt, pepper and cream. Pour the sauce over the fish. Arrange the mushrooms on top. Serve at once.

## Brill with Courgette [Zucchini]

*An easy and uncomplicated way to cook brill, this is, nevertheless, an elegant enough dish to serve as part of a main course for a lunch or dinner party. Turbot may be substituted if brill is not available.*

4 SERVINGS

3 oz. [$\frac{3}{8}$ cup] butter
2 lb. brill fillets
1 teaspoon lemon juice
1 lb. courgettes [zucchinis], peeled and sliced
$\frac{3}{4}$ teaspoon salt
$\frac{1}{2}$ teaspoon black pepper
$\frac{1}{2}$ teaspoon dried basil
4 tablespoons flour
10 fl. oz. [$1\frac{1}{4}$ cups] milk
1 tablespoon grated cheese

Preheat the oven to moderate 350°F (Gas Mark 4, 180°C).

Grease a shallow baking dish with 1 tablespoon butter. Put the fish fillets in the baking dish and pour in the lemon juice and enough water to barely cover

them. Poach the fillets in the oven for 15 to 20 minutes, or until the fish flakes easily.

Transfer the fish to a flameproof serving dish and keep warm. Strain the liquid from the baking dish and reserve it.

While the fish is cooking, melt 2 tablespoons of the butter in a medium-sized saucepan over moderate heat. Add the courgette [zucchini] slices to it. Stir, cover and simmer for about 8 minutes, or until they are just tender. Stir in $\frac{1}{2}$ teaspoon salt, pepper and basil. Place to one side and keep hot.

Preheat the grill [broiler] to moderate.

Melt the remaining butter in another medium-sized saucepan over moderate heat. Remove the saucepan from the heat and stir in the flour with a wooden spoon. Add the milk and the liquid from the fish, stirring continuously until the

*Garnished with tomatoes and mushrooms, Brill with Aubergine in a creamy sauce, is a superb dinner party dish.*

mixture is smooth. Replace the pan on the heat and bring the sauce to the boil. Stirring continuously, boil the sauce for 5 minutes. Stir in the remaining salt. Taste the sauce and add more salt if necessary.

Put the fish fillets in a flameproof serving dish. Cover with the sauce. Sprinkle on the cheese and brown under the grill [broiler]. Surround with the drained courgette [zucchini] slices and serve.

## Brill à la Dugléré

BAKED BRILL WITH TOMATOES, ONIONS AND WHITE WINE

*A simple and fairly quick dish to prepare, Brill à la Dugléré (bree ah-lah doo-glay-ray) is ideal for an informal lunch or dinner party. Serve it with boiled new potatoes and a green vegetable.*

4 SERVINGS

3 oz. [⅜ cup] butter
1 lb. tomatoes, blanched, peeled, seeded and chopped
1 onion, very finely chopped
1 tablespoon tomato purée
2 lb. brill fillets
  bouquet garni, consisting of 4 parsley sprigs, 1 thyme spray and 1 small bay leaf tied together
4 fl. oz. [½ cup[ white wine
4 fl. oz. [½ cup] fish stock
2 tablespoons beurre manié
½ teaspoon salt
¼ teaspoon white pepper
¼ teaspoon cayenne
1 tablespoon chopped parsley

Preheat the oven to hot 425°F (Gas Mark 7, 220°C). Grease a large flameproof dish with 2 tablespoons of butter.

Put half the chopped tomatoes and onion into the dish with the tomato purée. Lay the fillets on top and cover them with the remaining tomatoes and onion. Tuck in the bouquet garni. Pour the wine and fish stock over the fish.

Cut 2 tablespoons of butter into very small pieces. Dot the fish mixture with the pieces of butter.

Place the dish over moderate heat for 3 to 4 minutes, or until the liquid boils. Remove the dish from the heat and place it in the oven. Bake for 15 to 20 minutes.

Take the dish out of the oven and transfer the fish fillets to a plate. Skin them and cover with aluminium foil to keep hot. Remove the bouquet garni from the dish and discard.

Pour the tomatoes, onion and liquid into a medium-sized saucepan and stir in

just enough beurre manié, a little at a time, to thicken the sauce. Cook over moderate heat for 5 minutes, stirring constantly.

Beat the remaining butter into the sauce with a wooden spoon. Add the salt, pepper and cayenne.

Return the fish fillets to the cooking dish, pour the sauce over the fish, sprinkle with parsley and serve at once.

## Brine

Brine is a solution of sea-salt and water to which is often added sugar, saltpetre and herbs and spices. The brine is boiled, cooled and then poured over the food which is to be preserved. Six days of soaking in brine are necessary in summer and eight in winter.

The proportion of salt to water will vary according to the type of food being preserved.

## Brioche

Made of yeast dough, a brioche (bree-yohsh) is a versatile bun that originated in France. Brioches may be baked in loaf or fluted tartlet tins, in the traditional round or ball shape with a round 'head', or they may be baked in a ring. Fresh brioches may be eaten with butter or jam. Stale brioches are delicious sliced and toasted.

Large brioches are often hollowed out and used as a container for sweet or savoury foods.

## Brioche—I

*The process used in making brioches is more complicated than that for most bread, and particular care must be taken in the early stages. Your efforts, however, will be rewarded, because brioches are the most delicious of buns. This traditional recipe may be used for either a Grosse Brioche à tête (grohs bree-yohsh ah tet) or the smaller individual Petites Brioches aux têtes (p'-teet bree-yohsh oh tet). Both have the classic 'heads'.*

1 LARGE BRIOCHE OR 8 SMALL BRIOCHES
3 oz. [⅜ cup] butter
8 oz. [2 cups] flour
½ oz. yeast
1 teaspoon salt
2 teaspoons castor sugar
2 eggs
2 to 3 tablespoons milk
GLAZE
1 egg, lightly beaten

Place the butter on a marble slab or on

a sheet of greaseproof or waxed paper on a board. Soften the butter by beating it with a rolling pin. Then spread it out with the heel of your hand until it is smooth and soft. Scrape the butter off the marble, or paper, with a knife and set it aside on a plate.

Clean the board or marble slab. Dry it thoroughly and then sift the flour on to it. Using your fingers, draw aside one-quarter of the flour and make a well in the centre. Crumble the yeast into the well and moisten it with only enough warm water to dissolve the yeast. Using your fingers, mix to a soft dough. Gather the dough into a ball and, with a knife, cut a cross in the top.

Slide the yeast ball into a bowl of lukewarm water. Be sure the water is not hot, or it will kill the yeast. Set the bowl aside for 8 minutes. In this time the yeast ball should rise to the surface and double in size. With your hand, scoop the yeast ball out of the bowl and drain it on a cloth. If your dough is not finished by the time the yeast ball is ready, cover it with an inverted mixing bowl until you are ready to use it.

Sprinkle the remaining flour with the salt and sugar. Make a well in the centre and into this break the eggs and add a little milk. Mix the eggs and milk together with your fingers and gradually draw in the flour. Continue mixing, adding more milk if necessary, until the mixture becomes a sticky dough.

Beat the dough with the fingers of one hand by drawing the dough up and then throwing it down again on to the board. Continue lifting, throwing, and scraping the dough back together again into a mass. After about 10 minutes of such beating, the dough should have enough elasticity and body so that it hardly sticks to your fingers.

Now begin to work the softened butter gradually into the dough. Add only about 2 tablespoons at a time. After each addition of butter, beat the dough, mix it vigorously with your fingers and smear it around on the board. When all the butter has been incorporated, the dough should be smooth and only barely sticky.

With your fingers, mix the drained yeast ball thoroughly into the dough. The consistency of the finished dough will be like that of stiffly whipped cream.

Scrape the dough off the board with a knife and gather it into a ball in your hands. Place it in a clean, lightly floured bowl that is large enough to allow the dough to double in size. Cover with a cloth and put the bowl in a warm place (80°F—85°F) for 3 hours.

*For Brioche, crumble the yeast into the flour, moistening with a little warm water to dissolve the yeast.*

*Gather the yeast dough into a compact ball and, with a sharp knife, cut a cross in the top.*

*Break the eggs into the remaining flour and gradually work in the milk to form a sticky dough.*

*Beat the dough for about 10 minutes, by drawing it up and throwing it down, until it is elastic.*

*Gradually work the butter into the dough, beating and mixing it vigorously, until it is smooth.*

*Mix the yeast ball into the dough and put the complete dough into a bowl. Cover the bowl and leave for 3 hours.*

*Place three-quarters of the dough in a brioche mould and, with your fingers, make a well in the centre.*

*Roll the remaining dough into a ball and firmly push it into the hole in the centre.*

259

At the end of this time, the dough will have doubled in bulk. Push the dough down with your fist, cover the bowl with aluminium foil and refrigerate for at least 4 hours, or overnight. An alternative method is to put the covered bowl directly into the refrigerator, instead of putting it in a warm place, and leaving it to rise for at least 12 hours.

Remove the bowl from the refrigerator. The dough will now be firm enough to handle and is ready to be shaped, proved and baked.

To make a large brioche, butter a fluted 1-pint brioche mould or a baking sheet. Turn the dough out of the bowl on to a lightly floured board or marble slab. Knead the dough lightly with the heel of your hand. Form the dough into a roll.

With a knife, cut off one-quarter of the dough and roll the remaining three-quarters into a ball. Place this ball in the mould or on the baking sheet. Make a hole in the centre of the ball by inserting three fingers into it.

Roll the remaining quarter of dough into a ball and taper one side into a point. Firmly push this 'tail' into the hole in the larger ball.

With a knife, make a few shallow incisions in the large ball close under the 'head'. Cover the mould or baking sheet and put it in a warm place. Leave to rise again (to prove) for 15 minutes. The proving may also be done on a rack over a tin of boiling water.

Preheat the oven to very hot 475°F (Gas Mark 9, 240°C).

After proving, brush the surface of the brioche with beaten egg. Bake in the centre of the oven for 20 minutes until the brioche has risen and is beginning to brown. Reduce the oven temperature to moderate 350°F (Gas Mark 4, 180°C) and continue baking for 30 minutes. The brioche is done when the surface is golden brown and a knife plunged down into the centre comes out clean.

Take the brioche out of the oven and transfer it to a wire rack. Cool the brioche for 25 minutes before lifting it out of the mould.

To make small individual brioches, butter 8 small brioche moulds (fluted, deep, tartlet moulds). After the dough has been removed from the refrigerator, lightly kneaded and shaped into a roll, divide it into 8 egg-sized portions. Cut off one-third of each 'egg' with a knife and roll the remaining two-thirds of each 'egg' into balls. Place the balls in the moulds and make an indentation in the top of each ball with one finger.

Shape the remaining one-third of dough into smaller balls, tapering into tails, and push one into the indentation in each large ball. Place the filled moulds on a baking sheet and prove in a warm place for 15 minutes.

Preheat the oven to hot 425°F (Gas Mark 7, 220°C).

After proving, brush each brioche with beaten egg. Bake in the centre of the oven for 15 minutes. When done, the tops will be golden brown. Remove the baking sheet from the oven and transfer the moulds to a wire rack. Cool the brioches for 20 minutes before turning out.

## Brioche—II

*This recipe for brioche dough is made with dried yeast, which is easier to use than fresh yeast.*

1 LARGE BRIOCHE

9 oz. [2¼ cups] strong white flour
1 sachet easy-blend dried yeast
3 tablespoons milk
  a large pinch of salt
2 teaspoons castor sugar
2 large eggs
3 oz. [6 tablespoons] butter, diced and softened
1 egg beaten with a few drops of water

Sift a quarter of the flour into a bowl and stir in the yeast. Add 2 tablespoons milk and mix to a firm dough, turn out and knead until smooth. Roll and cut a cross in the top, drop in a bowl of warm water and leave to rise and become spongy.

Make the brioche paste; sift remaining flour with salt and castor sugar on to a cold surface. Make a well in the centre. Add the eggs and a tablespoon milk and mix to a sticky paste, adding the remaining milk if the paste is stiff.

Using only one hand, lift the paste, then throw it down sharply with a flick of the wrist. Repeat for about 10 minutes. Gradually work in the butter.

Drain the spongy yeast dough and work it into the paste with your fingers. Shape the dough into a ball and place in a floured bowl. Sprinkle the top with flour, then cover with greased polythene and leave to rise in the refrigerator for at least 6 hours or overnight.

Grease a 2-2¼ pint [5½ cups] brioche mould.

Turn out the risen dough on to a floured surface and knead for 1 minute. Reserve a quarter of the dough. Shape the rest into a ball and place in prepared mould. Make a well in the centre.

Form the rest of the dough into a ball,

place it on top of the dough in the mould and press in place. Cover with greased polythene and leave to prove in a warm place for about 15 minutes. Preheat the oven to hot 425°F (Gas Mark 7, 220°C).

Uncover the dough and brush with the egg, then bake about 15 minutes, until risen, golden and just firm to the touch. Cool for a few seconds, then turn out. Leave on a wire rack until cold.

## Brioche aux Fraises avec Moussade Framboises

BRIOCHE WITH STRAWBERRIES AND RASPBERRY CREAM FILLING

*Brioche aux Fraises avec Moussade Framboises* (bree-yohsh oh frehz ah-vek moose-ahd fram-bwahz) *is a sophisticated dessert for a special dinner party.*

6 SERVINGS

1 large brioche, freshly baked and cooled
2 tablespoons framboise liqueur
4 oz. [½ cup] granulated sugar
1 tablespoon water
5 fl. oz. double cream [⅝ cup heavy cream]
1 teaspoon vanilla essence
1 tablespoon icing [confectioners'] sugar
6 oz. fresh or frozen raspberries, puréed and sweetened to taste
6 oz. fresh or frozen strawberries

Lift or cut off the head of the brioche and set it aside. With a metal spoon hollow out the centre of the brioche, leaving about a ½-inch shell of bread around the sides and bottom. Moisten the inside of the hollowed-out brioche with the framboise liqueur. Set the brioche aside.

Put the sugar and water into a medium-sized, heavy saucepan. Over moderate heat, bring the water to a boil, stirring it with a metal spoon to dissolve the sugar. Boil the sugar-and-water syrup, without stirring, until it begins to change colour. Then remove from the heat. With a pastry brush, coat the outside of the brioche with the caramelized syrup. Allow the caramel to harden, then transfer the brioche to a serving dish.

Pour the cream into a small bowl. Using a wire whisk, beat the cream until it is almost stiff. Then beat in the vanilla and icing [confectioners'] sugar. Fold in the raspberry purée.

*A luscious dessert, Brioche aux Fraises avec Moussade Framboises is rich with strawberries and raspberries.*

Spoon the raspberry-flavoured cream into the hollowed-out brioche. Decorate the top with half the strawberries and arrange the remaining strawberries around the base of the brioche. If you like, replace the head of the brioche on a slant.

Serve immediately.

## Brioche Mousseline

⭐ ⭐ ⭐ ① 𝕏 𝕏 𝕏

*Brioche Mousseline (bree-yohsh moos-leen) is a large, cylinder-shaped brioche which is baked in a plain, round mould. The butter in this recipe is in much greater proportion to the flour than in the basic brioche recipe, although the method of preparation is the same.*

1 LARGE BRIOCHE

7 oz. [⅞ cup] butter
9 oz. [2¼ cups] flour
½ oz. yeast
   warm water
¾ teaspoon salt
2 tablespoons castor sugar
3 eggs
1 beaten egg for brushing

Place the butter on a marble slab or on a sheet of greaseproof or waxed paper on a board. Soften the butter by beating it with a rolling pin. Then spread it out with the heel of your hand until it is smooth and soft. Scrape the butter off the marble or paper with a knife and set it aside on a plate.

Clean the board or marble slab. Dry it thoroughly and then sift the flour on to it. Using your fingers, draw aside one-quarter of the flour and make a well in the centre. Into this crumble the yeast and moisten it with only enough warm water to dissolve the yeast. Using your fingers, mix to a soft dough. Gather the dough into a ball and with a knife cut a cross in the top.

Slide the yeast ball into a bowl of lukewarm water. Be sure the water is not hot or it will kill the yeast. Set the bowl aside for 8 minutes. In this time the yeast ball should rise to the surface and double in size. With your hand scoop the yeast ball of out the bowl and drain it on a cloth. If your dough is not finished by the time the yeast ball is ready, cover it with an inverted bowl until you are ready to use it.

Sprinkle the remaining flour with the salt and sugar. Make a well in the centre and into this break the eggs. Mix the eggs together with your fingers and gradually draw in the flour. Continue mixing until it becomes a sticky dough.

Beat the dough with the fingers of one hand by drawing the dough up and then throwing it down again on to the board. Continue lifting and throwing. After about 10 minutes of such beating the dough should be elastic and smooth.

Now begin to work the softened butter gradually into the dough. Add only about 2 tablespoons at a time. After each addition of butter, beat the dough, stir it vigorously with your fingers and smear it around on the board. When half the butter has been incorporated, add the remainder all at once and beat it thoroughly. The dough should now be quite smooth.

With your fingers, mix the drained yeast ball thoroughly into the dough. The consistency of the finished dough will be like that of stiffly whipped cream.

With a knife scrape the dough off the board and gather it into a ball in your hands. Place it in a clean, lightly floured bowl that is large enough to allow the dough to double in size. Cover the bowl with a cloth and leave to rise in a warm place (80°F—85°F) for at least 1 hour.

At the end of this time the dough will have doubled in bulk. Push the dough down with your fist, cover the bowl with aluminium foil, and refrigerate for 12 hours or overnight.

Remove the bowl from the refrigerator. The dough will now be firm enough to handle.

Butter a large, plain, tall, round mould and wrap around it a piece of buttered greaseproof or waxed paper that will double the height of the mould. Tie on the paper with a piece of string.

Turn the dough out of the bowl on to a lightly floured board or marble slab and knead the dough lightly with the heel of your hand. Form the dough into a ball and place it in the mould. Cover the mould and put it in a warm place to rise again (to prove) for 15 minutes. The proving may be done on a rack over a tin of boiling water.

Preheat the oven to moderate 350°F (Gas Mark 4, 180°C).

After proving, brush the surface of the brioche with beaten egg and bake in the oven for 1 hour. The brioche is done when the surface is golden brown and a knife plunged down into the centre comes out clean.

Take the brioche out of the oven and transfer it to a wire rack. Cool the brioche for 25 minutes before lifting it out of the mould.

## Brisket of Beef

In England and in Europe, the cut of beef known as brisket is the best rib or the meat covering the breastbone. As it is a relatively tough and fatty piece of meat, a brisket of beef is inexpensive. It is generally boiled, braised or stewed or salted and pickled in brine.

## Brisket of Beef with Jelly

⭐ ① 𝕏 𝕏 𝕏

*It is best to buy a large piece of brisket for this dish as a smaller one may be too fatty. You will then have a piece of meat with a fine flavour. The natural aspic jelly, if not all eaten at one meal, should be melted down again, boiled and poured into a clean bowl. When cool, it can be kept, covered, in the refrigerator.*

12 SERVINGS

3 tablespoons vegetable oil
5-6 lb. fresh brisket of beef, boned, rolled and tied
2 calf's feet or 3 pig's feet, split
12 fl. oz. [1½ cups] sweet, white wine
1½ pints [3¾ cups] water
   bouquet garni, consisting of 3 parsley sprigs, 2 bay leaves, 2 thyme sprays and 1 crushed garlic clove tied in a piece of cheesecloth
2 teaspoons salt

Preheat the oven to warm 325°F (Gas Mark 3, 170°C).

In a large, heavy, flameproof casserole heat the oil over moderately high heat until it is hot. Put in the brisket and brown it well on all sides. Tuck in the calf's or pig's feet. Pour in the wine and water. The liquid should be just level with the top of the meat, so add more water if necessary. Add the bouquet garni and the salt. Cover the pot with aluminium foil and then with the lid. Put it in the oven and cook for 5 hours.

Remove the casserole from the oven, take out the meat and set it aside on a platter. When the meat is cold enough to handle, wrap it in aluminium foil and place it in the refrigerator. Boil the liquid in the casserole until it is reduced by half. Strain the liquid into a bowl and, when it is cool, cover and refrigerate overnight.

The next day, remove the meat from the refrigerator at least 1 hour before serving. Slice it and arrange the slices on a serving platter. Take the now solidified cooking liquid from the refrigerator and lift and discard the fat from the top. Chop the brown jelly and pile it in the centre of the meat slices. Garnish with watercress or parsley.

## Brisling

Resembling a sardine, the brisling is a small Norwegian fish of the herring family.

*Tasty and economical, cold Brisket of Beef with Jelly is ideal for a family lunch or supper.*

## Bristol Milk

Bristol Milk is the name used by some wine merchants in Bristol, England, for fine sweet sherries that they blend. Bristol Milk is generally sweeter than other sherries.

## Broad Beans

This is a variety of bean grown in Europe. The pods are long and grey-green in colour, and the beans inside a paler green. They have a fairly short season, early June to the beginning of August and like all summer vegetables they are at their best when young and tender.

To prepare them, slit the pods along the edge and remove the beans. The pods are tough but make excellent flavouring for soups. The beans are cooked in boiling salted water for 10 to 20 minutes depending on size and age. To serve them plain, drain well and serve with a knob of butter and sprinkled with chopped parsley.

Broad beans in a white sauce are the traditional accompaniment to boiled bacon [ham].

Broad beans are also available frozen or canned.

## Broad Beans Vinaigrette

Cook the broad beans, drain and leave to cool. Chop 2 to 3 spring onions [scallions] and mix into the beans. Drip a little French dressing through the bean mixture, then chill in the refrigerator. Serve as part of an hors d'oeuvre or on its own with cold meat or ham.

## Broad Beans à la Crème

Cook the broad beans, drain and return to the saucepan. For every pound of beans, beat 1 egg yolk with 5 fluid ounces single cream [$\frac{5}{8}$ cup light cream] and stir into the broad beans. Cook over low heat, stirring gently with a wooden spoon for 2 minutes. Season with freshly ground pepper.

## Broad Bean Soup

*Thick and creamy, Broad Bean Soup is inexpensive and easy to prepare. It may be garnished with chopped parsley and served with hot French bread.*

4 SERVINGS

1 lb. broad beans, weighed after shelling
1½ oz. [3 tablespoons] butter

2 tablespoons lean bacon scraps and rinds
1 onion, coarsely chopped
1 pint [2½ cups] chicken stock or stock made with chicken stock cubes
2 savory sprigs
1 teaspoon salt
½ teaspoon white pepper
1 teaspoon arrowroot
5 fl. oz. [$\frac{5}{8}$ cup] milk
4 drops fresh lemon juice

Unless the broad beans are very young, the skins will give a bitter taste to the soup and make it an unattractive colour. So, blanch the beans in boiling salted water for 10 minutes. Drain them and remove the skins with a sharp pointed knife, so that only the delicate green inside is left.

In a large deep saucepan melt 1 tablespoon of butter over moderate heat. Add the bacon and onion and fry for 10 minutes. Add the stock and savory. When the stock boils, add the beans. Simmer the liquid, uncovered, for 20 minutes, or until the beans are tender.

Remove the pan from the heat, drain the beans and reserve the liquid, plus 6 of the best beans for garnish. Rub the remaining beans through a strainer with a wooden spoon. Return the bean purée to the saucepan with the cooking stock.

## Broccoli with Capers

Sprinkle capers and 2 tablespoons of melted butter, mixed with a little of the juice from the capers, over the hot broccoli.

## Broccoli alla Siciliana

Heat 4 tablespoons of olive oil, 2 crushed garlic cloves and 3 chopped anchovy fillets in a saucepan. Add the cooked broccoli, cover and simmer over low heat for 5 to 10 minutes. Sprinkle over a little lemon juice and serve at once.

## Broccoli Salad

Chill the cooked, drained broccoli and marinate in vinaigrette dressing for at least 1 hour. Arrange crisp lettuce leaves in a large salad bowl. Place the marinated broccoli on the lettuce leaves. Spoon mayonnaise over the broccoli and garnish with black olives.

## Broccoli with Black Olives

*Try this unusual way of serving broccoli—with black olives and garlic and Parmesan cheese. Green olives may be used instead of black, but the colour of the dish will not be as interesting.*

4 SERVINGS

1½ lb. broccoli
10 fl. oz. [1¼ cups] water
2 teaspoons salt
3 tablespoons olive oil
1 garlic clove, finely chopped
6 grindings black pepper
2 oz. [¾ cup] stoned black olives, halved
4 tablespoons grated Parmesan cheese

Wash the broccoli, remove the leaves and break the flowerets into fairly large bunches.

In a large saucepan, bring the water to the boil. Add 1 teaspoon of salt and the broccoli. Cover the pan and cook the broccoli for 10 minutes over moderately high heat. Drain the broccoli. Reserve the water in which it was cooked.

Heat the oil in a large frying-pan. Add the garlic and fry over low heat for 5 minutes. Add the broccoli and season with the remaining salt and the pepper. Cook the broccoli for 10 minutes, stirring frequently. Add some of the water in which the broccoli was cooked if the pan gets too dry.

Add the olives to the pan and cook for another 2 minutes. Turn the broccoli and olives into a warmed serving dish. Sprinkle with Parmesan cheese and serve at once.

Bring the soup to the boil, add the salt and pepper and simmer for 10 to 15 minutes over moderately low heat, skimming frequently.

Mix the arrowroot with the milk in a small bowl and stir it into the soup. Raise the heat and boil the soup for 2 minutes.

Cut the remaining butter into small pieces and stir these into the soup with the lemon juice and the reserved broad beans. When the butter has melted, pour the soup into a tureen. Serve at once.

## Broccoli

A vegetable of the same species as the cauliflower, broccoli is native to southern Europe and was introduced into England from Italy in the early eighteenth century. There are a number of varieties of broccoli, of which the most interesting and common is Calabresse, an Italian green sprouting broccoli. Once available only in the spring it is now in the shops most of the year. It is noted for its fine, delicate flavour and is often eaten like asparagus with melted butter.

To prepare and cook Italian broccoli cut off the lower, tough part of the stalks. Peel the stalks from the butt of the stem upwards and remove all wilted leaves. Split the large bunches in half lengthways so that all the stalks are of uniform thickness. Make a ½-inch slit in the butt end of the stalks.

Soak the prepared broccoli for 15 minutes in cold, salted water to draw out any small insects.

Put enough salted water in a large pan to cover the broccoli and bring it to

*Broccoli with Almonds is an attractive and unusual vegetable to serve with roast meat.*

the boil. Add the broccoli, lower the heat and simmer, uncovered, until the stalks are tender when pierced with a fork. The cooking time should not exceed 15 minutes. If you overcook the broccoli, the heads will become mushy. Because the heads are more tender than the stalks, Italian broccoli is sometimes cooked like asparagus, tied in bundles and cooked with the heads out of the water. Or the heads are cut off and cooked separately.

When the broccoli is cooked, drain it in a colander. Turn the broccoli into a warmed serving dish and dot it with butter. Serve it at once.

Other types of broccoli include a white variety which resembles a small cauliflower and which is cooked in a similar way. The other sprouting varieties, purple, green and white, may be cooked like the Italian broccoli or they may be first blanched and then dipped in batter and deep-fried.

The following recipes may be made with any type of broccoli. Allow 1½ pounds of broccoli for 4 people.
Note: If you cannot buy fresh broccoli, frozen broccoli can be used in these recipes.

## Broccoli with Almonds

Dot the hot broccoli with 2 tablespoons of butter. Sprinkle 2 tablespoons of chopped toasted almonds and 1 tablespoon of freshly squeezed lemon juice over the broccoli.

## Broccoli with Cheese Sauce

*This is a novel way to prepare broccoli. Serve it with steak, chicken or fish.*

6 SERVINGS

1½ to 2 lb. broccoli, washed and trimmed
1 teaspoon salt
SAUCE
1 oz. [2 tablespoons] butter
4 tablespoons flour
10 fl. oz. [1¼ cups] milk
¼ teaspoon white pepper
2 oz. [½ cup] Parmesan cheese, grated
6 anchovies, chopped, plus 4 anchovies for garnish

Break the broccoli flowerets into medium-sized clusters. Place them in a pan with the salt and about 10 fluid ounces [1¼ cups] of boiling water. Bring the water back to the boil over moderately high heat and cook the broccoli uncovered for 5 minutes. Then cover the pan and cook for 10 to 15 minutes more.

While the broccoli is cooking, prepare the sauce. Melt the butter in a small saucepan over moderate heat. Stir in the flour with a wooden spoon. Cook for 2 minutes, stirring constantly. Remove the pan from the heat and slowly add the milk, a little at a time, stirring constantly. Return the pan to the heat and cook until the sauce is thick. Add the pepper, cheese and chopped anchovies and continue stirring until the cheese has melted.

Drain the broccoli in a colander and arrange it on a warmed serving dish. Pour the sauce over the broccoli, garnish with the remaining anchovies and serve at once.

## Broccoli, Chinese-style

*A superb Chinese way to cook broccoli, Chao-chieh-ts'ai, as it is known in Chinese, takes a little more time to prepare than the usual method of serving broccoli, but the compliments you will receive when you serve it will make the effort worthwhile.*

4 SERVINGS

2 lb. broccoli
6 tablespoons peanut or vegetable oil
1 teaspoon salt
½ teaspoon sugar
10 fl. oz. [1¼ cups] chicken stock
2 teaspoons cornflour [cornstarch] mixed with 1 tablespoon cold water

Wash the broccoli and drain well. Using a small, sharp knife, remove the broccoli flowerets from the stalks in fairly large clusters and place them in a bowl. Peel the stalks and then slice them diagonally in 1-inch pieces. Place them in another bowl. Discard the tough ends of the stalks.

Heat the oil in a large frying-pan over moderate heat and add the sliced broccoli stalks. Fry them in the oil for 1 minute, stirring continuously. Add the flowerets to the pan and continue frying and stirring for 1 more minute. Add the salt, sugar and chicken stock. Stir well, cover the pan and cook for about 8 minutes over moderate heat, or until the broccoli is tender but still crisp.

Pour the cornflour [cornstarch] mixture into the pan. Stir for 1 minute, or until the sauce thickens and is translucent.

Transfer the broccoli and sauce to a warmed serving dish and serve at once.

## Broccoli with Green Peppers

*Broccoli cooked with tomatoes, celery, onion and green pepper is a colourful vegetable dish.*

6 SERVINGS

1 oz. [2 tablespoons] butter
4 tomatoes, blanched, peeled, seeded and coarsely chopped
3 celery stalks, diced
1 garlic clove, crushed
1 small onion, chopped
2 green peppers, seeds and white pith removed and chopped
1 teaspoon salt
½ teaspoon dried basil
4 grindings black pepper
2 lb. broccoli, washed and trimmed
1 teaspoon cornflour [cornstarch]

*Low Cal*

Melt the butter in a large saucepan over moderate heat. Add the tomatoes, celery, garlic, onion, green peppers, salt, basil and pepper. Stir well and cook for 2 minutes. Remove the pan from the heat. Place the broccoli on top of the other vegetables. Return the pan to the heat, cover and cook for 15 to 20 minutes, or until the broccoli is tender.

Remove the broccoli from the pan and place it on a warmed serving dish. Keep hot.

Stir the cornflour [cornstarch] into the vegetable mixture in the pan and cook until the liquid has thickened slightly. Pour the sauce over the broccoli and serve at once.

---

***Broccoli with black olives and garlic and sprinkled with Parmesan cheese - this is an unusual vegetable dish.***

## Broccoli à la Polonaise

BROCCOLI WITH FRIED BREADCRUMBS
AND CHOPPED EGG

*A more elaborate way of serving broccoli, Broccoli à la Polonaise (ah lah poh-low-naze) may be served as a first course or as a special vegetable dish.*

4 SERVINGS

4 oz. [½ cup] butter
1 oz. [⅓ cup] fresh white breadcrumbs
1 teaspoon salt
6 grindings black pepper
1½ to 2 lb. broccoli, prepared, washed
   and cooked
1 hard-boiled egg, finely chopped
1 tablespoon chopped parsley

Melt the butter in a small saucepan over moderate heat. Add the breadcrumbs. Fry them, stirring frequently, for 2 to 3 minutes or until the crumbs are lightly browned. Stir in the salt and pepper. Remove the pan from the heat and cover it with the lid or aluminium foil to keep the breadcrumbs hot.

   Drain the broccoli well and arrange it in rows on a warmed serving dish. Mix the chopped egg with the breadcrumbs, gently reheat them for 1 minute and then sprinkle them over the broccoli with the parsley. Serve at once.

## Broccoli Soufflé

*A tasty and attractive dish, Broccoli Soufflé may be filled with tiny, new boiled potatoes and served with almost any meat or fish dish.*

6 SERVINGS

1½ oz. [3 tablespoons] butter
2 oz. [½ cup] plus 1 tablespoon flour
10 fl. oz. [1¼ cups] water
1½ teaspoons salt
1½ lb. broccoli, trimmed, washed
   and cut into small pieces
1 garlic clove
8 fl. oz. double cream [1 cup heavy
   cream]
4 eggs, separated and the yolks
   lightly beaten
6 grindings black pepper
2 oz. [⅔ cup] Parmesan cheese,
   grated

Grease a 2-pint ring mould with 1 table-spoon of butter and lightly coat the mould with 1 tablespoon of flour. Knock out any excess flour and set the mould aside.

   In a large saucepan bring the water, with 1 teaspoon salt, to a boil. Place the broccoli and garlic in the water, bring the water back to the boil, cover the pan and cook the broccoli over moderate heat for 15 minutes. Discard the garlic.

*An attractive vegetable dish, Broccoli Soufflé filled with new potatoes, goes well with meat or fish.*

Drain the broccoli, chop it finely and set it aside in a large bowl.

   Preheat the oven to moderate 350°F (Gas Mark 4, 180°C).

   In a medium-sized saucepan melt the remaining butter over low heat. Stir in the flour. Cook for 1 minute, stirring constantly. Slowly add the cream, stirring constantly with a wooden spoon. When the sauce is thick and smooth, stir in the broccoli. Remove the pan from the heat and stir in the beaten egg yolks, the remaining ½ teaspoon of salt and the pepper.

   In a medium-sized mixing bowl, use a wire whisk to beat the egg whites until they are thick and stiff. With a metal spoon, carefully fold the egg whites into the broccoli mixture. Turn the mixture into the buttered mould. Stand the mould in a pan of boiling water and bake it in the oven for 35 to 40 minutes, or until the soufflé is puffed and set.

   Remove the mould from the oven and loosen the soufflé with a knife. Place a serving platter upside-down on the mould and reverse the two. The soufflé should slide easily out of the mould. Sprinkle with Parmesan cheese and serve.

# Brochette

Brochette (*broh-shet*) is the French name for a small skewer on to which pieces of meat, fish, or vegetables are threaded and then cooked under a grill [broiler] or on a barbeque.

## Brochettes Amalfi

KIDNEY AND CHICKEN LIVER BROCHETTES

*A tempting combination of chicken livers, kidneys, ham, onions and green peppers grilled [broiled] on skewers, Brochettes Amalfi is a satisfying, meaty dish. Serve it with baked potatoes and a mixed salad.*

4 TO 6 SERVINGS

1 oz. [2 tablespoons] butter
1½ lb. chicken livers
1 lb. lamb kidneys, trimmed of fat, skin and gristle and cut in half
1 lb. cooked ham, cut into 1-inch cubes
6 medium-sized onions, peeled and quartered
2 green peppers, white pith and seeds removed and cut into 1-inch squares
4 oz. [½ cup] melted butter

Melt the butter in a medium-sized frying-pan. Add the chicken livers and fry them over moderate heat for 2 to 3 minutes. With a slotted spoon, remove the chicken livers from the pan. Drain them on kitchen paper towels and allow the livers to cool.

Preheat the grill [broiler] to high.

Thread the chicken livers, kidneys, ham cubes, onion quarters and green pepper squares on the skewers.

Using a pastry brush, coat the brochettes with half the melted butter. Place the brochettes under the grill [broiler] and cook them for 4 minutes on each side, brushing them with melted butter again when you turn them. Serve the brochettes immediately.

## Brochettes Italiennes

LIVER AND SAUSAGE BROCHETTES

*An unusual and exceptionally tasty dish, Brochettes Italiennes (broh-shet ee-tal-ee-en) consist of bite-sized pieces of liver, chipolata sausages, mushrooms, tomatoes and bay leaves threaded on skewers and quickly grilled [broiled]. Sprays of thyme may be substituted for the bay leaves, and pieces of onion or green pepper may also be added. The brochettes are served on a bed of rice and may be accompanied by a mixed green salad.*

4 SERVINGS

1 lb. calf's liver
1 lb. small chipolata sausages
8 oz. button mushrooms, wiped clean
6 oz. [¾ cup] butter, melted
6 grindings black pepper
24 bay leaves
6 large tomatoes, quartered or 24 tiny tomatoes

Preheat the grill [broiler] to moderate.

Cut the liver into 1-inch cubes. Leave the sausages and mushrooms whole.

Pour the melted butter into a shallow bowl and roll the liver cubes in it. Season the cubes with the black pepper.

Squeeze the centre of each sausage. Twist the sausage to form two smaller sausages.

---

*Colourful and tasty ingredients make Brochettes Italiennes an excellent dinner party dish.*

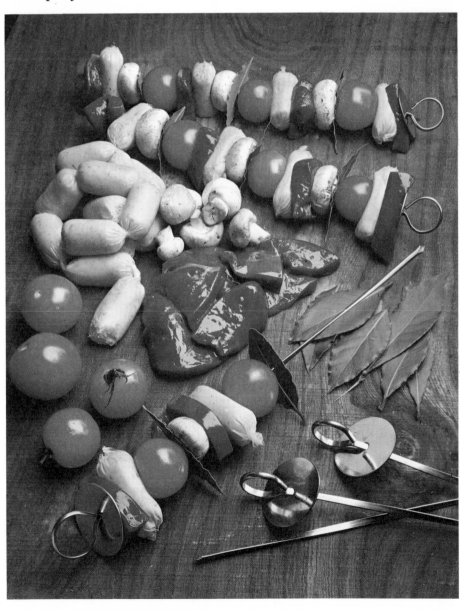

Thread the liver cubes, sausages, mushrooms, bay leaves and small tomatoes or tomato quarters on eight 12-inch skewers in alternating order.

Using a pastry brush, coat the brochettes with half of the remaining melted butter.

Place the skewers under the grill [broiler] and cook them for 6 to 8 minutes on each side, brushing them with the remaining butter when you turn them over.

Transfer the brochettes to a plate of rice and serve at once.

## Brochettes de Porc

PORK BROCHETTES

*Simple to cook yet elegant to serve, Brochettes de Porc (broh-shet d'por) make an attractive summer luncheon dish. Serve with boiled new potatoes and a green salad and a well chilled rosé wine. Great care must be taken to ensure that the*

pork is completely cooked, so be sure that the grill [broiler] is thoroughly heated before you start to cook the brochettes.

4 SERVINGS

- 4 tablespoons cooking oil
- 6 tablespoons vinegar
- 1 teaspoon salt
- ¼ teaspoon freshly ground black pepper
- 2 tablespoons chopped rosemary leaves
- 2 lb. lean loin or fillet of pork, cut into 1-inch cubes

In a large, fairly shallow bowl, mix together the oil, vinegar, salt, pepper and rosemary. Add the cubes of pork and spoon the liquid over them so that they are completely moistened. Leave the pork to marinate at room temperature for at least 6 hours, basting the pork occasionally with the marinating liquid to keep the meat moist.

Preheat the grill [broiler] to moderate.

Thread the pork cubes on to skewers (allowing 2 skewers per person). Cook the brochettes under the grill [broiler] for about 20 minutes, turning them from time to time, until the meat is well done and tender.

Serve the brochettes immediately.

## Brochettes de Rognons et Foie de Mouton

KIDNEY AND LAMB'S LIVER BROCHETTES

*An easy and inexpensive variation on beef or pork brochettes, Brochettes de Rognons et Foie de Mouton (broh-shet d'rohn-yohn ay fwah d'moo-tohn) make an excellent luncheon or supper dish.*

4 SERVINGS

- 4 tablespoons olive oil
- 6 tablespoons dry red wine
- 1 teaspoon dried thyme
- ½ teaspoon salt
- 6 grindings black pepper
- 1 lb. veal kidneys, cubed
- 1 lb. lamb's liver, cut in 1-inch thick slices and cubed

In a large, fairly shallow bowl, mix the olive oil, red wine, thyme, salt and pepper together. Add the kidney and liver cubes and leave them to marinate at room temperature for at least 4 hours.

Preheat the grill [broiler] to high.

Thread the kidney and liver cubes alternately on to skewers. Cook under the grill [broiler] for 4 minutes on each side or until the cubes are cooked. Baste once with the marinating liquid.

*Kidneys and liver marinated in red wine and served with rice - this is a tempting, economical dish which is ideal for a family supper.*

## Brochettes de Veau aux Champignons

VEAL, BACON, AND MUSHROOM BROCHETTES

*Brochettes de Veau aux Champignons (broh-shet d'voh oh sham-peen-yohn) blend veal with bacon and mushrooms for an unusual flavour. The brochettes may be accompanied by grilled [broiled] tomatoes and rice. The brochettes can be cooked on an outdoor barbeque. If an outdoor barbeque is used, make sure that it is hot before putting the brochettes on the rack and that the meat is turned frequently to cook completely.*

4 SERVINGS

MARINADE

- 6 tablespoons olive oil
- 6 tablespoons lemon juice
- 1 teaspoon dried thyme
- 1 teaspoon dried basil
- 1 bay leaf
- ½ teaspoon salt
- 4 grindings black pepper

MEAT AND MUSHROOMS
    1 lb. shoulder or flank of veal, cut
      into 1-inch cubes
    8 oz. bacon, sliced
   16 medium-sized mushroom caps
    1 teaspoon lemon juice

In a large, fairly shallow bowl, mix together the olive oil, lemon juice, thyme, basil, bay leaf, salt and pepper. Put the veal cubes into the bowl and spoon the liquid over them so that they are completely moistened. Roll up the bacon slices and place them carefully in the bowl. Leave the veal and bacon to marinate for at least 6 hours at room temperature, basting occasionally.

Wipe the mushroom caps with damp kitchen paper towels. Place the mushrooms in a small bowl and sprinkle them with the lemon juice. Set the bowl aside.

Preheat the grill [broiler] to moderate.

On each skewer (allowing two skewers per person) thread a mushroom cap, a veal cube and a bacon roll. Continue threading on the mushroom caps, veal cubes and bacon rolls until the skewers are full. Cook the brochettes under the grill [broiler] for about 15 minutes, turning them gently and sprinkling from time to time with the marinade, until the veal is tender when pierced with the point of a sharp knife.

Serve the brochettes immediately.

## Brodet Dubrovna
DALMATIAN FISH STEW

*A delicately flavoured, lightly spiced dish, Brodet Dubrovna [broh-det doo-brov-nah] is an unusual way to serve any firm, white-fleshed fish. The fish may be served with plain boiled rice and spinach.*

4 SERVINGS

    2 oz. [¼ cup] butter
    2 tablespoons vegetable oil
    2 medium-sized onions, thinly
      sliced
    1 lb. tomatoes, blanched, peeled,
      seeded and chopped or 14 oz.
      canned peeled tomatoes, drained
    3 fl. oz. [⅜ cup] white wine
    1 tablespoon white wine vinegar
    1 teaspoon chilli sauce
    4 grindings black pepper
    1½ teaspoons salt
    ½ teaspoon dried tarragon
    2 tablespoons flour
    4 x 8 oz. steaks of any firm white fish

In a medium-sized saucepan, melt 2 tablespoons of the butter and heat 1 tablespoon of the oil over moderate heat. When the butter foam subsides, add the onions.

Fry them for 5 to 6 minutes and add the tomatoes, wine, wine vinegar, chilli sauce, pepper, ½ teaspoon salt and tarragon. Bring to the boil, cover, reduce the heat and simmer gently for at least 30 minutes, stirring occasionally.

While the sauce is simmering, combine the remaining salt and flour together on a plate. Dip the fish steaks in the mixture and coat them well on both sides.

Ten minutes before the end of the sauce's cooking time, melt the remaining butter and oil in large frying-pan over moderate heat. When the butter foam subsides add the salted, floured fish to the pan. Cook for 5 to 6 minutes on each side, or until the steaks are lightly browned, adding more butter and oil if necessary. Transfer the fish steaks to a warmed serving dish and spoon the sauce over them. Serve at once.

## Broiler

A broiler is a small chicken, weighing two and a half to three pounds, and about 12 weeks old. Since broilers are so young when they are killed they have little flavour. They should always be well-seasoned and are delicious and tender if cooked in a distinctive, highly flavoured sauce.

## Broiling

Broiling is the American term for GRILLING.

## The Bronx

*This potent, refreshing cocktail is said to have originated in the borough of the Bronx in New York City. It is an ideal pre-dinner drink on a warm, summer's evening.*

1 COCKTAIL

    ½ fl. oz. sweet vermouth
    ½ fl. oz. dry vermouth
    2 fl. oz. gin
    2 tablespoons orange juice
    1 piece orange rind
    3 ice cubes

Put the sweet and dry vermouths, gin, orange juice, orange rind and the ice cubes in a cocktail shaker or covered container. Cover and shake well. Remove the top and pour through a strainer into a cocktail glass.

## Broth

A broth is a soup made from beef, mutton, veal or chicken stock to which vegetables, additional meat, or such grains as rice or barley are added.

## Brown-Bean Sauce

Made from fermented yellow beans, flour and salt, this thick sauce is sold in cans in Chinese provision stores. After opening the can, brown-bean sauce will keep for months in the refrigerator.

## Brown Chaudfroid Sauce
JELLIED BROWN SAUCE WITH MADEIRA

*This rich sauce is served cold as an accompaniment to game, duck or cutlets. The basis of Brown Chaudfroid Sauce (show-fwah) is the traditional demi-glace sauce with Madeira. It should be used when it is just on the point of setting.*

ABOUT 1 PINT

    1 tablespoon beef or vegetable fat
    1 medium-sized onion, finely
      chopped
    2 bacon slices, rind removed and
      diced
    1 tablespoon flour
    1 tablespoon tomato purée
    2 oz. mushrooms, wiped and finely
      chopped
    1 pint [2½ cups] home-made beef
      stock or stock made with a beef
      stock cube
    ¼ teaspoon salt
    ½ teaspoon freshly ground black
      pepper
    ½ teaspoon dried parsley
    ½ teaspoon dried thyme
    5 fl. oz. [⅝ cup] aspic jelly
    ¼ oz. gelatine
    3 fl. oz. [⅜ cup] Madeira, sherry or
      port

To make the demi-glace sauce, melt the fat in a heavy, medium-sized saucepan over moderate heat. Add the onion and bacon and, stirring occasionally with a wooden spoon, cook until brown. Add the flour and, stirring constantly, cook until the flour colours.

Remove the pan from the heat and stir in the tomato purée, mushrooms, beef stock or consommé, salt, pepper and herbs. Return the pan to moderate heat and bring to the boil. Reduce the heat to low and simmer for 20 minutes, stirring occasionally. Remove the pan from the heat and place to one side.

Heat the aspic jelly in a small saucepan over low heat and dissolve the gelatine in it, stirring continuously with a wooden spoon. Add the dissolved aspic mixture and the Madeira, sherry or port to the demi-glace sauce and stir to mix. Pour into a sauce boat. Put the sauce boat in the refrigerator.

When the sauce is on the point of setting it is ready to serve.

## Brown Chicken Fricassée

*An attractive dish that takes only a short time to prepare, Brown Chicken Fricassée is perfect for an informal dinner party. It may be served with rice or boiled new potatoes and buttered peas.*

4 SERVINGS

2 tablespoons flour
½ teaspoon salt
4 grindings black pepper
8 chicken pieces
3 oz. [⅜ cup] butter
1 onion, sliced
1 bay leaf
½ teaspoon dried thyme
1½ pints [3¾ cups] chicken stock
6 fl. oz. double cream [¾ cup heavy cream]
2 tablespoons beurre manié (optional)

Mix the flour with the salt and pepper on a plate and coat the chicken pieces in it.

Melt the butter in a flameproof casserole over moderate heat. When the butter foam subsides, add the floured chicken pieces and brown them on all sides. As the chicken pieces brown, remove them from the pan and set them aside on a plate. Add the onion to the pan and fry it for 8 minutes or until it is lightly brown. Return the chicken pieces to the pan. Add the bay leaf, thyme and stock and bring the mixture to the boil. Reduce the heat, cover and simmer for 1 hour, or until the chicken is tender.

Remove the chicken from the casserole and set aside on a plate. Cover the chicken with aluminium foil to keep it hot.

Boil the liquid in the casserole over high heat until it has reduced by half. Strain the liquid and return it to the casserole. Bring it to the boil again, reduce the heat to low and stir in the

*Quickly browned chicken in a creamy onion sauce, Brown Chicken Fricassée takes only a short time to prepare.*

cream. Heat the sauce gently. If it is too thin, stir in the beurre manié, a small piece at a time. Return the chicken pieces to the pan. Cook for 1 to 2 minutes and serve.

## Brownies
CHOCOLATE NUT SQUARES

*A great American favourite, Brownies are nutty chocolate squares. They may be served for lunch or with vanilla ice-cream for dessert. They are very easy to make and are best when they are slightly moist and chewy.*

12 BROWNIES

5 oz. [5 squares] plain dessert chocolate
2 tablespoons water
4 oz. [½ cup] butter, plus extra for greasing
5 oz. [⅝ cup] soft brown sugar
1 teaspoon vanilla essence
4 oz. [1 cup] self-raising flour
1 teaspoon salt

2 eggs, beaten
2 oz. [½ cup] chopped walnuts
   icing [confectioner's] sugar for
   dusting

Preheat the oven to warm 325°F (Gas Mark 3, 170°C). Place a shelf above centre. Grease a 7-inch square sandwich tin.

Put the chocolate, water and butter in a pan and melt over low heat, to blend.

Remove from the heat and stir in the sugar and vanilla. Leave to cool to room temperature.

Sift the flour and salt into a bowl and gradually stir in the cooled chocolate mixture, then the beaten eggs and nuts. Stir until the mixture is evenly blended.

Baked for 30-35 minutes. Leave in tin for 5 minutes, then turn out on to a wire rack and cut into 12 squares and sprinkle with sugar, if wished, when cold. Store in an airtight container for 1 week.

## Browning

Most recipes for stews or casseroles require the meat to be browned before the other ingredients are added so that the meat juices are sealed in and the stew has a good colour. The meat is browned by quickly frying it in hot fat.

Browning also refers to placing already cooked food under a hot grill [broiler], or in a hot oven, for a few minutes, to give it a golden-brown colour.

## Brown Sauce

*A strong, rich-flavoured sauce which may accompany steak, vegetables, game or eggs, Brown Sauce is sometimes called Sauce Espagnole.*

3 PINTS

4 oz. [½ cup] vegetable fat
1 medium-sized onion, sliced
1 medium-sized carrot, finely sliced
2 oz. lean veal, finely chopped
2 oz. lean ham, finely chopped
4 parsley sprigs, chopped
3 oz. [¾ cup] flour
4 pints [10 cups] home-made beef stock or canned beef consommé
2 tablespoons mushroom peelings
2 cloves
2 bay leaves
15 fl. oz. [2 cups] white wine
½ teaspoon salt
½ teaspoon black pepper

Heat the vegetable fat over moderate heat in a heavy, medium-sized saucepan. Add the onion, carrot, veal, ham and parsley. Cook, uncovered, stirring occasionally, for 15 minutes, or until the vegetables are tender. Sprinkle on the flour and stir well with a wooden spoon. Reduce the heat to low and cook the flour for 12 to 15 minutes or until it is brown, stirring occasionally.

Gradually add the stock or consommé, stirring continuously. Continue stirring and bring the liquid to a boil over moderate heat. Add the mushroom peelings.

Reduce the heat to very low and add the cloves, bay leaves, white wine, salt and pepper. Simmer very gently for 1 hour, stirring occasionally. With a slotted spoon regularly skim off the scum and fat.

Strain the sauce through a strainer lined with several layers of cheesecloth and placed over a bowl. Press and rub the vegetables with the back of a spoon, to press through the juice.

Rinse out the saucepan and return the

*A great American favourite, Brownies are delicious for tea or with ice-cream as a tempting dessert.*

strained sauce to it. Bring to the boil over moderate heat. Reduce the heat and simmer. As the fat rises to the surface remove it with a metal spoon (as much fat as possible should be removed from the sauce). When all the fat has been skimmed off the sauce will be semi-clear. Taste and add more salt and pepper if necessary. Pour into a sauce boat.

## Brown Sauce Diable

SPICY BROWN SAUCE

*Another variation of the traditional Brown Sauce, the piquant flavour of Brown Sauce Diable complements steak or chicken.*

1 PINT

1 tablespoon butter
1 onion, finely chopped
2 garlic cloves, crushed
½ teaspoon salt
½ teaspoon freshly ground black pepper
⅛ teaspoon cayenne pepper
3 teaspoons French mustard
1 tablespoon vinegar
1 tablespoon mango chutney
1 tablespoon Worcestershire sauce
2 tablespoons tomato ketchup
½ teaspoon dried tarragon
½ teaspoon dried thyme
1 pint [2½ cups] brown sauce

Melt the butter in a medium-sized frying-pan over moderate heat. Add the onion and garlic and fry them for 8 minutes, or until they are soft. Using a slotted spoon, transfer the onion and garlic to a medium-sized saucepan.

Stir in all the other ingredients and cook the sauce for 25 minutes over moderately low heat, stirring occasionally.

Pour the sauce into a warmed sauce-boat and serve.

## Brown Stock

*Brown stock is the base for sauces, and gravies. In fact, stocks are so important in French cookery that in France they are called* fonds *which literally means bases. In making stock you break several cooking rules. Instead of using young and tender things, a stock calls for mature vegetables and meat and bones from older animals because they have more flavour.*

4 PINTS

6 lb. veal and beef shin and marrow bones, broken or sawn into pieces
8 pints [5 quarts] cold water
6 peppercorns
6 cloves
   bouquet garni, consisting of 4 parsley sprigs, 1 thyme spray and 1 bay leaf tied together
1 carrot, diced
4 celery stalks, diced
1 onion, diced
1 turnip, diced

Preheat the oven to moderate 350°F (Gas Mark 4, 180°C).

Place the bones on a baking sheet and put them in the oven to brown for about 45 minutes.

Remove the baking sheet from the oven and, using a pair of tongs, transfer the bones to a large stock pot or saucepan. Add all the remaining ingredients.

Place the pot over high heat and bring the liquid to a· boil. As the stock heats, quite a lot of scum will rise to the surface of the stock. Use a slotted spoon periodically to skim off the scum and discard it.

After the stock has reached boiling point reduce the heat to low. Simmer the stock, partially covered with the lid at an angle, for 2½ to 3 hours, or until the stock has reduced to half the original quantity.

Strain the stock into a large bowl. Leave the stock to cool to room temperature before covering the bowl tightly with aluminium foil. Store the bowl in the refrigerator.

When the stock is completely cold a layer of fat will have formed on the top. This protective covering should not be removed until you are ready to reheat the stock for use.

The stock will keep in the refrigerator for 3 days. If you want to keep it for a longer period, remove the stock from the refrigerator and pour it into the stock pot or saucepan. Slowly bring the stock to a boil over moderately high heat and then allow it to cool before returning it to the refrigerator.

## Brown Sugar Tart

*A rich dessert with a strong hint of brandy, Brown Sugar Tart may be served hot or cold with whipped, unsweetened cream.*

8 SERVINGS

PIECRUST
6 oz. [1½ cups] flour
½ teaspoon salt
1½ oz. [3 tablespoons] vegetable fat
1½ oz. [3 tablespoons] butter
2 tablespoons water
FILLING
4 oz. [½ cup] butter, at room temperature
8 oz. [1 cup] light brown sugar
3 eggs, separated
2 fl. oz. [¼ cup] brandy

Sift the flour and salt into a medium-sized mixing bowl. Add the fat and butter and cut it into small pieces with a knife. Then with your fingertips rub the fat into the flour until the mixture resembles coarse breadcrumbs. Sprinkle on the water, 1 tablespoon at a time, and stir with a fork. Knead the dough until it is smooth and gather it into a ball.

Lightly flour a marble slab or board and roll out the dough to a circle of about 10½-inches in diameter.

Line a 9-inch pie tin with the pastry. Cover the tin with foil and put it in the refrigerator while you are making the filling.

Preheat the oven to fairly hot 375°F (Gas Mark 5, 190°C).

Put the butter in a medium-sized mixing bowl and cream it with a wooden spoon. Add the brown sugar a little at a time and beat well. Add the egg yolks one at a time, beating well between each addition. Then stir in the brandy.

In another bowl, beat the egg whites with a wire whisk until they form stiff peaks. Fold them gently into the sugar mixture. Pour the mixture into the pastry-lined pie tin.

Bake on the lower shelf of the oven for 45 minutes or until the crust is lightly browned.

Remove the tart from the oven and serve at once or allow it to cool to room temperature and chill it in the refrigerator for 30 minutes before serving.

## Brunswick Stew

*This famous American stew, which is ideal for a family lunch or dinner, may be served with hot crusty bread. The stew may appear to have a buttery film on the surface, but when you add the* beurre manié, *this will disappear.*

4 SERVINGS

2 oz. [¼ cup] butter
8 chicken pieces
1 large onion, sliced
1 green pepper, white pith removed, seeded and coarsely chopped
10 fl. oz. [1¼ cups] chicken stock or stock made with a stock cube
14 oz. canned peeled tomatoes, drained
½ teaspoon salt
¼ teaspoon cayenne pepper
1 tablespoon Worcestershire sauce
8 oz. canned and drained or frozen and thawed whole kernel corn
1 lb. canned and drained or frozen and thawed lima beans or 1 lb. broad beans
2 tablespoons beurre manié

In a medium-sized casserole, heat the butter over moderate heat. Add the chicken pieces and fry them for 2 to 3 minutes on each side or until they are golden brown. Remove the chicken pieces and set them aside on a plate.

Add the onion and green pepper to the casserole and cook for 8 to 10 minutes, or until the onion is soft and transparent.

Add the stock, tomatoes, salt, cayenne and Worcestershire sauce. Stir to mix and bring to the boil. Return the chicken to the casserole and cover. Reduce the heat to low. Simmer gently for 40 minutes.

Add the corn and lima beans or broad beans. Recover the casserole and continue to simmer for another 15 minutes.

Form the beurre manié into small balls and drop them, one at a time, into the stew, stirring constantly. Cook, stirring, for 10 minutes.

Serve at once.

## Brush

To brush is to coat thinly with milk or egg to form a glaze on pastry, or with butter or fat to keep grilled [broiled] and fried foods moist. A small brush is used, but if the bristles are nylon take care not to dip it into the hot fat.

## Brussels Sprouts

A variety of cabbage which was brought from Belgium to Britain in the nineteenth century, Brussels sprouts, which resemble miniature cabbages, grow in clusters on the stem of the Brussels sprouts plant.

Brussels sprouts are winter season plants and are a good source of Vitamin C.

Ideally, Brussels sprouts should be small and solid, with the leaves closely curled, green and very fresh.

To prepare Brussels sprouts, cut the base of the stalks and remove the tough outer leaves. Wash them well. With a sharp knife cut a cross in the base of each sprout. Cook, uncovered, in boiling salted water for 10 minutes, or until tender, but still crisp. Drain well. Alternatively the sprouts may be steamed in a

---

*Brunswick Stew is a warming and economical winter dish of chicken, beans, corn, tomatoes and onions.*

perforated steamer. They are now ready to be used to make other dishes.

If the sprouts are to be served plain, put them back in the dried pan with a large piece of butter, pepper and salt and, over low heat, toss them until they are lightly covered with butter.

## Brussels Sprouts with Bacon

*In France vegetables are often served as a separate course and Brussels sprouts cooked this way are tasty enough to serve alone.*

6 SERVINGS

1½ lb. Brussels sprouts
10 fl. oz. [1¼ cups] home-made chicken stock or stock made with a chicken stock cube

2 tablespoons butter
½ teaspoon salt
¼ teaspoon freshly ground black pepper
2 bacon slices, diced and fried

Wash the sprouts thoroughly. Trim off the tough outer leaves. With a sharp knife cut a cross in the base of each sprout.

Bring the chicken stock to a boil in a medium-sized saucepan over moderate heat. Add the sprouts. Bring the stock to the boil again and simmer the sprouts uncovered, for 3 minutes.

Cover the pan and reduce the heat to moderately low. Cook for 10 to 15 minutes or until the sprouts are just tender. Drain off the liquid and stir in the butter, salt and pepper.

Transfer the sprouts to a warmed serving dish, sprinkle the bacon over the top and serve immediately.

## Brussels Sprouts with Chestnuts

*An interesting vegetable dish, Brussels Sprouts with Chestnuts go well with roast chicken, turkey, goose or duck. In this recipe the Brussels sprouts are blanched, plunged in cold water and drained to prevent them losing their flavour and colour.*

6 SERVINGS

1½ lb. Brussels sprouts
2 teaspoons salt
24 chestnuts
2 tablespoons arrowroot
1 tablespoon port or water
15 fl. oz. [2 cups] beef stock
2 oz. [¼ cup] butter
½ teaspoon black pepper
2 oz. [¼ cup] butter, melted

Preheat the oven to warm 325°F (Gas Mark 3, 170°C).

With a sharp knife, trim the base of each Brussels sprout and cut a cross in it. Wash and drain the sprouts, and remove any yellow or wilted leaves.

Fill a large saucepan with water, add 1 teaspoon of salt and bring to the boil over high heat. When the water is boiling, drop in the sprouts and bring the water back to the boil.

Reduce the heat to moderate and simmer the sprouts slowly for 6 to 8 minutes, or until they are almost tender. Drain off the water and place the saucepan full of sprouts under cold, running water for 3 minutes. Drain again and place to one side.

Using a sharp knife split the skins of the chestnuts at the pointed end. Put the chestnuts in a medium-sized pan, cover with water and bring them to the boil. Boil for 30 seconds, then drain and peel the chestnuts with a sharp knife.

Put the peeled chestnuts in a large flameproof casserole or baking dish. In a small bowl, mix the arrowroot with the port or water. Then pour in the stock and mix well. Pour this liquid over the chestnuts. Add 3 tablespoons of butter. The chestnuts should be well covered with the liquid. If there is not enough, add a little water.

Place the casserole over moderate heat and bring to simmering point. Then cover the pot and place it in the lower part of the oven. Cook for 45 to 60 minutes or until the chestnuts are tender. (Test them with a sharp pointed knife.)

Take the casserole out of the oven and raise the heat to moderate 350°F (Gas Mark 4, 180°C). Lift the chestnuts out of the casserole with a slotted spoon and discard the cooking liquid. Replace the chestnuts and add the Brussels

---

*A simple dish, Brussels Sprouts Creole blends sprouts with green pepper and tomatoes for colourful vegetable accompaniment.*

sprouts. Sprinkle with the remaining salt and pepper and the melted butter.

With the remaining butter grease a sheet of greaseproof or waxed paper and cover the casserole with it. Bake in the oven for 20 minutes then turn the vegetables into a serving dish and serve immediately.

## Brussels Sprouts Creole
BRUSSELS SPROUTS WITH GREEN PEPPER AND TOMATOES

*This simple recipe makes a colourful change from plain, boiled Brussels sprouts. It may be served with any savoury dish from an omelet to the Sunday roast.*

4 SERVINGS

1½ lb. Brussels sprouts
1½ oz. [3 tablespoons] butter
1 large onion, finely chopped
1 garlic clove, crushed
1 green pepper, white pith removed, seeded and chopped
1 lb. tomatoes, blanched, peeled and chopped
½ teaspoon freshly ground black pepper
¼ teaspoon dried basil
1 teaspoon salt

With a sharp knife, trim any tough or discoloured outer leaves from the sprouts, and wash them thoroughly. Cut a cross in the base of each sprout.

Melt the butter in a heavy, medium-sized saucepan over moderate heat. Add the onion, garlic and green pepper. Cook them, stirring occasionally, for 8 minutes. Add the tomatoes, sprouts, black pepper, basil and salt. Taste the mixture and add more salt and pepper if necessary.

Reduce the heat to low, cover the pan and cook for 15 to 20 minutes, or until the sprouts are tender. Turn the mixture into a warmed serving dish.

Serve at once.

## Brussels Sprouts with Grapes

*Brussels Sprouts with Grapes is a surprising and fresh-tasting combination which makes an excellent accompaniment to roast chicken or turkey. The sprouts should be small and firm.*

4 SERVINGS

1½ teaspoons salt
1½ lb. Brussels sprouts
2 oz. [¼ cup] butter
½ teaspoon white pepper
¾ lb. seedless green grapes

Half fill a large saucepan with water. Add 1 teaspoon of the salt and bring the water to the boil over moderately high heat. Add the sprouts. When the water boils again, cover the pan, reduce the heat to low and simmer for 8 minutes or until the sprouts are just tender. Drain the sprouts thoroughly in a colander and set them aside.

In a medium-sized saucepan melt the butter over moderate heat. Add the sprouts, pepper and the remaining salt. Mix well so that the sprouts are well coated with the butter.

Add the grapes and cook gently until the grapes and sprouts are thoroughly heated.

Serve immediately.

## Brussels Sprouts with Ham

*Brussels Sprouts with Ham make a good accompaniment to roast meat and fowl. If the amount of ham is increased it may also be served as a main dish.*

4 SERVINGS

1½ lb. Brussels sprouts, washed and prepared for cooking
3 oz. [⅜ cup] butter
6 tablespoons flour
1 pint [2½ cups] milk
2 teaspoons salt
½ teaspoon white pepper
12 oz. cooked ham, diced
1 lb. tomatoes, blanched, peeled and sliced
3 tablespoons grated Parmesan cheese

Preheat the oven to fairly hot 400°F (Gas Mark 6, 200°C).

Steam or boil the Brussels sprouts until they are almost tender. Drain them well. (The sprouts should be quite dry.) Put them in a baking dish and set aside.

In a medium-sized saucepan melt half of the butter over moderate heat. Add the flour and stir to mix with a wooden spoon. Remove the pan from the heat and, stirring continuously, add the milk a little at a time. When all the milk has been added and the mixture is smooth return the pan to the heat. Stirring continuously, cook the sauce for 2 minutes until it is thick and smooth. Add the salt and pepper. Taste the sauce and add more salt if necessary.

Sprinkle the ham on top of the Brussels sprouts. Pour the sauce over the ham. Lay the tomato slices evenly on top. Sprinkle with the cheese.

Cut the remaining butter into small pieces and dot the top of the Brussels sprouts mixture with them. Put the dish

into the centre of the oven and bake for 25 to 30 minutes or until the vegetables are thoroughly heated and the top is browned. Serve at once.

## Brussels Sprouts Mould

*Finely chopped Brussels sprouts cooked with eggs, milk, cheese and breadcrumbs make an unusual and excellent dish for a vegetarian meal. Brussels Sprouts Mould may be served in the soufflé dish in which it is cooked.*

6 SERVINGS

1½ lb. Brussels sprouts
1 tablespoon vegetable oil
2 oz. [¼ cup] plus 1 tablespoon butter
1 small onion, finely chopped
¼ teaspoon white pepper
½ teaspoon salt
⅛ teaspoon celery salt
3 oz. [¾ cup] Gruyère cheese, grated
1½ oz. [½ cup] fresh breadcrumbs
4 eggs
10 fl. oz. [1¼ cups] milk
SAUCE
10 fl. oz. [1¼ cups] dry white wine
3 tablespoons chopped fresh tarragon
2 tablespoons chopped fresh chervil
2 tablespoons chopped fresh parsley
2 shallots, finely chopped
15 fl. oz. [2 cups] béchamel sauce
1 tablespoon butter

With a sharp knife, trim the sprouts and wash them thoroughly. Cut a cross in the base of each sprout.

Fill a large saucepan with water and bring to a boil over moderately high heat. Add the sprouts and bring the water to a boil again. Reduce the heat and cook the sprouts for 8 minutes, or until they are almost tender when pierced with a fork. Drain the Brussels sprouts, chop them finely and put aside.

Preheat the oven to warm 325°F (Gas Mark 3, 170°C).

Using a pastry brush, grease a medium-sized soufflé dish with the vegetable oil.

In a medium-sized saucepan, melt 1 tablespoon butter over moderate heat. Add the onion and fry it for 10 minutes, stirring occasionally with a wooden spoon. Put the onion into a medium-sized mixing bowl. Add the pepper, salt, celery salt, grated cheese, breadcrumbs and the eggs to the onions. Beat well with a wire whisk.

Pour the milk into a large saucepan and heat it over moderate heat. Stir in the remaining butter. Continue stirring until the butter melts. Let the milk cool for 5 minutes and then pour it in a thin stream into the egg mixture, beating continuously. Fold in the chopped sprouts. Taste the mixture and add more salt and pepper if necesssary. Pour the mixture into the greased soufflé dish.

Half fill a baking tin, large enough to hold the soufflé dish, with boiling water. Place the soufflé dish in it and put it in the centre of the oven. Bake for 40 to 60 minutes or until a knife plunged into the centre of the mould comes out clean.

While the mould is cooking make the sauce. Put the wine, 2 tablespoons of tarragon, 1 tablespoon chervil, 1 tablespoon of parsley and the chopped shallots in a small enamel saucepan. Boil slowly over moderately high heat for 20 minutes, or until the liquid has reduced to about 3 tablespoons.

Have the béchamel sauce ready in another saucepan and place a strainer over it. Pour the wine-and-herb liquid through the strainer, pressing the juice out of the herbs with the back of a wooden spoon. Mix well and simmer gently over low heat for 3 minutes, stirring with a wooden spoon to incorporate the wine.

---

*Topped with hard-boiled eggs and crispy breadcrumbs, Brussels Sprouts Polonaise goes well with roast meat.*

Remove the sauce from the heat and stir in the remaining tarragon, chervil, parsley and the butter. When the butter has melted, pour the sauce into a warmed sauceboat.

Serve the mould straight from the soufflé dish with the sauce.

## Brussels Sprouts Polonaise
BRUSSELS SPROUTS WITH HARD-BOILED EGGS, PARSLEY AND BREADCRUMBS

*Brussels sprouts served in this way are a tasty accompaniment to roast lamb, beef or pork.*

4 SERVINGS

1½ lb. Brussels sprouts
1¼ teaspoons salt
2 hard-boiled eggs, finely chopped
2 tablespoons chopped parsley
¼ teaspoon freshly ground black pepper
1½ oz. [3 tablespoons] butter
2 oz. [⅔ cup] fresh white breadcrumbs

With a sharp knife, trim any old or discoloured leaves from the sprouts and wash them thoroughly. Cut a cross in the base of each sprout.

Half-fill a medium-sized saucepan with water and add 1 teaspoon of the salt. Bring the water to a boil over moderately

high heat. Add the sprouts. Bring the water back to the boil and cook the sprouts uncovered for 5 minutes. Cover the pan and cook the sprouts for 10 minutes longer or until they are tender, but still crisp.

Drain the sprouts and transfer them to a heated serving dish. Sprinkle them with the eggs, parsley, pepper and remaining salt. Set the dish aside in a warm place.

Melt the butter in a small saucepan over moderate heat. Add the breadcrumbs. Cook the mixture for 10 minutes, or until the breadcrumbs are golden, stirring occasionally with a wooden spoon.

Sprinkle the browned breadcrumbs over the sprouts and serve at once.

## Brown-baked Potato Slices

*A Swedish dish, Brown-baked Potato Slices have the golden crispness of deep-fried potatoes, but instead of being fried they are parboiled and then baked in the oven. These potatoes are especially good served with roast meat or poultry.*

4 SERVINGS

2 oz. [¼ cup] butter, melted
4 large potatoes, peeled
1 pint [2½ cups] water
1 teaspoon salt

Preheat the oven to very hot 450°F (Gas Mark 8, 230°C). Using a pastry brush, grease a large baking sheet with 1 tablespoon of the butter and set it aside.

Using a sharp knife cut the potatoes in quarters lengthways, and slice each quarter in half lengthways.

Bring the water to a boil in a medium-sized saucepan over moderately high heat. Add the potato slices and blanch them for 3 minutes. With a slotted spoon remove the slices from the pan and pat them dry with kitchen paper towels.

Place the potato slices, side by side, in a single layer on the baking sheet. Use a pastry brush to brush half the remaining melted butter over the slices and sprinkle them with half the salt.

Place the potatoes in the oven and bake them for 30 minutes. Halfway through baking, use a spatula to turn the potato slices over. Brush the slices with the rest of the melted butter and sprinkle them with salt.

Remove the potatoes from the oven and turn into a warmed serving dish.

## Bubble and Squeak

*This traditional English dish was originally made from leftover boiled beef, mixed with cold mashed potatoes and greens and then fried. Its name comes from the noise it makes when frying. Today, however, the meat is usually omitted and Bubble and Squeak consists only of leftover mashed potatoes and greens. The quantities of each*

*should be approximately equal, but it really depends on how much you have left over. Bubble and Squeak may be served with any light main dish or snack.*

4 SERVINGS

½ lb. cold mashed potatoes
½ lb. cooked, cold greens (cabbage, Brussels sprouts, winter greens)
½ teaspoon salt
4 grindings black pepper
2 oz. [¼ cup] butter
1 teaspoon vinegar

*(Low Cal)*

In a large mixing bowl use a fork to mix the potatoes and greens together. Season with the salt and pepper.

Melt the butter in a large, deep frying-pan over moderately high heat. Add the potato-and-greens mixture. Cook for 5 to 6 minutes, or until the potatoes and greens mixture is thoroughly hot, stirring frequently.

Sprinkle the vinegar on top of the mixture. Remove the pan from the heat and turn the Bubble and Squeak into a warmed serving dish.

Serve at once.

## Bublanina

SPONGE CAKE WITH CHERRIES

*An easy-to-prepare Czechoslovakian sponge cake, rich with luscious black cherries, Bublanina (boo-blah-nyee-na) is a cake that may be served at any time. The cherries sink to the bottom of the cake to form a moist and juicy layer.*

*From Czechoslovakia, Bublanina is an easy to make sponge cake with a layer of black cherries.*

ONE 9-INCH CAKE

1 teaspoon butter
4 eggs, separated
5 oz. [⅝ cup] sugar
  grated rind of 1 small lemon
2 teaspoons lemon juice
½ teaspoon vanilla essence
4 oz. [1 cup] self-raising flour, sifted
6 oz. canned cherries, stoned and drained

Preheat the oven to moderate 350°F (Gas Mark 4, 180°C). Lightly grease a 9-inch cake tin with the butter.

In a large mixing bowl beat the egg yolks with a wire whisk, or rotary beater, until they are pale yellow. Beat in the sugar, lemon rind, lemon juice and vanilla essence. With a wooden spoon lightly fold in the flour.

In a separate mixing bowl beat the egg whites with a wire whisk until they stand in stiff peaks.

With a metal spoon, lightly fold the beaten egg whites into the egg yolk mixture. Fold in the drained cherries.

Pour the batter into the greased cake tin and place it in the centre of the oven. Bake for 45 to 50 minutes, or until the top of the cake is golden brown and a skewer inserted into the cake comes out clean.

Take the cake from the oven and leave it to cool on a wire rack before removing it from the tin.

# Buchteln

VIENNESE JAM PUFFS

*Buchteln* (BOOKH-teln), *buttery jam puffs, are traditionally Viennese. It is said that the recipe originated sometime during the early nineteenth century and was handed down from mother to daughter to the present day.*

*Buchteln are especially delicious served warm with coffee.*

16 PUFFS

½ oz. yeast
4 oz. [½ cup] plus 1 teaspoon sugar
1 tablespoon lukewarm water
5 fl. oz. [⅝ cup] milk
6 oz. [¾ cup] butter
14 oz. [3½ cups] flour
¼ teaspoon salt
1 egg plus 2 egg yolks, lightly
  beaten together
  grated rind of 1 lemon
  strawberry jam

In a small bowl, mash the yeast with the teaspoon of sugar and lukewarm water. Set the bowl aside in a warm, draught-free place for 20 minutes, or until the mixture is frothy and has doubled in bulk.

Pour the milk into a medium-sized saucepan. Place the pan over moderate heat to scald the milk (bring it to just under boiling point).

Reduce the heat to low and stir in 4 ounces [½ cup] of the butter and 2 ounces [¼ cup] of the sugar. Stir constantly until the sugar dissolves. Remove the pan from the heat and cool the milk-and-butter mixture to lukewarm. Stir in the yeast mixture.

Sift the flour and salt into a large, warmed mixing bowl. Make a well in the flour and into it pour the yeast-and-milk mixture, the whole egg, egg yolks and lemon rind. Stir the ingredients with a wooden spoon until all the flour is worked in and the mixture becomes a medium-firm dough. If the dough is too wet, stir in a little more flour.

With your hands, shape the dough into a ball and place it in a large, lightly buttered bowl. Sprinkle the ball of dough lightly with flour, cover the bowl with a cloth and place it in a warm, draught-free place for 1 hour.

Preheat the oven to moderate 350°F (Gas Mark 4, 180°C).

Turn the dough out of the bowl on to a lightly floured working surface. With your fist punch the dough to remove the air. Knead the dough for about 10 minutes, or until it is smooth and elastic.

With a rolling pin roll out the dough into a rectangle, about ¼-inch thick. Trim the edges of the dough with a knife to square off the sides and cut it into 16 squares.

Place a teaspoon of the jam in the centre of each square. Gather up the sides of each square over the jam and press them together with your fingers to form a small bundle.

Melt the remaining butter in a small saucepan over low heat. Dip each bundle into the melted butter. Put the bundles, seam side down, in a 9-inch cake tin, with a removable bottom or sides, arranging the bundles in circles and working inwards from the side of the tin.

Dribble any leftover butter over the bundles. Cover the tin with a cloth and stand it in a warm, draught-free place for 15 minutes.

Uncover the tin and place it in the oven. Bake for 30 minutes, or until all the bundles are golden brown and have puffed up so much as to completely fill the tin.

Remove the tin from the oven, release the bottom or sides and sprinkle the puffs with the remaining sugar. Break the puffs apart before serving.

## Buckling

Buckling are herrings which are beheaded and brined or dry-salted before being smoked and cooked simultaneously. Buckling, skinned and filleted, can be used in the same way as smoked trout.

*For Buchteln, roll the dough into a rectangle and cut it into 16 small squares.*

*Gather up the sides of each square over the jam and press them together to form a small bundle.*

## Buckwheat

Also called Saracen corn, Saracen wheat, and beechwheat, buckwheat is an herbaceous plant which will grow in poor soil. Because its seeds yield a flour from which bread can be made, it is often considered a cereal. Rarely used in Great Britain, buckwheat is grown extensively in Russia and in parts of France, Italy, Holland and the United States. It is used to make a kind of porridge, pancakes and bread.

## Bulb Baster

Particularly helpful in the basting process as they prevent splashing of fat, the best bulb basters are made of heat-resistant glass, as plastic can melt in very hot fat or liquid.

## Bullace

The name of a small, wild tree and its fruit, bullace is related to the damson plum. Rare in the United States, bullace is native to Europe, where it is traditionally used in making jams.

*Place a small teaspoonful of strawberry jam in the centre of each square of dough.*

*Coat each bundle with melted butter and lay them, seam side down, in a 9-inch cake tin.*

## Bully Beef

Another name for CORNED BEEF, Bully Beef originated from the French *bouilli*, or boiled beef, which was issued as rations to French troops in the Franco-Prussian war of 1870-71. It became British Army slang, bully beef or just bully, in World Wars I and II.

## Burgers in Red Wine

☆ ① ⧖

*Served with a red wine sauce, these beef-burgers are rather special. This dish is ideal for an informal dinner. The burgers may be served with fried potatoes and peas or broccoli.*

8 BURGERS

- 4 oz. [$\frac{1}{2}$ cup] butter
- 2 onions, finely chopped
- 2 celery stalks, finely chopped
- 2 lb. minced [ground] beef
- 2 teaspoons tomato purée
- 1 teaspoon dried oregano
- $\frac{1}{4}$ teaspoon dried thyme
- $\frac{1}{2}$ teaspoon salt
- 6 grindings black pepper
- 4 fl. oz. [$\frac{1}{2}$ cup] dry red wine

In a large frying-pan melt half of the butter over moderate heat. Add the onions and celery and fry them for 6 to 8 minutes, or until the onions are soft and translucent.

With a slotted spoon, remove the onions and celery from the pan and place them in a large mixing bowl. Using a fork, combine the meat with the onion and celery and mix in the tomato purée, oregano, thyme, salt and pepper.

With your hands, shape the mixture into 8 patties. Melt the remaining butter in the frying-pan over high heat. Place the patties in the pan and sauté them for 1 minute on each side.

Reduce the heat to moderate and add the wine to the pan. Continue cooking the patties for about 8 to 10 minutes, turning them over halfway through cooking.

Transfer the burgers to a warmed serving dish. Taste the wine sauce and, if necessary, add more salt and pepper. Spoon the sauce over the burgers and serve them at once.

## Burgundy Wines

Burgundy is a narrow strip of land in eastern France, bounded by the Saône, the Loire and the upper Seine rivers, which produces, with Bordeaux, some of the finest wines in the world.

Burgundy wines can be red or white. The reds are, generally, full-bodied, dry and deep, rich ruby in colour. The whites (with the exception of Chablis) are strong, slightly woody and dry to taste and a greenish pale gold in colour.

Burgundy produces relatively little wine, an average of only eight million gallons per year as compared to Bordeaux which produces one hundred million gallons per year. This is partly because of the stringent *appellation contrôlée* laws passed in the 1930's which strictly define the quality, and thereby the quantity of wine produced. But mostly it is because of the multiple ownership system existing in the Burgundy region.

Most vineyards are owned by several, and sometimes many, different owners, all of whom work their own areas in their own way and at their own pace. A wide fluctuation in quality of even a single wine is a natural consequence.

The multiple ownership system also meant in the past that many burgundies were blends of several types of wine, since many of the small growers simply passed their product to *négociants* who organized bottling and shipping. Today, however, more and more burgundy is being estate-bottled, with the guarantee of quality that that implies. *Mis en*

*bouteille au domaine*, or *mis en bouteille à la propriété* are the burgundian equivalents of *mis en bouteille au château* (château-bottled) Bordeaux.

Burgundy is divided into four main wine-producing areas—the Côte d'Or to the north, Côte de Chalonnais and Côte Mâconnais in the middle and, to the south, Côte de Beaujolais. Chablis, situated to the northwest of the Côte d'Or is not, strictly speaking, in Burgundy, but the pale golden wine it produces is considered to be a Burgundy wine.

The Côte d'Or produces most of the truly superlative wines of Burgundy and, perhaps as a result, has, with the exception of Chablis, the most clearly identifiable system of quality control in the region. Wine produced here is divided into three categories. The first, *village* wine, a sort of superior *vin ordinaire*, is identified only by the name of the village within which the vineyard is located (Chambolle-Musigny, for example). The second, *premier cru* (first growth) is identified by both the village and the vineyard name (Chambolle-Musigny/Les Amoureuses). And, at the very top, a few *grands crus* are identified by their vineyard alone. (Musigny, for example, is a Chambolle-Musigny wine.)

The northern part of the Côte d'Or is called the Côte de Nuits and stretches from just south of Dijon to the village of Nuits St. Georges. It produces some of the great red wines of Burgundy. Chambertin, reputed to be Napoleon's favourite red wine, Romanée-Conti and Clos de Vougeot are the three most distinguished. Even the *village* wines are superior and Nuits St. Georges is an excellent example.

Côte de Beaune makes up the southern half of the Côte d'Or and produces one great red wine, several good ones and most of the best white wine of the region. Corton is the great red with, on a more modest scale, some very drinkable reds from Beaune and Pommard. The three greatest whites are Montrachet, Corton-Charlemagne and Meursault.

The middle areas, Chalonnais and Mâconnais, also produce some good, and underrated, wines. Givry and Montagny are the best-known areas of Chalonnais, while the soft, fragrant Pouilly-Fuissé is, perhaps, the most popular of several excellent white Mâcons.

Beaujolais produces light fresh red wine best drunk when very young. Moulin-à-Vent and Brouilly are two of the better ones.

Chablis is, after Beaujolais, probably the most imitated wine of Burgundy and, in its pure state, is the traditional accompaniment to oysters. It is sold under four categories—*grand cru*, *premier cru*, Chablis and *petit* Chablis.

Four vineyards in Chablis have earned the right to call themselves *grands crus*. Vaudésir is probably the best-known of these.

Red burgundies go well with roasts, steaks and such poultry as duck and goose, and they are often served with game. Chablis and Pouilly-Fuissé can be served with fish or a light salad.

Côte de Beaune whites complement anything but go particularly well with such white meats as veal and pork, and such poultry as chicken.

*Clarified butter is used mostly for sealing potted shrimps and pâtés.*

# Butter

Butter is an entirely natural food, free of all preservatives, made with cream (solidified milk fats). The average composition of butter is 81.5 per cent milk fat, 15.9 per cent water, up to 2.5 per cent salt and up to 2.0 per cent milk protein and other residues. One pound of butter requires the cream from at least 18 pints of milk. Almost one-third of all the milk produced in the world is made into butter.

Butter, a concentrated high energy food, rich in calories and Vitamin A, also contains amounts of calcium and Vitamin D. The principal uses of butter are as a spread and a cooking fat.

Butter is mentioned in the Bible, but how it was discovered is unknown. One story is that wandering herdsmen carrying milk in goatskins found that the swinging skins, acting as miniature churns, turned the milk into butter.

There are two main kinds of butter. The first, sweet cream butters, are made from fresh cream in New Zealand, Australia, Denmark, Eire, the British Isles and the United States. The second, lactic butters, come mainly from Europe and are made from ripened cream, that is, cream to which special bacterial cultures have been added to enhance the butter flavour and develop a mild acidity.

Sweet cream butter is mild and delicately flavoured. Its texture is firm, waxy and smooth. This makes it an ideal ingredient for pastry and biscuits, where the dough has to be rolled. Lactic butter has a full flavour and a very fine texture. It creams easily and so it is an excellent ingredient for all kinds of cakes, especially for spicy cakes such as Ginger or Dundee. Lactic butter is also used for making fudge, caramels and toffees. Both types of butter may have a limited amount of salt added for flavour.

CLARIFIED BUTTER

Butter contains salt and water which must be removed if the fat required is to be pure. The process of removing the salt and water is known as clarifying.

The butter to be clarified should be melted in a saucepan over moderate heat and gently cooked, without browning, until all bubbling stops. This shows that the water has been drawn off. The pan is then removed from the heat and allowed to stand for 2 to 3 minutes while the salt and any sediment settle. Finally, the butter is strained through cheesecloth into a bowl.

Clarified butter is used by perfectionists in many recipes and in Indian cooking, where it is known as *ghee*, it is used almost exclusively. It is also used for sealing potted shrimps, pâtés and terrines.

It is not necessary to clarify unsalted butter as the fresh taste will be lost.

DRAWN BUTTER

In the United States, drawn butter is another name for clarified butter, but in Britain it is melted butter used as a form of dressing for such foods as asparagus, corn on the cob, globe artichokes and some fish dishes. Allowing 2 tablespoons of butter per person, the butter is melted in a bowl set in hot water to prevent it from browning, and then served in a heated sauce boat.

FOAMING BUTTER

When butter begins to melt in a pan, the liquids in the butter evaporate and cause the butter to foam. While it is foaming, the butter is still not very hot, but when the liquids have almost evaporated, it is possible to see the foam subsiding. Butter, mixed with oil, will heat to a higher temperature before burning and browning than plain butter, but the signs are the same. Therefore, the point at which the eggs, meat or vegetables are added to the pan is when the foam begins to subside and when the butter is at its hottest.